On Torture

On Torture

Edited by
Thomas C. Hilde

The Johns Hopkins University Press | *Baltimore*

© 2008 The Johns Hopkins University Press
All rights reserved. Published 2008
Printed in the United States of America on acid-free paper
9 8 7 6 5 4 3 2 1

The Johns Hopkins University Press
2715 North Charles Street
Baltimore, Maryland 21218-4363
www.press.jhu.edu

ISBN-13: 978-0-8018-9026-0
ISBN-10: 0-8018-9026-8

Library of Congress Control Number: 2008924410

A catalog record for this book is available from the British Library.

Special discounts are available for bulk purchases of this book. For more information, please contact Special Sales at 410-516-6936 or specialsales@press .jhu.edu.

The Johns Hopkins University Press uses environmentally friendly book materials, including recycled text paper that is composed of at least 30 percent post-consumer waste, whenever possible. All of our book papers are acid-free, and our jackets and covers are printed on paper with recycled content.

For more information about *South Central Review,* please see:
www.press.jhu.edu/journals/south_central_review/

Contents

About the Cover Photograph

Paula Luttringer, photographer

"I went down about twenty or thirty steps and I heard big iron doors being shut. I imagined that the place was underground, that it was big, because you could hear people's voices echoing and the airplanes taxiing overhead or nearby. The noise drove you mad. One of the men said to me: so you're a psychologist? Well, bitch, like all the psychologists, here you're really going to find out what's good. And he began to punch me in the stomach." MARTA CANDELORO WAS ABDUCTED ON JUNE 7, 1977, IN NEUQUEN. SHE WAS THEN TAKEN TO THE DETENTION CENTER, 'LA CUEVA.'

From the series, *El Lamento de los Muros, 2000–2005*. Digital print on fine arts paper.

Paula Luttringer is an Argentinean who lives in Paris. She was "disappeared" for more than five months during Argentina's Dirty War. Her photographic series, *El Lamento de los Muros*, from which the cover photograph is taken, documents some of the hundreds of secret detention centers in Argentina during the 1970s and 1980s and some of the thousands of women who were disappeared, tortured, and often murdered in the centers.

On Torture

Introduction

Thomas C. Hilde

> [T]he term "torture" means any act by which severe pain or suffering, whether physical or mental, is intentionally inflicted on a person for such purposes as obtaining from him or a third person information or a confession, punishing him for an act he or a third person has committed or is suspected of having committed, or intimidating or coercing him or a third person, or for any reason based on discrimination of any kind [. . .] No exceptional circumstances whatsoever, whether a state of war or a threat of war, internal political instability or any other public emergency, may be invoked as a justification of torture.
>
> —*Convention against Torture and Other Cruel,*
> *Inhuman or Degrading Treatment or Punishment*, 1984

IF CRUELTY IS THE WORST THING that humans do to each other, torture being the most extreme expression of human cruelty, then the very existence of torture forces us to confront basic presuppositions about morality, law, and ourselves. The present so-called "torture debate," prompted by the radical instrumentality of U.S. treatment of its captives in the "war on terror," ostensibly revisits this discussion. The current debate, however, is framed wrongly from the outset, and remains largely sealed off from a broader public which is nonetheless implicated in the debate's outcomes. Ariel Dorfman writes that the moral and practical arguments against torture are myriad, but "I cannot bring myself to use them, for fear of honoring the debate by participating in it."[1] Dorfman has long struggled against human abuses, and his work reflects deep moral commitments. He is perhaps expressing the deeper, widely-shared frustration of discussing torture in our world, especially torture committed in the name of securing modern liberal democracy. Torture has no ethical justification and little practical use, at least in its stated use as a means of information-gathering (although it might be effective as an instrument of oppression). Why, then, do we return to condemning the logic and practices of torture? Why do we choose to do so?

It is crucial to think of participation in the "torture debate" in terms other than those set before us by the present discourse. The current debate sets up an opposition between legalistic apologists and the morally outraged; between a *crude* instrumentalist utilitarianism and cost-benefit expediency on one hand, and moral absolutism on the other. For the crude utilitarian, torture may be justified if it leads to a better aggregative end; for the absolutist, torture is wrong, period, as a basic human rights matter if not a function of deep-seated Christian or Kantian principles. In this form of debate, one is forced to choose between an untenable absolutism and the reduction of torture to a regrettable instrumentality of war. The absolutist maintains that respect for human dignity is a universal principle at the core of all moral systems. Torture is the most fundamental violation of that principle. Seeking to justify torture is tantamount to seeking to justify the moral relativism of power. The crude utilitarian asks what the absolutist is to do when faced with a scenario in which committing torture against one individual would save many other individuals. The absolutist is then caught in the trap of weighing moral costs and benefits. He is thus now faced with the impossible choice of violating one individual's or many individuals' dignity and/or rights, counting heads and considering exceptions. He is no longer an absolutist regarding torture. Once the sanction against torture is broken, what remains is to examine the potential benefits attained through torture.

Furthermore, some political opinion leaders actively encourage the collective moral imagination to draw a new version of an old picture of the world in which good is pitted against evil. These dualisms combined yield a whirlpool of rhetorical gestures; they lack legal and moral concreteness. Human cruelty, especially cruelty committed in one's own name, becomes an abstraction, an evasive matter of metaphysical infantilism and arbitrary loyalties. The ambiguity, distance, and basic difficulty of the torture question is then exploited in the "torture debate" through specious arguments such as the famous "ticking time bomb" hypothesis or through legalistic quibbles over which physical and psychological abuses constitute torture under "exceptional circumstances."[2] You say "waterboarding," I say "bobbing for apples."

What is at stake is radical. The radicalism of the present moment reveals itself in the disruption of a common and habitual aversion to torture, even when we are simply ignoring its existence. Now, it is impossible to avert the eyes from the disquieting Abu Ghraib photographs. Many states—including liberal democratic ones, which hold the principle of no-harm as the keystone of their moral systems—have engaged in torture out of the public eye while condemning it publicly. Michel Foucault wrote on precisely this Janus-faced approach of modern societies' increasingly clever means of concealing the beasts that we know we truly are through increasingly antiseptic penal institutions.[3] It is a mistake to think that the large liberal democracies have not been involved in abuses in the past and that the present radicalism is a product of exceptional times. The torture practices at Abu Ghraib and Guantánamo, Baghram and "The Salt Pit," and other sites, are not simply due to the sadism of a few soldiers in times of extreme stress. These practices, and especially the refinement of psychological techniques, come straight from the CIA's 1963 *KUBARK: Counterintelligence Interrogation* manual, and the CIA's "Human Resources Exploitation Manual—1983," as well as previous studies on psychological torture since at least the 1950s.[4] The famous Bybee Memo of 2002 is itself a masterpiece of the genre of legalistic quibbling over torture methods, defining torture as the experience of pain equivalent to "serious physical injury so severe that death, organ failure, or permanent damage resulting in a loss of significant body function will likely result."[5] Apart from seeming to allow any abuse short of death, this statement avoids mention of the perfection and institutionalization of techniques such as stress positions, extreme isolation, and sensory deprivation, largely equating psychological torture with physical abuse. As a matter of technique, however, we don't need the kind of gruesome physical spectacle depicted in the famous opening pages of Foucault's *Discipline and Punish*. In Foucault's account, Damiens is publicly drawn and quartered in 1757, his limbs hacked at the ligaments in order to complete the task, and the living torso thrown onto the pyre. Today, we have American treatment of the now "mentally incompetent" Jose Padilla.

> According to court papers filed by Padilla's lawyers, for the first two years of his confinement, Padilla was held in total isolation. He heard no voice except his interrogator's. His 9-by-7 foot cell had nothing in it: no window even to the corridor, no clock or watch to orient him in time.
>
> Padilla's meals were delivered through a slot in the door. He was either in bright light for days on end or in total darkness. He had no mattress or pillow on his steel pallet; loud noises interrupted his attempts to sleep.
>
> Sometimes it was very cold, sometimes hot. He had nothing to read or to look at. Even a mirror was taken away. When he was transported, he was blindfolded and his ears were covered with headphones to screen out all sound. In short, Padilla experienced total sensory deprivation.
>
> During lengthy interrogations, his lawyers allege, Padilla was forced to sit or stand for long periods in stress positions. They say he was hooded and threatened with death. The isolation was so extreme that, according to court papers, even military personnel at the prison expressed great concern about Padilla's mental status . . .

> Padilla's lawyers contend that as a result of his isolation and interrogation, their client is so mentally damaged that he is unable to assist in his own defense. He is so passive and fearful now, they maintain, that he is "like a piece of furniture . . ."
>
> . . . there are even some within the government who think it might be best if Padilla were declared incompetent and sent to a psychiatric prison facility. As one high-ranking official put it, "the objective of the government always has been to incapacitate this person."[6]

This is a product of what the 1963 CIA manual calls "homeostatic derangement," "the debility-dependence-dread state" that causes intense fear and anxiety, as well as a sense of extreme guilt.[7] The technique is designed to turn a human life into pure instrumentality. This form of torture has the political advantage of naturally concealing itself from a public still accustomed to spectacle. Indeed, this is one of the objectives. There is nothing to see in a barren room inside a human mind driven mad. The spectacle is itself coldly instrumental without object.

What expands this radicalism is that an alleged hard-nosed "realism" about political economy and human relations in which anything goes reveals itself again as somehow necessary and natural, a basic guide in the conduct of human beings, as if the liberal veil had dropped from the state of nature. "Don't you understand the supreme danger we face?" the realists say. "Don't you understand that 9-11 changed everything?" One implication of these politicized questions is the concomitant effect of belying human ideals of a more tolerant, less cruel future. At the political core of the current framework is the assertion that the *state of exception* involves not only international and domestic law, but also the very grounds of morality and decency.[8] This exceptionalism is not new—most powerful nations or groups have at some time in their history claimed special moral and legal privileges over other nations and peoples. State cruelty has usually functioned in the name of goals articulated exclusively by the state. What is new is the overt legal institutionalization of torture by a state that traditionally purports to be the opposite of tyranny. Torture has often been an instrument for achieving political and economic goals. In the present case, however, the assumed certainty of the exception is such as to attempt legally and technically to define "torture" out of existence, to "disappear" torture from the normative landscape.

The distinguished authors in the present collection have taken up the grim task of recasting the framework and content of the torture discourse, some at the risk of their own well-being. Indeed, this collection is a product of profound dismay—but not hopelessness—at the extant moral, political, and legal language of torture, the practice itself, its aesthetic, current politicized attempts to write and rewrite the history of our present and our collective future, and the overt and covert institutionalization of torture, especially by the largest liberal democracy the world has known. This collection is also, then, a product of larger questions about the struggles over and distortions of language, value, and historical reality.

The authors each decided which facets of torture to discuss for this collection. Notice that none of the authors chose to write about early practices of torture, but to consider our contemporary predicament. The literature and jurisprudence of torture extends at least from Roman canon-law, 13th- through 17th-century reports of legal disputes, accounts of Christian martyrs and ingenious torture techniques,[9] to discussions of modern techniques. Practices of cruelty in the 20th century were no less cruel and gruesome than the horrors of medieval punishment even if the particular methods are more refined and concealed. Over the past several decades, torture has been practiced from Burma to El Salvador, Chile to Vietnam, Iraq to Algeria, Saudi Arabia to Sierra Leone, Rwanda to Romania, Israel to Guantánamo, Argentina to the Philippines, and so on. The photographs from Abu Ghraib have brought a long history of torture once again to the forefront of our consciousness.

The authors reside around the globe and speak from their knowledge, experience, and histories. Although I have focused on the American case in this introduction, it is important that readers understand that we are discussing torture as a phenomenon that is rather widely practiced. This is not a collection simply about the United States. It is about a practice. This is not a collection that is simply about a political issue. It is about a moral issue.

These essays were not easy to write. Torture is not an easy topic to discuss. For those who have been witness to or victims of torture, to write about or photograph this cruelest of human practices is an effort of courage. For those who live comfortably outside of the immediate practice, the struggle to write is a function of attempting to extend the moral imagination to the worst that humans do, knowing that, as Jonathan Glover writes, "real cultivation of the moral imagination is a threat to many comforting conventional attitudes."[10] Sympathy alone, however, can be a way of distancing oneself from a problem or from victims of the problem in that one proclaims one's own innocence.[11] The thing about torture is that, once we understand that its logic entails its institutionalization rather than only the production of individual victims, we are all complicit in its perpetuation. Sympathy with distant individuals can become self-indulgence in something that remains unreal even in its cruelty, a mere corollary to "conventional attitudes." Torture demands sophisticated sympathy, but it also demands much more: the disruption not only of the crude utilitarian's hard-nosed pseudo-realism—which is a reductive flight from the issue—but also of idealistic attitudes about the absolute sanction against torture. Once these flawed moral positions are disposed of, we are morally disoriented and faced again with reconstructing simple humanity.

This collection of essays is principally structured in chronological form. It begins with a discussion of four historical and present cases of state torture: Nazi Germany, French Algeria, Palestine, and Colombia. It then turns to the rhetoric of torture, followed by several essays on the morality, politics, and legality of torture in the "war on terror" and the Iraq War. It concludes with essays on the representation of the torturer and the aesthetics of torture. It is a mistake, however, to conclude from the chronological order that the relations among these different essays are not overlapping and continuous. The contributors to this collection develop several entry points into the discussion of torture: historical lessons (Todorov, Wittmann, and Ophir), the human capacity for cruelty and sadism (Calveiro and Subirats), the politics of language (Athey and Britt Arredondo), legal contortions (Castresana and Hatfield), moral argument (Dorfman), the literature of cruelty (Subirats), individual identities of torturers and victims (Ehrenreich, Britt Arredondo, and Calveiro), torture as an institution (Rejali and Hilde), torture and information (Hilde), torture as an instrument of submission (Lingis and Ophir), and torture as a facet of a larger political and economic environment or project (Serje). These diverse points of entry collectively suggest that the "torture debate" is far from settled.

We *return* to the issue of torture precisely because it is an institutional practice. It is a moral issue, but also a policy issue, where policy is understood not as a simple calculation of costs and benefits but as the discussion over values we collectively wish to project into a better future through their institutionalization. An increased tolerance for and normalization of human cruelty is not a future we should prefer. It is our hope that this collection contributes to a history of the present that recasts the distorted dialogue about the future.

NOTES

The idea for this collection began several years ago during a breakfast discussion in Washington, DC, with Richard J. Golsan, professor and editor of *South Central Review*. His kind support provided the opportunity and space to put together this special issue.

Discussions about the project with Christopher Britt have been invaluable—I am indebted to "Kitú" for his assistance and am deeply grateful for his friendship. I am also grateful to Eduardo Subirats, my UMD colleague Peter Levine, Cali Ruchala, Michael Hatfield, Drew Sullivan, and Darius Rejali for their critical discussions about the project. Paula Luttringer, a wonderful photographer, generously contributed the cover photograph. Nick Lawrence, editorial assistant at *SCR,* has made the editing job a breeze. This has been a special project from the outset, generated not merely out of scholarly interest in the dark subject of torture, but also from genuine, humane commitment on the part of the contributors and photographer. I wish to thank all of them for their participation, as well as the translators and, of course, Ines for the cover design.

1. Ariel Dorfman, "Are We Really So Fearful?" *The Washington Post.* Sunday, September 24th. Page B01 2006. Reprinted in the present collection.

2. See Todorov and Hilde, this collection, for explanation of the "ticking time bomb" hypothesis.

3. Michel Foucault, *Discipline and Punish* (New York: Vintage, 1979).

4. See this discussion and documentation in Alfred W. McCoy, *A Question of Torture* (New York: Henry Holt and Company, 2006).

5. "Memo: Jay S. Bybee to Alberto Gonzales," August 1, 2002. Reprinted in Mark Danner, *Torture and Truth* (New York: New York Review of Books, 2004). 126. For further discussion of the legal memos and debates, see Hatfield's and Rejali's essays in this collection as well as David Luban's "Liberalism, Torture, and the Ticking Bomb," *Virginia Law Review* 91 (2005): 1425–1461.

6. Nina Totenberg, "U.S. Faces Major Hurdles in Prosecuting Padilla." *NPR.* January 6, 2007. *http://www.npr.org/templates/story/story.php?storyId=6682846.* As this article discusses, Padilla was originally accused publicly by the United States government of planning a "dirty bomb" nuclear attack. This accusation was later downgraded and shuffled in sequential steps along with his legal status. Padilla is now under indictment for allegedly helping to plan Chechen rebel attacks on Russian troops.

7. Danner, *Torture and Truth,* 17–19.

8. *State of exception* is a phrase developed by Carl Schmitt in his *Political Theology* (Cambridge: MIT University Press, 1985 [originally 1922]), and popularized more recently by Giorgio Agamben in his *State of Exception* (Chicago: University of Chicago Press, 2005). Several of the present authors also make reference to this idea. The *state of exception* involves, very briefly, a complex and ambiguous "no-man's land between public law and political fact, and between the juridical order and life" (Agamben).

9. See, for instance, Antonio Gallonio, *Tortures and Torments of the Christian Martyrs* (Los Angeles: Feral House, 2004 [published first in Italian in 1591; translated into Latin, 1594; this English version, 1904]). See also John Foxe's *Acts and Monuments of the English Martyrs, 1563.*

10. Jonathan Glover, *Humanity.* (New Haven: Yale University Press, 1999). 410.

11. This point is adapted from Susan Sontag. See her *Regarding the Pain of Others* (New York: Farrar, Straus and Giroux, 2003).

I

Torture on Trial: Prosecuting Sadists and the Obfuscation of Systemic Crime

Rebecca Wittmann

WITH WAR COME WAR CRIMES. There is no documented war not accompanied by atrocities, torture, and excessive cruelty toward innocent civilians. After the dust of battle settled and casualty counts were taken, atrocity crimes were documented in both world wars, the French-Algerian War, the Vietnam War, the war in Bosnia-Herzegovina, and the war in Iraq, to name but a few. Since the appalling and sensational example of the Abu Ghraib scandal, journalists and scholars have unearthed documentary evidence proving that torture, in the guise of "enhanced interrogation methods," is standard US military policy in the so-called war on terror. In fact, the CIA began developing sophisticated forms of torture in the 1960s which they continue to use today.[1] As I write, President Bush and the Senate are in a heated debate not about whether torture occurs, but about which methods of torture should be acceptable within the Geneva Convention in the American military's quest for intelligence.

I am less interested here in whether states condone torture and whether it is actively applied policy. We know that states condone torture—from Algeria to Abu Ghraib—whether they admit it or not. What interests me more is the way that governments—specifically democratic ones—deny their use of torture, after the fact, by staging trials. The official, public condemnation of a few "bad apples" is the preferred mode of catharsis that governments offer to their citizens. In general, the public is ready and willing to swallow this mendacious message.

Why do we so quickly distance ourselves from the reality of torture? Why do we allow ourselves to be estranged from the truth? We are all horrified by the images of torture we see splattered across the newspapers, and we demand inquiries. But we then settle for the typical explanation: it was a few sadistic people acting out their dark fantasies. And although we are aghast, we cannot look away. A liberating, breast-beating, collective "that is not us" belies a deeper, voyeuristic "of course that is us," which we quickly, defensively, deny. This is our modern charade: our spurious reaction to the notion of Human Rights, the Geneva Convention, the perceived societal duty to seek justice. We pretend to want to get to the bottom of torture; we stage trials which supposedly exact justice. But they do nothing of the sort.

In the wake of the Second World War, and the atrocities committed by the Germans and the Japanese, the newly formed United Nations impressed upon democratic nations the need to investigate, prosecute, and punish crimes of excessive cruelty, torture, and atrocity occurring within the framework of war.[2] Prosecutors throughout postwar democratic West Germany undertook a massive program of investigation and legal proceedings against former Nazis suspected of committing heinous crimes. From the outside, this appeared to be an earnest attempt to confront the past and properly condemn the unspeakable crimes of the "Final Solution." A closer look, however, shows us that the judiciary deliberately attempted to normalize systemic Nazi crimes by focusing legal attention and public moral outrage on the crimes of a few "excess perpetrators." The public learned to gasp at the crimes of a few sadists, while distancing itself from the system in which so many members of this very same public had been enmeshed. Although Nazism had fallen and West Germany was on its bright new democratic path, the legal system was not so quick to embrace democratic ideals when judging its own past. Postwar judges created a legal system that suited them well and pleased the public too.

In the case of Nazi Germany, war included a systematic genocide, whose machinery took almost 6 million Jewish lives outside of the framework of the *Blitzkrieg* and the front. Rightfully, war crimes and crimes against humanity became the focus of criminal prosecution after the war. The "Trial of the Major War Criminals" at Nuremberg, conducted jointly by the Allies, and the subsequent Nuremberg Trials held by the Americans, set new and bold standards for how war crimes could be prosecuted. The introduction of Control Council Law #10 and its four key charges (Crimes against Peace, War Crimes, Conspiracy to commit War Crimes, and Crimes against Humanity) remains the most important development in international criminal law to this day. These charges continue to be used at the International Criminal Court and they represent the best attempt that we have to address the crimes not only of individuals but also of government systems. Control Council Law #10, however, did not sit well with the newly formed West German state, and the Ministry of Justice decided not to adopt it in their criminal code (unlike France or Israel, for example). The national humiliation brought on by the Nuremberg trials smacked of victor's justice, used *ex post facto* laws that did not exist at the time that the crimes were committed, and forbade the Germans from pointing out Allied atrocities such as the fire-bombing of German cities and the Soviet massacre of 10,000 Polish officers at Katyn. These factors left the newly formed German justice system—not to mention much of the German population—with a bad taste in its mouth. So trials of Nazis would be conducted according to the regular German penal code after 1949. The Adenauer government wanted to show that it could deal with its own past through its own laws, laws which were in existence throughout the Nazi period and which would demonstrate Nazi actions to have been criminal from beginning to end. The German Penal Code had been in existence since unification in 1871, and the Justice Ministry felt that it was perfectly adequate to deal with Nazi crimes using the regular murder charge.

The West Germans brought some 6500 former Nazis to trial between 1949 and the present, for their participation in the "Final Solution to the Jewish Question," as camp guards, members of killing squads, and "desk killers." State attorneys' offices had high hopes for these trials: at the Frankfurt Auschwitz Trial, Attorney General of Hesse, Fritz Bauer, intended to put the whole "Auschwitz Complex" on trial. The Berlin prosecutors at the planned RSHA trial—a massive legal proceeding against the high command of the Main Reich Security Office, responsible for the SS, police, camp system, and in general the Nazi genocide—hoped to condemn the bureaucrats in charge of the Holocaust, whose pen strokes and signatures sanctioned the murder of millions. And yet, the trials changed course. In the case of the Auschwitz Trial, the majority of defendants received mild sentences because they did not show individual initiative. The Berlin investigation of the RSHA fell apart after jurists introduced an amendment into the penal code which prevented prosecutors from trying suspects whose base motives—such as racial hatred—could not be proven. The real crime—the methodical murder of innocent men, women, and children in the gas chambers and by the killing commandos—receded into the background, while the full force of the law came down only on the "monsters" on the stand who had created their own instruments of torture, lived out their evil fantasies, and committed crimes so heinous that even the Nazis had investigated them for their excesses. The law and the courts neglected the system that had allowed these men and women to flourish, encouraged their racism and taught them to view Jews, gypsies, the handicapped, homosexuals, and "asocials" as parasites, leeches on the German body politic. The vast majority of participants in the Nazi racial program came out of the courtroom looking like reluctant, decent people who had gotten confusedly caught up in a madness over which they had no control. The Nazi system ultimately escaped censure when prosecutors had to use as evidence actual Nazi investigations of excessive brutality or corruption in order to get a conviction of perpetrating murder. In the end, only those who had gone above and beyond the call of duty in the Nazi period were convicted of serious crimes.

Upon first glance, this appears to have been an inevitability. After all, how successful could a nation be in bringing to trial and punishing all those who had participated in the Holocaust? This was a crime committed by hundreds of thousands of participants, for an endless number of motives: antisemitism, careerism, opportunism, financial gain, militarism, nationalism, and so on. Could it really be possible to find justice? The answer, usually, was, "we are doing the best we can." And yet a closer examination shows that they were not. The judiciary and the public apparently did not want to punish those who had been responsible, which would have meant ultimately pointing the finger at themselves. On the contrary: the judiciary concertedly attempted to *shape* and *distort* the public understanding of what Nazi crime was, and to normalize the crimes of the vast majority, including the elite: doctors, scientists, professors, civil servants, and most importantly, lawyers and judges. Laws were twisted and bent so that the most important factor in convicting a defendant of perpetrating murder (and leading to a sentence of life in prison) was proof of individual initiative and inner motivation, such as sadism, lust for killing, sexual drive for killing, or other "base motives." Despite the fact that the West German government insisted that the Nazi state itself was criminal, and that murder was never legal, only those who went cruelly beyond the call of duty were convicted of murder.

Wilhelm Boger provides a good example of the kind of Nazi perpetrator most harshly condemned by the West German judiciary. Boger was an SS officer and a member of the Political Department at Auschwitz from 1942 to 1945. The Political Department was responsible for registering and "interrogating" political prisoners who were suspected of being Communists, Socialists, or members of the resistance. Prisoners who were subjected to the horrors of the Political Department were usually Poles and Ukrainians, but also sometimes Jews. Wilhelm Boger was brought to trial in Frankfurt from 1963 to 1965, where he was accused of many hundreds of counts of murder. Witnesses described Boger as the "devil of Birkenau," universally feared for his sadistic ways, which included murdering children in front of their mothers. But Boger became most famous for his "Boger swing"—a primitive torture device on which prisoners had to swing by their hands and knees while Boger whipped them during what he called "intensified interrogations." Boger's swing led to the death, disfigurement, and castration of countless men, and was of great interest to the courtroom in Frankfurt and of course to the press covering the trial. What became most important for the judges was not that Boger was a volunteer SS guard murdering innocent people at Auschwitz (as was every single defendant in Frankfurt), but whether or not the swing had been authorized by Boger's bosses in Berlin.

Why did this matter, if the whole system was perverse and criminal? In order to demonstrate that Boger had individual initiative and sadistic motivation, the court showed that Boger's swing was *not* in fact approved by a former SS judge named Konrad Morgen—a postwar lawyer in Frankfurt—who had been part of an SS commission to investigate corruption and excessive brutality at Auschwitz in 1943. Morgen testified that Boger's swing was not authorized. The authorities in Berlin had in fact condemned Boger for not following the rules. It is clearly absurd that the SS was investigating "excessive brutality" at a place of mass murder, and in the vast majority of cases torture, cruelty, and sadism went unchecked by the Nazi authorities. However, the Gestapo used people like Boger as a warning to the rest of the lower ranked camp guards who thought of overstepping their authority. Morgen therefore punitively transferred Boger from Auschwitz to a smaller camp where he had less power. The Frankfurt courtroom, where prosecutors had initially hoped to show that anyone who worked at Auschwitz was a murderer, ended up legitimating Nazi standards of criminality. The press loved the Boger case because of the sensational and best-selling headlines his grotesque crimes produced. The public wagged its collective finger in horror at his crimes and breathed a collective sigh of relief (along with the rest of the defendants on the stand) that the system itself—and their role in it—was not going to be under the spotlight. Only a few troubled commentators noticed the absurdity of this. Martin Walser, then a left-wing novelist, journalist, literary critic and general muckraker in conservative postwar West Germany wrote at the end of the trial:

> One has to imagine the death-factory without the properties and peculiarities that the defendants are now accused of: without Kaduk's walking cane; without Boger's swing; without Broad's wish to shoot the most beautiful women first; . . . without Baretski's deadly "special blow" with the side of the hand . . . without Klehr's longing to play the doctor; without Bednarek's desire to beat people to death with chairs. . . . Auschwitz without these "colors" is the real Auschwitz. Selections on the platform, transport into the gas chambers, Cyclon B, crematoria. . . . Auschwitz was not hell, it was a German concentration camp.[3]

To Walser's dismay, Auschwitz remained "hell" in postwar Germany. The Auschwitz Trial, like many hundreds of other trials, did not judge the system which created these monsters and devils. This leads to the obvious question: why would representatives of the successful, peaceful, democratic West Germany want to obfuscate the crimes of the Nazi regime? In the US, the reasons for obfuscation are logical: the government still in charge could be implicated. But why the Federal Republic of Germany, which could have used the trials as an opportunity to condemn the whole Nazi period, as they explicitly argued they intended to do? According to Alfred McCoy, it is typical for post-authoritarian societies—such as those in Latin America—to be silent about the subject of torture. Why? Because Nazi functionaries remained in elite positions in the post-authoritarian state: in academia, medicine, media, bureaucracy and the judiciary. Eight million party members remained in Germany after the war, many in positions of authority that required a high level of education and training—invaluable skills and experience for a devastated country. The Americans recognized this too, and made it policy to grant amnesty to former Nazis. After all, it was a priority for the United States to quickly turn its former enemy into an ally against the new great threat, the Soviets. And so, one by one, most professions in West Germany were restocked with old Nazis. The judiciary is the most glaring example: approximately 80% of judges in 1960s West Germany were former Nazi judges. In fact, the man responsible for the amendment which led to the dissolution of the RSHA trial (and the chief author of criminal law reform in the 1960s), Edward Dreher, was also a prosecutor at the Innsbruck *Sondergericht*. This was one of hundreds of "special courts" created by the Nazis to persecute political opponents: innocent men and women were sentenced to death in brief, farcical trials and summarily executed. Dreher had reason to want to shape the law so that people like him—who could not be proven to be openly antisemitic or sadistic, but only "doing their jobs"—would not become the target of legal investigations conducted by young and critical prosecutors.

It is well known—and was the subject of harsh criticism and outrage by the New Left in Germany during the 1960s and 1970s—that much of postwar West German society was built on the foundations of old Nazi structures. Nowhere was this more obvious than in the Nazi trials. Judges did everything they could to draw attention away from their own crimes—crimes that the Allies, in Nuremberg, had put in the spotlight—and towards the actions of the "small men"—camp guards, local police, members of the *Einsatzgruppen*—who had acted brutally. The crimes of these underlings—all volunteer members of the racially, ideologically driven SS, after all—should of course not be ignored. But the West German judiciary failed miserably—and purposefully—in showing the systemic nature of Nazi crime.

What relevance does this have for current discussions of torture and war crimes? When we take the prison guards at Abu Ghraib, we are not dealing with soldiers within a genocidal dictatorship, volunteers working at death camps designed especially for extermination. But the soldiers who engaged in the tortuous crimes at that prison have been demonized and held up as monstrous animals whom we condemn for their brutality and inhumanity. The US military publicly prosecutes them as examples of exactly what it does *not* want among its ranks. They will be punished, justice will be served, and the good war can go on. And yet these soldiers did not appear out of nowhere; they are fighters in an ideological battle against "evil." They have learned to see their prisoners as potential threats to our "way of life" and have been instructed to destroy this enemy—but only after they have extracted intelligence from them. The soldiers interrogated, humiliated, and tortured their enemy, all smilingly in front of the camera. This photographing highlights two important things. First, these soldiers believed they would be cheered for their actions, for they otherwise would not have documented their "crimes"; second, as Mark Danner correctly points out, humiliating the enemy has always been shown to be an effective way to break them, and the US military was exploiting Arab sensitivities to public humiliation of a sexual nature. The cameras served that purpose perfectly, as did the "stress positions," "water-boarding," "hooding," and "light and sleep deprivation" that the International Committee of the Red Cross documented as "routine" and "systematic" in their 2004 report on the "coalition" prisons in Iraq.[4] The soldiers who carried out these "methods and techniques" to "soften up" detainees did not demonstrate *mens rea*, a covert, sadistic desire to do harm to others. These prison guards did what their military expected of them in order to "set the conditions for successful exploitation of the internees."[5] Mark Danner calls them "amateur stooges of 'the process.'" They were crude and caught, perhaps *not* because they had acted out of order, but more likely because the exigencies of this supposedly long war had strapped the military to the maximum and put soldiers with "little or no training" into the position of interrogators.[6] But their trials sent a completely different message: the army and society would not tolerate such horrors, especially when they became public. In fact, the actions of the prison guards at Abu Ghraib were tolerated and ordered. But the trials of Lynndie England and her colleagues did nothing to address the systemic problems which created the atmosphere at Abu Ghraib.

There is a lesson to be learned here about the tendency, in democratic societies, to condemn only the most extreme perpetrators of violence and torture and to turn a blind eye to the system that created them. Why do we accept the message that the US government is horrified by these actions, when we have proof that they were deeply involved? Perhaps the problem lies with our inability to accept our own responsibility for bringing into office people capable of ordering such barbarities. In that sense, postwar democratic West Germany is no different from the United States today, except that the West German judiciary was implicated in crimes that took place twenty years beforehand, not just twenty weeks beforehand. We desperately want to believe that the laws of our country are being defined, applied, and upheld in a humane and moral way—after all, the laws of a democratic society are supposed to and generally do reflect the will of the people—and we show this through our tacit acceptance of the decisions and pronouncements of our lawmakers. But we need to recognize that when we place such unquestioned trust in the legal system, in the motives of our governments, we allow them to define for us what is "normal" and "abnormal" and a vacuum is created in which the public loses its ability to see that justice is not served. Even worse, we accept the message that the "enemy" is threatening our "way of life." We therefore stage trials that lend us an air of morality while shielding us from the need for systemic change, simply because we are frightened that it might drive oil prices even higher and hence disrupt our comfortable lives.

Perhaps the scandalous use of torture *does* ultimately delegitimize government; scholarly probing *does* lead to wider public criticism, no matter how much a government and its courts feign abhorrence of this crime. In 1968, for example, students in West Germany mounted increasing opposition to their parents' conservatism and obfuscations, insisting that society's institutions be dismantled and built up anew. The student movement and the New Left succeeded in overturning deeply conservative university policy by insisting that old Nazi professors be removed, and that German history from 1933 to 1945 finally be taught in the classroom. And yet, the refusal of authorities in the "system" to own up to their crimes led to a distinctly unhealthy relationship to the crimes of Nazism. The next generation was left with what Hans Ulrich Gumbrecht has so sagely recognized as a kind of "free-floating guilt" that was never dealt with in the courtrooms of postwar West Germany. The young adopted this guilt as their own, berated their parents for their refusal to acknowledge responsibility, and displayed what Gumbrecht calls "moral rigidity"—finger pointing, arrogant, righteous indignation, that was bound to lead to a backlash, as it did with opponents of the New Left who argued that supporting Communist regimes in Eastern Europe was as morally repugnant as what their parents had done.[7] Could it be that we are seeing the same thing in the US today? There is an ever growing suspicion of US governmental policy in its "detention centres" and with its "enhanced interrogation methods." Many Americans now view the scandalous treatment of "enemy combatants" in Afghanistan and Guantánamo, and prisoners of war in Abu Ghraib, critically, despite the protestations of George Bush, Donald Rumsfeld and others ultimately responsible. The finger pointing has begun. But the uneasiness that torture brings out in all of us could be precisely what allows many Americans who supported the idea of war—those who are now not so sure—to erase from their memories their own gullibility, culpability, and responsibility for the actions of their government.[8] The solution is elusive; it requires *immediate* recognition of guilt, responsibility, complicity, and commitment to change not only the effects of atrocious policies but the causes. The decision to support war will always, ultimately, be a decision to support war crimes. It makes no sense to imagine that torture is only the provenance of a few "bad apples"—it is a fundamental element of war in which "we" attempt to understand, undermine, and eradicate "them." To relegate torture to the margins, to the exceptional, and to the crime of a few sadists is to willfully ignore the nature of war. What a depressing development it is that the Americans, so determined and so successful in putting the masterminds of aggressive war and war crimes on trial at Nuremberg, now refuse to be held to the same legal standards. Robert Jackson, chief prosecutor at the first Nuremberg trial, proudly declared in his opening statement that subjecting the architects of crimes against peace to the rule of law was "one of the most significant tributes that Power ever has paid to Reason." Where is reason now?

NOTES

1. See Mark Danner, *Torture and Truth: America, Abu Ghraib, and the War on Terror* (New York: New York Review of Books, 2004); this book contains hundreds of pages of classified documents recording discussions between military and governmental authorities about how best to proceed with interrogations at Guantánamo and Abu Ghraib. See also Alfred McCoy, *A Question of Torture: CIA Interrogation from the Cold War to the War on Terror* (New York: Henry Holt and Co., 2006).

2. The push for the establishment of an international court to deal with crimes that domestic courts refused to prosecute came only during the 1990s, after the genocides in the former Yugoslavia and Rwanda. Before this, only a handful of jurists and politicians actively pursued the creation of such a court—including such advocates as Benjamin Ferencz, former prosecutor at the subsequent Nuremberg trial of the *Einsatzgruppen*.

3. Martin Walser, "Unser Auschwitz," in *Heimatkunde: Aufsätze und Reden* (Frankfurt-am-Main: Suhrkamp Verlag, 1968), 12, 11.

4. "Report of the International Committee of the Red Cross (ICRC) on the Treatment by the Coalition Forces of Prisoners of War and Other Protected Persons by the Geneva Convention in Iraq during Arrest, Internment and Interrogation," February 2004, in Danner, *Torture and Truth*, 251–275. It is important to note that the prisoners at Abu Ghraib were *not* categorized as "enemy combatants" and therefore incontrovertibly protected by the Geneva Convention. At the time of writing, the question of protection for enemy combatants is under fierce debate between President Bush and the Senate.

5. Danner, *Torture and Truth*, 8.

6. Danner, *Torture and Truth*, 8–9.

7. Hans Ulrich Gumbrecht, "On the Decent Uses of History," in *History and Theory*, vol. 40, no.1 (February 2001), 125–127.

8. See McCoy, *A Question of Torture*, 6–7.

2

Torture in the Algerian War

Tzvetan Todorov
(Translated by Arthur Denner)

IN MARCH 2002, France marked the fortieth anniversary of the Evian Accords, the agreement that ended the war in Algeria. Numerous popular articles and books about the war came out that year, and a number of French television documentaries carried the war into the country's living rooms. Interest in this episode in their history had already begun to awaken among the French several years before, after decades of relative quiescence. In France, traumatic events seem to require about a third of a century to work their way up into the national collective consciousness. A case in point: the Second World War did not become a major topic of analysis and representation in France until after 1975. It is as if our war veterans cannot speak freely and examine their consciences until they have gone into retirement and suddenly find themselves with enough time on their hands to have to look their grown children in the eye. Does this mean that today's debates on the Algerian War will help France get over its long and lingering obsession with World War II? One would hope so, but it's still too early to tell.

Among the topics that came up during the commemorations, one in particular—the French army's use of torture—took center stage. Some of the interest in the subject may be purely voyeuristic, but whatever the reasons for all the recent attention, it affords us the opportunity to look more closely at this ubiquitous and deplorable practice and perhaps come to a better understanding of it. One of those television documentaries from 2002, Patrick Rotman's *The Intimate Enemy* (*L'ennemi intime*), will guide us in our reflections on this painful subject. Composed of interviews with French soldiers who fought in that war, it was broadcast over three successive evenings on French public television. A book by the same title came out at the same time as a companion edition to the program (Seuil, 2002).

Rotman's film asks many questions, but one question it does not ask is whether torture took place. We know that it did. During the war and afterwards, while the French civil and military authorities were denying the practice, the torture victims—both Algerian and French—spoke publicly about the abuses they suffered. More recently, high-ranking military officers like army generals Jacques Massu and Paul Aussaresses (*The Battle of the Casbah: Terrorism and Counter-Terrorism in Algeria, 1955–1957*; Enigma, 2004) have confirmed the victims' irrefutable testimony. Academic researchers such as Ralphaëlle Branche in *La torture et l'armée pendant la guerre d'Algérie—1954–62* have established the wide extent of the use of torture. The object of Rotman's questions through the course of the interviews, then, is not the fact of the matter but rather the cause. What could allow this officially dismissed and universally deplored practice to take place on such a massive scale? How could so many people who had lived the lives of quiet French citizens before the Algerian war—and later returned to those lives when the war was over—how could such people so easily and so willingly consent to become torturers? The great merit of Rotman's project is that its objective is not to judge the actors but rather to understand their actions, to answer the question: what made it possible for them to do what they did?

The standard answer to this question, formulated many years ago by military leaders who decided that they would no longer try to conceal what had been done, is that torture was the only way to win the war. The Algerian war was not a traditional war, they explained; the enemy did not engage them on a mutually recognized battlefield that both sides had agreed to beforehand. This was a civil war and the army did not know who its enemy was. The French were being ambushed and violently attacked, but by whom? And who was giving aid and comfort to these invisible adversaries? The army needed to know, and for this they needed information; if no one was offering it voluntarily or for a price, then it had to be coerced—through torture, if it came down to that.

Those who try to justify torture in this way have a favorite example that they like to bring to their argument: What do you do, they ask, if you know of an impending attack and it is up to you to prevent it? Colonel Roger Trinquier (in a different film, *Une civilisation de la torture*) expounds on this example at great length. Imagine, he says, that you have just arrested a bomber who has planted five time bombs and you find out that they have been set to go off in three hours. Basically, you have a choice: you can be polite and ask the bomber nicely to tell you where he put the bombs, but if you do that, you may wind up with forty dead and two hundred wounded people on your hands; or you can torture him to find out where the bombs are so that you can deactivate them. "If it's up to me, I'm going to interrogate him until he tells me what I want to know."

There are two problems with this argument. The first is that torture is almost never used in such circumstances; bombers are rarely caught before their bombs go off. The main use of torture is to identify and eliminate the enemy; it is far more commonly used for that purpose than to prevent an imminent attack (although admittedly, one can make a more compelling case, at least rhetorically, by citing the latter goal). The second problem with the argument that Trinquier and so many others have made concerns the principle itself that torture was "the only way to win the war." France lost that war; torture was *not* the way to win it. Torture, summary executions, and other acts of violence by the military had the effect of turning the entire Algerian population into sworn enemies of France virtually overnight. For every man struck down, ten rose up to take his place. The rational argument for using torture simply does not hold, and so once again we have to ask why French soldiers were so willing to use it? How did they manage to anesthetize not their faculties of reason (which is not difficult at all) but their conscience?

Let us first lay out a set of circumstances that, if they do not shed light on the motivations of a person who becomes a torturer, will at least help us grasp what makes it easier for him to put aside the inhibitions that, under different circumstances, would not allow him to become one; what we are looking for, in other words, is not the driving forces but the favorable conditions, as it were. So, to begin with, who were these people who committed acts of torture? Many were young draftees with no political experience or knowledge of history, boys from the provinces who shipped out to Algeria directly from their native town or village. They believed, for they had been told, that this land where they were being sent was French soil and that the rebels were a tiny, criminal minority that had to be eliminated, the sooner the better. Once they arrived, the soldiers were cut off from the outside world: the mail was slow and letters were censored; the local French press, in the meantime, was calling for harsher and harsher measures. Armies are rigid hierarchies in which disobedience is immediately punished; one needs a strong personality and firm convictions to be able to refuse an order and risk harassment or punishment. But an even more important factor than pressure from above is peer pressure: if everyone else in my platoon is willing to participate, how can I not? By refusing to go along with the others, I expose myself to ridicule, put my virility into question, and show myself to be soft and weak.

As for the people I'm fighting, it is easy to paint them as less than human; in this way, I can legitimize my inhumane treatment of them. They live in destitution and deprivation; simple tasks and techniques, things that any Frenchman can do with his eyes closed, escape them; apparently, they can't even speak French. How can someone identify with such people? As General Bollardière explained, "We didn't refer to the Algerians as human beings. We called them rats. Or *bougnouls*.[1] And it's easy to torture a *bougnoul*, because you figure he's not a human being" (in a 1984 film, *The Algerian War*). At the same time, your enemies are also particularly cruel, and thus deserving of whatever cruelty they encounter at your hands. One hears this argument again and again in accounts of French war veterans: our enemy's heinous acts cry out for vengeance. Those who use this argument don't really care that it was the French "ultras," not the Algerian rebels, who struck first; once the cycle of attack and counter-attack has been set into motion, there's no reason to stop, it seems. They slaughtered some of ours, why shouldn't we slaughter some of theirs? "The rebels were acting like savages; why couldn't we?" (102). They have no pity; neither will we. That is how the escalation begins: they kill one of ours, we kill ten of theirs. And for some career soldiers, Algeria was an opportunity to avenge their defeat in Indochina in 1953.

One of the men Rotman interviews calls our attention to another feature of the process of transformation experienced by many who were sent to fight in Algeria: to shield themselves against their own feelings, those who perform acts of torture and those who stand by watching as those acts are carried out recast the world around them as fiction, begin to treat it as spectacle. "I was a spectator . . . I didn't feel that I was actually there. . . . It felt to me as though I were watching a film. Everything was more or less unreal. It was a game for us." Why this transmutation of reality into fiction? Because the reality was unbearable. "You change the situation into something acceptable" (57–59). The border between the real and the virtual can be crossed from either direction: we can make living beings out of literary characters and live with them as though they were people we knew; but it is also within our capacity to treat acts that we have actually committed as though they were fictions and feel as though we are standing apart from what we do, that we are watching "from the outside" as a story unfolds in which we ourselves play no part.

But if we can speak of conditions "favorable" to one's becoming a torturer, are there not perhaps also systematically *unfavorable* conditions, circumstances that ensure a rejection of these practices? We like to think, optimistically, that such conditions exist, but in fact there are no such guarantees: culture, education and knowledge, none of these provides any protection at all. Nor does religion: most of the French recruits who fought in Algeria had a religious upbringing, yet this did not stop them from torturing and killing; the French army, moreover, had chaplains who counseled the use of "efficient, but not sadistic, interrogation techniques" (cited in Massu, *La vraie bataille d'Alger*, Plon 1971).

Nor is the memory of having been the victim of torture enough to prevent a person from taking part in torture, though it may cause second thoughts. Cases of victims turned into torturers or silent accomplices to torture are not uncommon: a good number of French officers came out of the ranks of the Resistance or had fought in the Free French Forces against the Nazis. Some of these men had suffered mistreatment by enemy hands, yet their experiences did not stop them from torturing or carrying out summary executions. Massu, the paratrooper general, Bigeard, the colonel under whom he served, and Aussaresses, chief of a torture unit, were all veterans of the fight against fascism, former Free French combatants. Robert Lacoste, France's governor general (*ministre résident*) in Algeria, supreme representative of political authority and thus the person most responsible for the use of torture (along with Prime Minister Guy Mollet), was a leader in the resistance. Captain Thomas, another of the men interviewed by Rotman, was a *Maquisard* and had fought with the Communist-backed FTP (Francs-Tireurs et Partisans) in central France; he remained in the army after the Liberation and fought in Indochina. In Algeria he performed acts of torture and participated in summary executions. One day, he was told to choose ten hostages to be executed by firing squad in retribution for an enemy attack and to deter such attacks in the future. He was devastated but he did what he was asked to do. Hofman, an enlisted man interviewed by Rotman, had been caught in a Nazi roundup as a child and sent to the Drancy transit camp, the last stop for French deportees on their way to Auschwitz. Having managed to escape the "Final Solution," he found himself in Algeria where he watched men being tortured. "How could I, with what I had personally lived through, not have acted in Algeria? That's the big question I ask myself" (195).

The similarity of the two situations, with the roles reversed, was not lost on the soldiers. One of them said, "If one day there's another Nuremberg trial, we'll all be convicted: every day there was another Oradour, and this time we were committing them."[2] An officer added, "Next to us, the Germans were schoolboys" (155). Sergeant Samson, the son of a Resistance fighter, mused: "The FLN guys, *they* were the Resistance" (220). These similarities, while acknowledged, did not prevent the men from doing their "job." There was another similarity, it is true, with which they shielded themselves from self-reproach (one can always find an excuse): in 1957, as in 1940, they were defending the country, working for the glory of France.

But it is not enough to say that the favorable conditions all came together, that the brakes that should have worked somehow malfunctioned; there had to be deeper and, dare we say, more positive reasons that allowed the torturer to derive satisfaction from his actions, that allowed him to ignore both the illogic of his arguments and the lessons of his own past. Here we must begin with the observation that in any human collectivity, there is a convinced, resolute minority who act, and a passive, indecisive majority who prefer to follow, and that the minority almost always prevails. Those who passionately despise and hate, say, "the Arabs," who openly enjoy the suffering of others, are few in number, yet they set the tone for everyone. The fanatics and the sadists are the ones who act, while the others, feeling either feeble indignation or guilty satisfaction, stand aside and let them do what they want. But why this *satisfaction*, which, even forty years after the fact, is difficult for people to admit to? Where does it come from?

One of Rotman's interviewees tries to get to the bottom of the feelings he had at the time. He remembers the barracks where the soldiers were billeted, the walls plastered with pornographic photos. He had witnessed a scene of unbearable brutality: after hours of torturing a man who refused to talk, the soldiers brought in his twelve-year-old daughter and forced her to torture her father with electric shocks. The former soldier continues: "What I felt was a kind of fascination. . . . You can feel a kind of jubilation in watching scenes that are so extreme. Today, I associate that feeling with the porno pictures on the walls over our bunks that we used to look at, and I say to myself, there's an obvious connection—in both cases, you have a body that's been instrumentalized . . . you're taking a body and you're doing what you want to it" (231).

Reducing another person to a state of complete powerlessness gives you the feeling of being supremely powerful, a feeling that torture provides better than murder does, because murder doesn't last: a dead person is an inert object that can no longer offer you that feeling of jubilation that comes from having completely triumphed over the will of another human being who continues to exist and, in his degradation, continues to reaffirm your triumph. Raping a woman while you force her husband, parents, or children to watch, torturing a child while you make the parents look on produces a feeling of omnipotence, of absolute sovereignty attained. During peacetime, such acts are considered criminal and those who commit them are punished by the law; in wartime, they are tolerated, even encouraged.

Does this mean that deep down, human beings are sadists and that it is only social convention that prevents us (most of the time) from indulging our instincts? Some former soldiers think so, and they fall back on the image of an animal lurking within each of us, ready at the first opportunity to rip through the thin veneer of civilization. "War brings out a human being's most primitive instincts," says one of them (234). "Deep within the human being is a kind of animal, a monstrous beast restrained by education and the environment," observes another. "I know that now man's animal is very present," concludes a third (239). Even Rotman, in the preface to his book, defines his project in similar terms: "To explore the vertiginous regions where the beast lurks, to search that dark zone that resists humanity" (8).

But why do we blame the animals? Strictly speaking, the behaviors we are talking about, if one stops and thinks for even an instant, are really not animal-like at all; on the contrary, they seem to offer a negative definition of the specifically human. What animal would dream up the idea of torturing children in front of their father in order to revel in his powerlessness? Acts of this sort do not seem particularly primitive either: there's nothing we know about the cavemen that would suggest the slightest knowledge on their part of these refinements of torture. The French army used torture far more than the Algerian fighters did, who confined themselves to massacring their enemies; should one conclude that the French were more primitive, or more civilized?

And in peacetime, is it really only our fear of the policeman that stops people (or, should I say, that stops males) from using torture and rape to satisfy their desires? That feeling of existence, which the torturer draws from the humiliation of his victim, can be obtained by other, better means, in the myriad daily interactions that form the web of our social lives. And what if war were not merely the circumstance that favored the liberation of "our most primitive instincts" but the reason that those drives, which in fact are not basic or inherent at all, erupted in the first place? When the other is no longer capable of giving us the recognition we desire, he must be killed or forced to submit. One of Rotman's war veterans speaks of the difficult time he had readjusting to his new life when he returned from Algeria. "Over there, I had the right to kill; here, I couldn't even steal a motorbike. I spent time in jail and, if not for Algeria, I wouldn't have" (251). War doesn't expose what had existed previously, in some hidden state; it creates something new. We don't need to hypothesize a "torture instinct" (or "death instinct") in order to understand the desire to torture, rape, and humiliate; it has the same source as our other desires but takes this violent form when the other paths to social recognition are blocked—hence in war.

Paul Teitgen, one of the rare high-ranking French government officials in those days who stood up against the use of torture, sees the act of torture as resulting from a breakdown in social interaction, from self-doubt fostered by not being recognized by others; he speaks (in the film *Une civilisation de la torture*) of "the hatred that people have for themselves, which they then inflict on those whom they torture."

We want to think that people who embody evil are fundamentally different from ourselves, but anyone who has seen evil up close knows the futility of such hopes. "All of us have the potential for evil," Teitgen says. "Put anyone in this sort of situation, and he can do the same thing," another witness believes (228). "We all have this fragility within us, this attraction to evil," observes another (232). Or as Rotman himself concludes, "Our intimate enemy is the one within us" (8). Within each of us? Paul Teitgen, secretary general of the police for the Algiers Prefecture, having ascertained that torture had been used on "suspects," resigned his position. He recognized on their bodies "the deep marks of abuse and torture that I myself was subjected to fourteen years ago in the basements of Nancy at the hands of the Gestapo" (137). General Bollardière, who (like Massu and Aussaresses) had fought the Germans throughout the war, publicly denounced the "appalling danger" to the nation that the generalized practice of torture represented; he served sixty days in a military prison for having heeded the voice of his conscience rather than the reason of the state. People like Teitgen and Bollardière were few and far between, but they did exist.

What should we do today, forty years later, as more and more former torturers are beginning to tell their stories? One thing we should not do is assume the mantle of moral superiority that only hindsight can provide and demand criminal convictions for the former torturers. Yet, this is precisely what happened to Aussaresses, who was brought to trial and convicted of "justifying war crimes" for having made a case in his memoirs for his use of torture. It was a dubious victory indeed for the three human rights groups that had pressed charges. Aussaresses was punished not for having tortured people; the statute of limitations on those crimes had run out, and in any case, he had acted under the orders of the French government, which ought to have been but never was held to account for these orders. What Aussaresses was punished for is having spoken about his actions publicly—and, of all the things he did, that was probably the only action for which he deserves any credit. Wouldn't the moral health of the French nation be better served by a pursuit of truth and an open, if unrepentant, confrontation with a shameful past, than by going after criminal convictions: a former torturer is unlikely to want to pursue the truth if he is likely to be imprisoned or fined for doing so. Freedom of expression is a necessary precondition of the quest for the truth, especially when that truth is liable to be a bitter one.

NOTES

1. A racist term, used to refer to Blacks, North Africans, or Arabs.
2. The 2nd Panzer division of the Waffen SS destroyed the town of Oradour-sur-Glane in 1944, killing 642 of its inhabitants.

3

There Are No Tortures in Gaza

Adi Ophir

WHEN SUFFERING IS INTOLERABLE and yet interminable, there comes torture. When pain is accumulating and one's body and soul cry "enough," and the thing—the torturing thing—goes on, there is torture. The thing colonizes one's space of experience, steals one's time, grabs one's expectations, and contracts one's span of emotions to a single yearning—a yearning for the thing to go away. But it stays. It grows out of proportion, detached from that to which it belongs—a body, an instrument, memories, its place in one's home or one's heart—and assumes an overwhelming presence, which becomes one with the presence of suffering itself and from which one cannot disengage.

The torturing thing may be anything. It requires no intention to torture, no human presence, not even an invisible hand. It may be the neighbor's dog that barks all night and drives you mad or a dripping faucet in the kitchen when you are too tired and weak to get up and shut it off. But even then, when torture is completely anonymous, the torturing thing is always too close. It is its closeness that is intolerable, its immediate presence, which soon becomes all too familiar. There is hardly any situation of torture without the propinquity of something very familiar, without the intimacy of a room, a neighbor, a friend, or a lover. Palestinian prisoners and detainees whose reports about their tortures have been collected diligently by various human rights organizations always know the names or nicknames (it does not really matter) of their torturers. They often know a lot more about them: the smell of their body or breath, the feeling of a sweating hand on one's skin, the way a face changes expressions from irony to rage or from concern to indifference. The torturers, obviously, know much more about their victims, and what they know they often put to use to manipulate their victims, intimidate, scare, and humiliate them, improve the method of their torture, extend its duration, and expand its impact. They know, and they care for details. Torture is not only a moment of proximity to the other but a form of care for the other.

The torturer comes very close, scraping or penetrating the surface of the victim's body, peering through the halls of his or her soul. Sometimes he is all over, sometimes he is inside, in-forming and de-forming, and even when he leaves, something of him refuses to go away. His is a very

27

special way of being with an other, which has its own conditions. Today, torture usually takes place behind closed doors, and even when it occurs in the open, in well-orchestrated ceremonial events or in unexpected bursts of violence, a kind of hallowed space separates the torturer(s) and their victim(s) from the spectators. Like games and art, the festival and the ritual, contemplation or prayer, the display of torture interrupts routine, everyday activities. Because it is violent it risks a stable economy of violence and threatens the political order that sustains it. Hence the site of torture must be secluded, and this seclusion should endure long enough. It usually takes time to torture; one blow is not enough. It is usually a matter of the lingering effects and their accumulation and of keeping the tortured from trying to take distance and disengage from the source of suffering.

Being together in a closed space over a relatively long period of time, the torturer and the victim become emotionally engaged with each other, although never in a symmetrical manner. A posture of indifference may be a means of torture, but the one who is really indifferent, oblivious to the situation of her victim or to his or her very existence, performs the role of torturer poorly. Torture requires close attention to the way a victim sits and stands, breathes and shouts, is looking at and listening to. The torturer must be present at the side of his victim, be next to and with him, at least for a while, in a relation of intimacy in which the one is falling apart while the other indulges in pleasure or is dutifully doing his job, bravely overcoming his shame and disgust.

The kinds of torture, types of motivation and justification for torture, conditions that make them possible, and effects they have on victims and victimizers vary and are relative to specific historical, political, and cultural circumstances. But across all of these differences, torture remains a form of care for another, a special concern for and interest in the victim's body and soul. At stake is first of all the life, even a certain well-being of the victim. Torture is not a burst of formless violence and it cannot take place if the victim dies too early; no justice, pleasure, or information would be gained or extracted. Hence, the exercise of violence must be well controlled and artfully limited (but not too constrained) in order to endure and to torture by its very endurance. The strictures of the law, disciplinary regulations, and physicians' instructions may all play a role in the art of torture by setting limits and forcing the imaginative torturer to play within them without stopping or losing the game.

The victim should not die too early. Once this is assured, concern for and interest in the tortured other go elsewhere. There is something else about him or her that matters, something about what he feels, knows, thinks, cares for, something about her identity and deeds, his sins or intentions, or simply something about her singular appearance. This something could not simply be taken away, grabbed or extracted from the other, either because he does not want to give it away or because the torturer takes all his pleasure or sense of justice from not immediately seizing it. Without a strong interest in and sometimes an attachment to this thing about the other, torture would soon end up in killing, forsaking, or indifference, putting an end to the other or to the special relation to the other. The victim of torture would then become just another person to be executed, expelled or excused, or simply sent back to his place among the rank and file. Torture is personal. It presupposes the recognition of the other as a singular individual; it needs the face of the other, her presence of mind, not only her body.

But not always, of course, not always. In front of some of the checkpoints the Israeli army planted throughout the West Bank in the Occupied Palestinian Territories, there are open waiting areas encircled by high fences. Those who operate the checkpoints often think of them as a kind of border control. One must pass through a gate with a rolling bar and then through the explosives detectors; then one must present one's documents to an Israeli soldier who sits behind a wall in a large hall and observes the passenger through a small screened opening from the height of his elevated seat. Only one person can cross the rolling bar at a time. Armed soldiers surround the closed waiting area and take positions within the hall where the check takes place.

Many women and elderly people are crowded in the waiting area—young men hardly try to pass for they rarely have permits—along with many babies and young children. Many people carry heavy sacks with their belongings. Passing through the gate is slow and interrupted quite often. There are times of the day and days of the year when the waiting area becomes very crowded. Those who enter it cannot go back, but neither can they move forward. In fact there are times they cannot move at all, and sometimes they can hardly breathe. The people who are caught inside try to help each other, up to a point, but there is not much they can do. They are squeezed, they are pushed, they are hurt by the fence or by objects other people carry. Their hearts go out to their screaming or crying children whom they cannot help and whom they often cannot carry any longer. They are thirsty and angry, humiliated and desperate. Every once in a while someone almost suffocates or faints. Time moves very slowly, and there is nothing they can do to release themselves from their cage. Every part of their body cries "stop it," and yet they hardly cry or shout or speak at all, not so much for fear of the soldiers as for respect for their suffering fellows. Their forced passivity and speechlessness only add to their agony. For many, suffering becomes so intense that they cannot take it any longer. It is absolutely intolerable, and yet it goes on. This is precisely the moment that suffering turns into torture.

The checkpoints are not meant to torture. No one gains anything—neither pleasure, nor justice, nor information—from the torturous process. When people are tortured at the checkpoints, it is not because someone who cares for someone in particular intended this to happen but because no one cares for anyone at all. The waiting area lacks the moment of recognition, the intimacy, and the particular interest in the victims that usually characterize torture. The soldiers and security agents that run the facility are quite indifferent to those who wait outside, at least as they remain within the closed area and pose no threat; they care only for those who have passed the rolling bar and then mainly for their papers and identity. The passengers' suspicious intentions or the hidden weapons and explosives they might carry become objects of concern only after the passengers have crossed the bar. While waiting in the closed space, people are completely ignored. They may be anyone, they may be happy or miserable, they may blow themselves up. No one really cares. But this is precisely the time and the site in which torture takes place.

This type of unintended torture happens occasionally in tightly controlled and closed spaces where people are forced to remain despite deteriorating conditions. Since the Second Intifada, and especially since the consolidation of the new regime of movement imposed on Palestinians in the Occupied Territories as part of Israel's response to the Intifada, scenes like this happen quite regularly. The gates in the fence that encircle Gaza are often closed completely. The West Bank was sliced into "cells" separated from each other, and permits of all kinds are required to move even between the cells, let alone to enter or leave the West Bank. Permits are given only to those who are not declared "prevented for security reasons" and who have permission to go to the few offices where permits are requested and distributed. Closed spaces, long, idle hours of waiting that disrupt everyday movement, crowded waiting zones, indifference of the soldiers at the checkpoints—these have all become part of the system. But this is not true for torture. Torture is an unintended consequence of the new regime of movement, like the agony of the sick and wounded forced to wait for hours or the deaths of newborns who die because their mothers were forced to wait or were even turned back while already in labor.

Complaints about the cruelty of the checkpoints mounted; local and international organizations, journalists, and diplomats filed numerous reports. The reports were mostly formulated in terms of human rights violations and the lack of proper means to deal with "humanitarian cases." Since Palestinians' movements within their territory—the daily walk to school, the drive to work or to visit friends—have all become dependent on the situation at the checkpoints and could be suspended at any moment, the right to move has become a humanitarian issue and the "humanitarianization" of one's situation has become the main reason for granting permits and a common strategy to get them. Since such requests have often been refused, legal appeals have been filed and accumulated.

The judicial regulation of the new regime of movement is no less part of the system than the security devices it employs. Since its inception, the Israeli regime of occupation has assumed the appearance of legality. Martial law and military decrees have been subject to judicial examination and often challenged in the Israeli Supreme Court of Appeals. In most of the cases, the decrees have been upheld and the appeals rejected. The very existence of a legal procedure, however, and the very few cases in which the court decided in favor of the Palestinian plaintiffs sufficed to create the needed façade of legality and created an arena for resistance to the Occupation shared by Palestinians and Israelis alike. Instead of alleviating the conditions of people living under occupation, the rights discourse has become part of the occupation structure. Several Supreme Court rulings on freedom of movement and the right of access to school and work insisted on "proportionality"—the need to balance security concerns and humanitarian needs. The occupier and the occupied are thus abstracted from the real context of their power relation and put "on a purportedly equal plane" in a way that enables the court to use the discourse of human rights to justify limiting Palestinians' rights "beyond the scope of a strict interpretation of International Humanitarian Law."[1]

In the specific context of torture, public pressure brought about a special committee of inquiry that looked at practices of torture used by the Israeli Security Service. This committee called for legalization of a special kind of "moderate physical pressure," which would not be considered as torture but would be tough enough on the detainees to yield the necessary information. After a long debate, the law was changed accordingly. New reports on torture have since been filed, but now the question is not whether torture has taken place but rather whether the physical pressure exercised on the detainees falls within the strictures of the new law. The law itself has established a gray area in which certain forms of torture have become barely distinguishable from the permissible use of force. But this was not the case with torture at the checkpoints.

This kind of torture had nothing to do with investigations of suspects in times of emergency. It had to be eliminated, for legality does matter.

The army has taken notice of the accumulating complaints and instead of asking for the legalization of a new questionable method, as it often does, has started changing the method. First it appointed "humanitarian officers" in charge of preventing unnecessary suffering at the checkpoints and gave crash courses in humanitarianism and human rights to some of the soldiers serving there. Then it devised new facilities for the main checkpoints. One of the first things to be arranged was a special "humanitarian queue" for the "humanitarian cases." But this did not solve the problem of waiting, the possibility of torture in the closed waiting zone. It was necessary to rationalize the checking mechanism for other reasons as well. It was not efficient, it caused too much friction, and it was bad public relations for Israel. A whole new set of border control facilities was therefore devised and constructed at the principal crossing areas on the main blocked roads. A better order has been established, the means of control and identification have been improved, waiting time has been somewhat shortened, and the density of the crowds has been reduced. Torture by means of herding a multitude of human beings into hermetically closed spaces has become rare indeed. In fact, torture has become almost impossible by virtue of the fact that, in the new facilities, nothing—and nobody—can get too close to a waiting person. Contact between the Palestinians asking to pass and the security personnel has been reduced to zero; the waiting zones and the halls are large enough, perhaps too large. In the new terminals, most of the soldiers now take positions on a second floor and are mostly invisible to the passengers. The soldier who actually checks the papers is seated too high and too far away to be clearly visible, and most of the communication is done by means of a set of loudspeakers through which orders and names are shouted, usually in Hebrew and often in a distorted and hardly decipherable voice.

With the "humanitarianization" of the terminals, torture in the waiting areas has decreased dramatically. At the same time, however, the fragmentation of space and the apartheid-like regime of movement that shatter the life-world of the Palestinians have been kept intact; in fact, fragmentation has advanced and the movement regime has been all the more consolidated. The regime is now capable of more qualified distinctions and differentiations, on the one hand, and of more devastating forms of closure and blockade, on the other hand. The construction of the "Separation Wall" and the improvement of the checkpoint system in the West Bank and the complete closure of the Gaza strip after "the disengagement" (the withdrawal of Israeli troops in August 2005 and the evacuation and destruction of the Israeli settlements there) are two different means that achieve similar results in different settings and conditions of domination: reduction of direct contact and other forms of "friction" between Israelis and Palestinians and abandonment of the Palestinian population left within its gated spaces. Movement of people and goods within these spaces remains tightly controlled, but now it is controlled at a distance.

The new system of rule includes specific "humanitarian arrangements," of course, which let the international community (NGOs, UN agencies, governmental agencies of donor countries) take most of the burden of caring for the Palestinians from the Israeli government and make sure that certain minimal basic provisions of food and medicine will be supplied. Dramatic proof of the efficiency of this arrangement came about in the first weeks after Hamas took hold of the Gaza Strip in June 2007, after a clear victory over Fatah forces. The gates to Gaza were completely closed, and the Hamas government, boycotted by almost every state on the globe, had to negotiate through mediators with the Red Cross and the UN Agency for Palestinian Refugees (UNRWA) for continued provision of basic food and medication through the gates. Israel cooperated willingly, showing the world that it would always stop short of creating a humanitarian catastrophe in the Occupied Territories while maintaining "catastrophization" as an efficient means of governance. Once again it has been demonstrated that the Occupied Territories are "on the verge of humanitarian catastrophe," as humanitarian experts often warn, but that this threshold is not going to be crossed. Boycotted Hamas has consolidated its grip in Gaza, and there is still no famine in the Strip, no epidemics, no mass killings; only an ever-growing shortage of everything except, apparently, explosives. And since armed resistance has not ended, new waves of "targeted killings" resume occasionally. In July 2007 about twenty Palestinians were killed. Most of them belonged to one of the Islamist militias; the low level of "collateral damage" may have to do with the fact that no air strikes were used and the forces were ground forces.

There is something that resembles torture in this process of deterioration, for the conditions of a chronic disaster and the infliction of suffering and losses must be constantly monitored and the ruling apparatus must be careful not to cross the imaginary line of a full-fledged catastrophe. But this resemblance is superficial. The great "merit" of the new regime of occupation Israel has established in the Occupied Territories, of which Gaza is the ultimate model, is minimal friction, distant control, the luxury of indifference to the plight of particular persons, and—in Gaza—warlike operations that give the acting forces more freedom from the constraints of the rule of law and its appearances. The violence with which Israel rules the Gaza Strip is not that of a sovereign who has declared an emergency and suspended the law; it is rather that of a sovereign who has become ever more indifferent to the plight of its subject population—it cares only to avoid crossing that imaginary threshold of humanitarian catastrophe—and to most of the system of law and its distinctions (e.g., between combatants and civilians, armed men in action and innocent bystanders)—it cares mainly for the legal authorization to use force in ways that no legal system can explicitly sanction. In Gaza, no sovereignty is infringed and no sovereignty is enforced; the withdrawal of the state apparatuses has enabled the state to exercise bare force on lives that became bare long ago, without, however, being engaged in war. Palestinian "suspects" are hunted like dangerous criminals, but the policing forces comprise soldiers who have nothing to do with the enforcement of the law.

Israel rules the Territories today through a combination of means: the fragmentation of space, a very tight control of movement between spatial cells, and scattered, unpredictable, but relentless and recurrent violent blows (usually in the forms of missile attacks from the air and sea and the pursuit of suspects by commando units on the ground). While the regulation of movement is still embedded in a system of decrees codified in a quasi-legal language and open to legal questioning in Israeli courts, the exercise of violence is usually conducted according to a hit list of people who are supposed to be involved somehow in "terrorist activity." The list often includes perpetrators and collaborators alike. During the first year after the Gaza disengagement in August 2005, there were weeks in which attacks of this kind happened almost daily. Temporary ceasefires and other contingent political considerations occasionally change the pace and scope of these attacks, but they have never been outlawed or ruled out. About half of the people injured or killed in these attacks were not on the list and were not targeted. Those who are targeted are selected according to information collected by different intelligence apparatuses. Apparently, there is a specific procedure for approving the killing of people on the list, and top-ranking military officers discuss this procedure with Israeli (Jewish) philosophers who, in this case, play the role of physicians in the torture halls—they draw an imaginary line that limits violence and legitimizes it at the same time, at least in the eyes of the perpetrators. But both the general procedure and the particular decisions made to add a person to the list and then to execute him at a particular time and place and in particular circumstances are practically immune to legal questioning.

In the camp called Gaza, killings are now regular. They may happen at any time—and yet they always arrive unexpectedly; they may happen anywhere, because no shelter is immune to Israeli attacks, and to anyone, because it is hard to know when one is standing or coming near a target. In 2006, the Israeli army added a hit list of houses to the hit list of individual suspects. Residents get a phone call that warns them of a coming attack and orders them to evacuate the house, which is hit by a missile shortly thereafter. The ongoing killing and destruction terrorize and traumatize tens of thousands who are not physically affected. These are people who mostly live in poverty, with average incomes of less than two dollars a day, in one of the most densely populated areas on the globe, and whose economic situation is in a constant state of deterioration. Less than 50% of the 1.3 million people in Gaza have some kind of work and income; about 60% receive food and medicine from humanitarian organizations. People have nowhere to go; there are fences all around, the gates are mostly closed, the beach has become too dangerous. The withdrawal of the Israeli ruling apparatus in August 2005 has not liberated Gaza but has turned it into a wasteland. But there is no war in Gaza, very little visible presence of Israeli forces, and no torture either.

The torture of Palestinian detainees was one of the symptoms of Israeli oppression during the first Intifada. During the Oslo years, the use of torture declined but it was also legalized after a long public and legal debate. Torture became popular again during the first years of the Second Intifada, but the number of reported cases dropped after 2003. Since the disengagement, in Gaza at least, there is no more torture (except, perhaps, for that exercised by Palestinian forces on Palestinian political prisoners). In the West Bank (in which "disengagement" has taken place only from a very small area in the Jenin area where hundreds of Jewish settlements thrive), hundreds are still detained without trial and dozens of detainees are still tortured. In Gaza, suspects are not arrested, detained, and tortured but rather systematically eliminated, mostly from a distance. Targeted killing has replaced torture as a special kind of state terror in which the use of violence is intimately linked to an intensive interest in designated individuals.

Indeed, the torture of detainees and the "targeted killings" of suspects (with their usual "collateral damage") are two different forms of state terror in which state authorities invest a great deal in coming to know their victims as private individuals, profiling them in detail, and learning about them whatever may seem relevant for establishing their relation to one of the active militias. In the first case, the intimate co-presence of the perpetrator, the torturer, and his victim produces knowledge that is then mobilized to extract information the detainee is supposed to conceal. In the second case, power has no personal encounter with its victims; they have become names on a list, images on a screen to be destroyed at a distance, like figures in a video game. Here information is not the goal but a means; the goal is "elimination." Moderation is exercised not to keep the victim alive but to keep his death as "clean" as possible, and "cleanliness" is not a matter of legality but of sheer efficiency and good public relations. One does not work here any longer in the shadow of a suspended law, on the other side of law, which is still defined by law, but in a sphere almost entirely detached from the law and mostly indifferent to it.

Torture stands out as an unusual form of state terror because it may still be challenged in court with certain positive results. State torture, associated as it is with clandestine operations and the darkness of secret, hidden rooms, is the shadow of suspended law and of indecency. Where torture exists—at least clandestine, hallowed torture—there is still shame that may be called upon, and there is law and decency that may be retraced and restored. "Targeted killings," or systematic "catastrophization" and its use as a means of governance, belong to a different realm of state terror (sometimes disguised as a "war on terror"). This is a realm beyond decency and indecency, mostly oblivious to the law, a realm in which security has become a name for a license to eliminate individuals and to rain havoc upon entire populations, reducing them to the conditions of bare life. Here there are neither shadows nor shame. Eliminations are carried out in the open, in front of the victims' families and neighbors, the public, and the camera. At the same time, the conditions of bare life are quickly monitored in order to save the victims from a "humanitarian catastrophe." In this new realm of state violence, the almost complete obsolescence of torture and the almost complete impotence of law go hand in hand.

Why then does state torture continue? Why these secret, hidden places for holding detainees and torturing them outside the reach of the law? Why the intense attention given to Abu Ghraib? Perhaps these are but signs of an effort to extend the shadows of law and legality into the new realm of state terror in a kind of desperate attempt to overcome the state's indifference to law. It is as if people believed that, where torture occurs, the law too can be retraced, and that by insisting on legal investigations of cases of torture they can force the state to re-introduce its violence into the legal sphere. Both the critics and the state authorities who respond to them seem to stick to an old faith in the double life of the law, as reasoned and enlightened ruling accompanied by an always excessive force. It is as if, when force is framed as excessive, law somehow reappears.

In this sense, Gaza is but a paradigm for a new modus operandi of state power that restructures the relation between law and violence in regions absent any form of sovereignty. The use of direct violence is not restrained by the law, it is not made possible by the suspension of the law, and it is not called for by interruption in law enforcement due to a declared state of emergency. Officially, the use of direct violence is related only to the armed resistance of the governed population, as it is defined by the governing power. This resistance is usually continuous with the very presence and existence—the life—of the governed. Violence is therefore not part of a system of law but of a system of bio-power. The "gentle" means for the suppression of resistance is the production of disaster through nonviolent means (enclosure, blockade, embargo, fragmentation of space, etc., which choke the economy and destroy the social infrastructure). Brutal means include the killing of suspects and those who happen to be near suspects at the time of an attack and the destruction of their houses and living environments. The two elements complement each other: a measured and relatively controlled production of death that never becomes mass killing accompanies and contributes to a relatively controlled production of disaster that never becomes a full-fledged catastrophe. Torture has not come to an end but remains external to this new form of state power; torture functions on the margins of this power or characterizes its relatively rare moments of excess. Both the practice of torture and its critique should be questioned in the framework of this new economy of state violence.

NOTE

1. Aeyal M. Gross, "Human Proportions: Are Human Rights the Emperor's New Clothes of the International Law of Occupation?" *European Journal of International Law.* 18 (2007): 1–35.

4

The Nation as Iron Maiden

Margarita Serje
(Translated by Ashley Caja, Rebecca Natolini, Laura Rexach,
and C. Britt Arredondo)

PUERTO INÍRIDA, GUAINÍA. JULY 20, 2006

IT IS INDEPENDENCE DAY in Colombia. The flight that I made today from
Bogotá to Puerto Inírida was run by Satena, the commercial airline of
Colombia's armed forces, which flies to "the most distant regions" of
the country, to places where other airlines won't go. We took off ahead of
schedule because the air space over Bogotá was about to be restricted in
order to make way for the military planes that were to feature in today's
traditional military parade. For this reason, the sight of a thoroughly
militarized capital did not seem strange to me as we took off and left
Bogotá behind. I was surprised however when I arrived at the airport in
Inírida, a small town in the middle of the jungle, near where the Guaviare
river flows into the great Orinoco, on the border with Venezuela. This
small airport, which was built according to the established canons of
modern international architecture, looks run down: plaster is falling off
the walls, mold is growing everywhere, and the glass dome is falling to
pieces. If it weren't for all the military activity, you would think we had
arrived at an archeological ruin of modern civilization . . . a civilization
made obsolete by the profuse vegetation of the jungle. As we got off the
plane we were met by a thick wall of humidity and a group of armed
men who had come to escort the passengers. Several military helicopters
were taking off, while others landed. The paved runway was surrounded
by trenches disguised by camouflage. Groups of men with different
uniforms—marines, army, and police—swarmed the military camps
that had been set up around the control tower. At that very moment they
were unloading an enormous cargo plane. A number of smaller planes,
used to fumigate, were waiting in line to reach the runway. It looked
like a scene out of Apocalypse Now. *And as tends to be the case in just*
about any airport in the world, we passengers from the third world were
treated as though we were terrorist suspects and were made to submit to
several searches by the customs and immigration officials; only that in

38

this case we weren't entering the industrialized world, we were entering the "Other Colombia."[1]

The modern nation, embedded in the development of the world economy, has historically been defined in contrast to what it opposes: by its alterity and its limits. It has been configured in opposition to those groups and landscapes that seem to be beyond the reach of the state and the rationality of the modern economy. These *others*, which to a certain extent have been invented with the purpose of giving meaning to its project, permanently haunt both the state's integrity and the nation's identity.

The current Colombian government has undertaken a policy of "territorial re-conquest" based on the idea that there is an "Other Colombia." This task of reclaiming the national territory, understood as the military occupation of the land, has been unabashedly celebrated as a "difficult and bloody act of reconquest" and as a "glorious campaign of national liberation."[2] This initiative seeks to integrate the country's "marginal periphery"—characterized as extensive wildlands, poor and vulnerable areas under the influence of illegal armed groups, and above all by being "outside of the control of the state." The current campaign to incorporate and redeem them is based on the premise that the military occupation of the national territory will guarantee increased presence of institutions and better provision of goods and services. Territorial occupation is then the "path to develop and exploit" this enormous tract of territory "still covered by jungles and therefore uninhabited."[3] This view arises from the belief that the nation's natural repository of wealth is being usurped by guerrillas and drug traffickers. At the same time it insists on forgetting that jungles have always been inhabited by indigenous and maroon communities and that these forests constitute the social landscapes these groups create.[4]

This quest for the conquest of the land—understood as a crucial part of the government's frontal attack on drugs and terrorism—has exacerbated the dividing lines that have historically delimited the internal geography of the country. It has transformed Colombia's urban centers into gated cities where life carries on in a perversely normal way. In these urban spaces, life keeps apace of the speedy transactions in commercial malls; it is attuned to the constant and uninterrupted programming on cable TV. Life in the gated cities of Colombia keeps its distance from the thousands of minefields and military trenches that characterize daily life out on the so-called periphery of the country. Colombia has labored under a state of exception for the last forty years. In the "marginal peripheries" it has been experienced as a permanent and uninterrupted state of conquest. Ever since the Spanish occupation, these regions have been conceived and managed as a theater for military operations; what is more, the inhabitants of these regions have typically been treated as little more than war booty.

No man's lands in Colombia have been represented through the same set of paradoxes.[5] On one hand they are seen as a promise of enormous wealth and opportunity. On the other, they represent danger and risk: rich in natural and mineral resources but inhabited by dark, backward, dangerous rebels. They constitute an object of desire—because of their exotic and luscious landscapes—and an object of contempt—because of their hot, humid, feverish climate plagued by disease and infested with insects and snakes. They are, at the same time, a haven for fugitives and rebels and a home of pristine nature and cultures. Nowadays they are seen as both a potential for development—for their biodiversity, water, and mineral reserves—and a threat to national stability—because of their seemingly constitutive violence, rebellion, and drug trafficking.

The people imagine these wild regions to be a reality outside the scope of civilization, beyond the reach of the nation. Marked by the sign of alterity, they are an "Other" reality. Not surprisingly, they are usually construed as *"la Otra Colombia,"* the "Other Colombia," problematic precisely because it is beyond the control of the state and its proclaimed *Libertad y Orden* ("Freedom and Order"). The state's alleged abandonment of vast areas is seen to have fueled many of Colombia's problems: poverty, underdevelopment, illegality, and particularly violence. Both in journalism and in academia, it is widely acknowledged that "in geographically marginalized regions where the presence of the state was almost nonexistent . . . violence became a form of resolving problems" (Obregón and Stavrapoulou 1998, 403). For this reason, Colombia has been listed by the Fund for Peace and Foreign Policy in their ranking of *failed states*. This classification groups sixty states considered to be the most precarious in the world because of "their vulnerability to violent internal conflict and societal dysfunction." Their defining trait as failing states is not having effective control of their territory.[6] Furthermore, the "absence of the State" has been considered to be one of the central traits of Colombia's political organization, ever since "the State developed having very little control over vast areas of its national territory. In the State's absence, its authority was substituted by local powers that not only control the dominant economic activities in the regions, but also define and implement justice in their own way" (Chernick 2003, 137).

What seems to be forgotten in this discussion is the relationship between these "local powers" and the state. Far from being a totalizing set of abstract institutions, the state is constituted by the visions, interests, and practices of particular groups. These groups, who have access to "being" the state, decide and speak in its name; they design its project; they control its structure and apparatus; they define its priorities and policies; and, above all, they fashion the legitimate way to read and understand reality. Thus, their vision becomes the official vision. These "local powers" are the de facto state.[7] Historically, the descendants of the *criollos*—literate, modern, urban, and preferably Andean elites—are the ones who have incarnated the state in Colombia. Since their imagination embodies what the nation is, it also defines the antonymous non-nation, the wild "Other" that is in need of taming.

Behind the screen of the alleged "absence of the state," there lies a definite and coherent line of action by means of which the state/local power groups have sought to gain dominance over Colombia's "wild regions." Throughout history these no man's lands have been maintained as large-scale red-light districts where all sorts of illegal practices have been pursued. These practices are related not only to marginal or criminal activities, such as smuggling or drug trafficking, but also to abusive modes of exploitation, of surplus extraction, and of enforced compliance. The state/local power groups, as they repeatedly turn a blind eye to these practices, have not just been passive beneficiaries; they have orchestrated and regulated them. The notion of the absence of the state makes this intertwining of the legal and the illegal possible. This popular notion functions as a smoke screen; it serves to cover up all sorts of intrusive interventions and abuses by the state/local power groups in the mythically lawless lands of Colombia.

The territorial conquest that is taking place today throughout Colombia actually constitutes what can be considered a new *peine forte et dure* addressed to the indigenous, Afro-descendant, and campesino populations who inhabit the country's marginalized regions. It intends to give continuity to the project of geographically constructing the nation, understanding its project as a process of pacifying territories to "open" them for commercial exploitation. "Pacify for business," as General Butler put it in his campaign to guarantee the operation of transnational companies in the wildlands of the planet (quoted in Bakan 2004, 86). This range of policies and interventions—which in Colombia include contention and physical violence, chemical poisoning and rape, confinement, forced displacement, and abandonment, as well as different forms of terror, psychological torment, and humiliation—can be understood as a device that generates a systematic process of collective abuse.

The modern nation-state is usually represented and embodied as a maiden, as a young, female body that must be cherished and protected.

As Parker et al. (1992, 6) have pointed out, "this trope of the nation-as-woman of course depends for its representational efficacy on a particular image of woman as chaste, dutiful, daughterly or maternal." Both the nation's territory and the state's actions may be visualized in the ambiguous terms of the relationship—of family, of love, and of protection—that is culturally associated in the West with the image of this maiden. If, however, we explore the practices and representations to which the nation subjects its "wild" and "Other" landscapes and populations, we realize what is really at stake in the relation with this virgin-mother. The nation then appears more like an iron maiden: a device that originates in the masculine imagination of a torturer, in which the external image of a Madonna conceals an interior covered with sharp spikes that slowly lacerate and bleed dry whomever is trapped inside. This is the bloody embrace that hides behind the amiable image of the maiden-nation.

CHENGUE, SUCRE. JANUARY 17, 2002

The witnesses testified to government investigators that various units from the Colombian military ignored the heavily armed group of paramilitaries who passed by while they were on their way to the village. The paramilitaries gathered the villagers into two groups and killed the men one by one, smashing their heads with heavy stones and a battering ram. When they were finished, twenty-four men were left lying dead in pools of blood. Two more were found in shallow graves. Upon leaving, the troops set fire to the village.[8] The Senate Human Rights Commission condemned the twenty-three massacres committed by the militia during this month, which accounted for 138 murdered people.[9]

There is nothing particularly novel about how today's militias, private armies, mercenaries, and armed groups annex territories and attempt to establish order by imposing "progress" and "civilization" on the people who live there. Since the colonial occupation in the Americas, the expansion of agricultural frontiers and extractive economies has been accompanied by armed men. The areas that presented the colonial enterprise with the most resistance to being "pacified" were ceded as concessions to entrepreneurs who had the ability to privately finance the needed military campaign through mercenaries and militias contracted by commercial firms (Serje 2005). Their profits were based on the forced labor of indigenous and African peoples. The expansion enterprise was thus accompanied by diverse forms of slavery, sustained by a system of overseers armed with whips and dogs, and complemented by the presence of private armies who were charged with committing whatever atrocities were deemed necessary to bring about the subjugation of Aboriginals and Africans.[10] Only in this way was it possible for the would-be conquering civilizers to change these people's traditional ways of life, which were based on livelihood systems and forms of commerce that were quite different from the logic of modern forms of production, where human labor is conceived as a "cost" that must be reduced to the bare minimum. The violence with which these regions have had to live is, in short, the result of the expansion of a modern economy.

Although the idealized image of contemporary globalization presents us with a liberating narrative of deterritorialized economic organization, globalization today is, among other things, a matter of consolidating at all costs a process of territorial occupation that, for the past five hundred years, has been devised to gain control over the land and impose order on its populations: "clean and hold."[11] Indeed, the control of vital resources such as oil, biodiversity,[12] water, and even oxygen—the new forms of "gold"—depends on territorial control. In Colombia, alarming statistics clearly illustrate this: only 15,273 people are owners of 61.2% of the land.[13] Surely, this panorama of the concentration of landed estates does not differ too much from what it had been in the eighteenth century.

This process of appropriation and exploitation of natural resources and the enslavement of the population has created a situation of perpetual terror in a history of almost uninterrupted atrocities.[14] This devouring impetus, which thrives in areas of expansion, is hidden behind the high level of violence that the entire country has suffered for the past forty years. During recent decades, it has become increasingly evident. Between January 1996 and May 2006, 212,515 homicides were reported in Colombia. If one starts counting from 1986, that number rises to 445,388 homicides,[15] which means that an average of 22,270 homicides were committed annually during the last twenty years.[16] These figures do not account only for the deaths directly related to the territorial conflict, but they also give an overall idea of the situation of fear that has been imposed on all realms of daily life in Colombia. The territorial conflict is better expressed by the 1,248 reported massacres that occurred during 1995–2005, which left behind 6,617 victims.[17] According to Amnesty International, the figures that encompass homicides, murders, and "disappearances" of noncombatants since 2003 continue to be higher than the average from the period 1991–2002. Moreover, a rise in recent years in certain types of abuses such as torture and forced disappearances has also been noted.[18] The sites scattered with mass graves that are being found today—farms that were used over the years by paramilitary groups, guerrillas, and drug lords to torture and hide their victims—are all located in zones along the "agricultural frontier." It is there where the most appalling events of the hidden history of the nation's outposts of progress are coming to light.

Thanks to the multifaceted terror that marks daily life in these regions (from the forced displacement and disintegration of families to persecution, threats, and uncertainty), the foremost public health problems in the country today are sadness, depression, anguish, and permanent fear: the emotional conditions related to those who suffer violence.[19] A few years ago in the heart of Magdalena Medio, one of the strongholds of the paramilitaries, I asked an adolescent during an interview what his expectations were for the future. He answered that what he wanted most from life was to be able to die from a shooting rather than from a chainsaw, the tool of choice among the paramilitaries during the massacres and homicides that had recently taken place in the region. "People have even lost the ability to hope."[20]

Bogotá. March 27, 2006

At six in the morning, despite the mist and chilly drizzle of the Andean high plateau, the city of Bogotá is fully awake. The dreadful traffic, constantly cursed by its inhabitants, is nearly at its peak. Along the Parque del Virrey, a line of trees flanks a canal whose stream flows down from the mountains. Commuters ignore a scene that has become quite common in the public spaces of this city of around seven million people: in the ravine's freezing gray waters, half-hidden by the canal's brick walls, a group of women and children, stiff with cold, wash themselves. Their clothes and their calentano traits[21] betray them as some of the millions of internal refugees that crowd most Colombian cities. After their private ritual in the stream, they head off to make good use of the hard-earned privilege of begging by a stoplight in one of the country's most opulent neighborhoods.[22] Every day I pass Aracely there; she, her sister, and her sister-in-law take turns begging and caring for the five children who arrived with them in Bogotá a few months ago. Before fleeing to Bogotá, Aracely was forced to watch as her husband and her brother were killed. She was beaten for hiding her children in the scrub and raped by a group of armed men in camouflage. "I was told afterwards they were paracos (paramilitary)." Aracely claims that things are going relatively well for her in Bogotá. For now she has found herself a good place to beg—though she has to pay someone, probably a cop or a security guard, a cut for it. She is grateful to have shelter against the cold. "Merely to spend the night, since sleeping is impossible. More often than not, we don't sleep at night. How can we forget the things we have seen, what has been done to us, what has been taken from us, the people that were killed?"

Displacement is merely one of the "externalities" in the process of "opening the frontiers" of the colonial-modern world. The first massive displacement in Colombian territory took place with the arrival of the Europeans, when the indigenous population was expelled from its lands and confined to *haciendas, reducciones,* and *pueblos de indios.* By the second half of the eighteenth century, when the system of Hispanic settlements experienced a notable demographic recovery, a significant part of the population was "expelled by the tensions inherent to the colonial agrarian structure in the 'empty territories' of the *tierra caliente*" (Gónzalez 1994, 14–15). The frontier "acted as a safety valve to relieve the tensions that existed in the countryside. [. . .] Disgruntled renters and sharecroppers did not have any reason to directly confront landowners because they could always migrate to the frontiers, where free lands were readily available" (Legrand 1988, 17). These "frontiers" or "empty territories" were, of course, "wildlands" inhabited by indigenous groups (which had also lived through a process of demographic recuperation after having their populations notably diminished by the conquest) and by Afro-descendant maroon populations.

The displacement movement pressed from the metropolitan centers to the peripheries: from the urban Andean zone integrated into the circuits of the modern metropolitan market toward the regions known as agricultural or colonial frontiers. This continuous process of displacement and colonization intensified in the twentieth century in various waves. The first wave—at the turn of the century—resulted from the conjunction of the "Thousand Days' War" and the establishment of the first large agro-industries, including the banana industry, as well as the expansion of exploitation of timber and other resources, such as petroleum. The second great wave occurred during the bloody decade known in Colombian history as "La Violencia" at midcentury, and the third occurred in the 1970s and the early 1980s with the introduction, expansion, and explosion of crops destined for the illicit drug economy. The drug economy fueled violence that opened the way for the "outposts of progress." By the beginning of the eighties, the various local power groups were already reaping the benefits of an increase not only in marijuana, coca leaf, and poppy production but also of the "licit" economies, including gas, coal, and agricultural products like banana and African palm. All of these industries have contributed to strengthening the guerrillas—through kidnapping and extortion—and the paramilitaries.[23] Since then, the violence inherent to these economies and to the War Against Drugs has shifted the direction of displacement; it pushes now from the peripheries to the center.

In this manner, the twentieth century's continuous displacement process has had a triple movement: the *campesinos*, expelled by the rigid land tenure structure in the central areas, became *colonos* and settled farming communities, clearing the rain forests and thus driving the indigenous and Afro-descendant communities away from their historic territories.[24] Now all groups—*colonos,* Afro-descendants, and aboriginals—are being dispossessed and are forced to seek sanctuary in slums and shantytowns. In many regions, *campesino* families have been displaced twice within one generation: from the central Andean region to the "frontier" and now from there to the urban centers. Many remember being children when they arrived with their parents on foot, clearing the path with a machete into the jungles of Guaviare, Urabá, Sierra Nevada, Arauca, or Putumayo.

After Sudan, Colombia has the second highest population of internally displaced persons in the world.[25] Most of them are women and children who have also been the victims of different forms of aggression and violence. They have lost their homes, their lands, their houses, their belongings, and everything that they had gained from years of hard work. Furthermore, they live in deplorable conditions, worse than even the poorest of the poor: in Colombia the mortality rate among the displaced population is six times higher than the national average, 92% of displaced persons lack the resources to satisfy their basic needs, 55% have high levels of anemia, and 88% live in such indigence that they did not have the money to eat in the past month.[26] However, what they demand is not money, but justice.[27]

Displacement has gone hand in hand with dispossession.[28] This process has escalated parallel to land ownership concentration because in Colombia people are displaced in order to be expropriated: millions of hectares of land have been usurped from them.[29] It is not by mere chance that the regions most affected by forced displacement (such as Chocó, Sierra Nevada, or the Amazon piedmont) are the stage of enclave exploitations of natural resources and mega-projects that are considered to be the spearhead of the modern world economy. The development of ecotourism is particularly telling. Urban-dwelling Colombians become familiar with these jungle regions through sport fishing programs, canoeing and rafting in the jungle's rivers, and adventure excursions with lodging in exotic hotels, the majority of which are "protected" by private armies and paramilitary groups.[30] The systematic use of violence, paramilitarism, and drug trafficking has permitted, in the words of an editorial from the newspaper *El Tiempo*, the consolidation of "a portfolio of bloody investments, which goes much farther than their original interest in lands and livestock and covers a wide geographic area."[31]

Resguardo Chimila, El Dificil, Magdalena. July 14, 2002

For years, the resguardo[32] has been like a concentration camp. No one enters or leaves without passing through paramilitary roadblocks. Everything is controlled by them. They decide who works, where, and for what wage. A few months ago, just before the last elections, the "paras" came to tell the head of the governor of the cabildo to collect all community members' identification cards (cédulas), which they needed to use in the election. It's very easy to commit an obvious fraud like that here, given that the majority of people here do not know how to sign their name. The cabildo collected them, but by the time the paras returned, the cédulas had mysteriously disappeared. For that, they killed him right there. In front of us. They rounded up the community members and explained that "we had a pending account that had to be paid" and that the cédulas had to appear. Then and there, a rumor began that some of the adolescent boys that work with the indigenous organization had the cards. Within a few days, they came to the school and took one of the boys. Three days later, he was found dead, his body destroyed by blows and torture, hanging from a hook in the market among the cows' and pigs' entrails. The community recovered his body; there never was an autopsy or an investigation by the municipality's authorities. This was a warning, a threat. Since around here no one enters or leaves the resguardo without the paramilitaries' permission, we were all terrified, just waiting. A few days later they took the second boy and the same thing happened. His body was also found at dawn, covered in blood, hanging from a hook among the meat in the market. When they took the third boy, one of the leaders succeeded in calling Bogotá so that someone would come and witness what happened [. . .] In total they tortured and killed six boys. The authorities never knew of their deaths, because no one dared to report them or denounce them formally. This case won't even make the statistics.[33]

The strategy of displacement works hand in hand with the strategy of forced confinement. In fact, displacement figures would be higher without the consolidation of this phenomenon, which is equally or more troubling. Currently all armed actors—the national army, the guerrillas, paramilitary groups, and private armies—impose situations of blockade and confinement.

There are a series of localities in the geography of the Colombian territorial conflict that have been converted into true enclaves of blockade. There, armed groups impose prohibitions and rationings of local foodstuffs—in certain regions they go as far as impeding both fishing and hunting—and make it impossible for people to receive income, correspondence, provisions, medicine, and even humanitarian aid. One of the most dramatic cases of blockade is on the Atrato River in Chocó, one of the most humid forested regions of the planet, which is inhabited by indigenous and Afro-descendant groups and is now being turned into huge oil palm plantations for biofuel. Transportation and commerce along the river have been paralyzed for the past nine years. Previously sixty embarkations set off on the river daily, but at present only ships that are escorted by armed men can travel the route.

Another implication of the blockades is a limitation of access to health services and humanitarian aid. Diseases that had been eradicated through enormous efforts have begun to resurge in certain areas that systematically suffer from blockades. Because of this, there has been a reemergence of cases of yellow fever (Sierra Nevada de Santa Marta, Catatumbo), leishmaniasis (Chocó, Tolima), and dengue fever and cholera (Nariño, Sur del Magdalena, Sur de Bolívar). According to the Colombian National Institute of Health, blockades are one of the contributing factors that explain why 640 of the 1,192 municipalities in Colombia have serious problems with health care coverage.[34]

The armed forces use control of medications as one of their strategies to ensure that such medications do not end up in the hands of the guerrillas. This applies mercilessly to drugs needed to treat common pathologies in jungle zones: serums and antidotes for snake bites, as well as drugs for malaria and leishmaniasis. Needless to say, the principal victims of this policy are civilians who do not have access to drugs through the black market.

While the practice of encircling a population with hunger and illness has the goal of terrorizing those suspected to be sympathetic to rival groups and of pressuring for the abandonment and forced sale of lands, the tactic of besiegement seeks to impose a relentless control over the population. Indigenous communities are perhaps the principal victims of this practice. This same tactic was one of the most effective methods to guarantee the control and subordination of the indigenous population throughout the course of the colonial occupation, when the indigenous people were concurrently exploited for labor and indoctrinated in catechism through the establishment of haciendas and missions. Armed actors have not stopped using this scheme of concentration of the population through violent means; now it is the order of the day. Entire *resguardos* have been besieged, and nearly twenty-two thousand aboriginals currently live in these conditions. There are cases in which the totality of members of an ethnic group are encircled by warfare: the *Coreguaje* in the Amazon, the *Kankuamo* in the Sierra Nevada of Santa Marta, the *Awa* on the western Pacific coast, the *Yuko-yukpa* of the mountains of Perija, and the *Chimila* in the Magdalena Valley are enclosed by a paramilitary siege that has transformed their *resguardos* into veritable concentration camps. By means of terror and cooptation, the paramilitaries control the population to guarantee them as a cheap or even enslaved source of labor for the hacienda and its modern descendants: the agro-industrial projects.

The situation of confinement is not restricted to war zones. Many displaced persons who arrive in the cities have to suffer once again the rigor of confinement, this time in neighborhoods where they are contained by both visible and invisible walls. One case of this is the "Valle de Lili," an urban neighborhood where Afro-Colombian populations have taken refuge. A 260-meter wall has been constructed around the settlement to physically isolate its inhabitants and, more importantly, visually erase them from the view of people living in the buildings and condominiums of one of the wealthiest zones in Cali.

SAN VICENTE DE CHUCURÍ. AUGUST 13, 2001

I used to be the leader of a vereda (campesino community) in the region of San Vicente. I had three children, two of whom were 12 and 14 years old. In March of 2001, my daughter—who was then 16 and pregnant—left in the morning to accompany my sister to the market in the town. On the way, they met a group of men in uniform, who stopped them and raped them. They slashed open my daughter's womb with a bayonet, took out the child, and left her lying there. They beat and wounded my sister, leaving her for dead. Later, some neighbors found her lying in agony. It was a miracle that she survived. My sister and I tried to denounce the rape and the murder of my daughter and grandchild, but the authorities themselves warned us that our lives would be in danger if we pursued the accusation. To protect ourselves, we came here with my other two children. Two weeks ago, the paramilitaries burnt down the house on my farm, and because of that we're now living under the protection of the church which is going to help us get to Bogotá.

Rape and sexual abuse have historically been tactics of war. Despite the fact that sexual abuse against women, girls, and boys has become a greater dimension in the Colombian armed conflict, it goes virtually unmentioned. Women and children constitute approximately 70% of the total displaced population,[35] and in many cases they have been victims and witnesses of the most brutal forms of violence: massacres, disembowelments, rapes, and tortures. According to the United Nations Special Rapporteur on Violence against Women (2002), all parties in the conflict have committed atrocities against women and children, and all armed groups are guilty of rape, assassination, torture, kidnapping, enslavement, forced prostitution, and sexual mutilation.[36]

Worst of all, these cases are neither investigated nor even reported. They do not appear in statistics. Despite the fact that numerous international organizations and NGOs have repeatedly shown that armed groups have been systematically using sexual violence as an instrument of terror and specifically targeting women and children, not even the smallest reference appears in official statistics.[37] After homicides and massacres, kidnappings and attacks on economic infrastructure are the crimes that receive the most attention. According to Amnesty International, "these rapes committed against civilian [women and children] and even against combatants belonging to the same armed group have remained behind a curtain of silence hidden by discrimination and impunity."[38] Official autopsies and forensic medical reports analyze the evidence only along previously set, established forms that omit innumerable aspects pertaining to gender and sexual violence.[39] Because of this, the entire gamut of sexual abuse and torture suffered by women and children in the war simply goes undocumented. Therefore, they are not even recognized, let alone investigated. As crimes they are easily ignored. Victims of rape and sexual abuse are threatened in the rare case that they denounce their attackers. Furthermore, accusations are not even processed. Instead of being treated as victims, accusers are many times viewed as instigators or as responsible for all that has happened to them.

The parties of Colombia's territorial conflict frequently attack female community leaders and their families, leaders who protect children and oppose recruitment of child soldiers, partners and families of combatants or members of community organizations, and anyone who appears to be a "sympathizer" of other groups, as well as the children of these "sympathizers." Women's organizations are sometimes the only ones working to bring aid, relief, and solidarity to the communities most affected by the war. Despite this fact—or maybe because of it—they have become a military target of all armed groups. In fact, the country's largest women's association, the National Association of Black, Peasant, and Indigenous Women of Colombia (ANUMCIC), besides being dubbed terrorist by the president himself, has also been the object of constant threats, aggressions, and murders.[40]

Adolescents and children, in addition to constantly being subjected to sexual violence, are frequently recruited as combatants. Human Rights Watch estimates that there are approximately eleven thousand child soldiers in Colombia—one of the highest rates in the world. Their 2003 report shows the conditions that these minors suffer: they are subjected to abusive deals; obligated to witness tortures, assassinations, rapes, and massacres; and forced to kill. Armed groups often recruit minors to use them as human shields in combat. Despite the existence of laws explicitly prohibiting it, even the public armed forces use children as informants, in propaganda campaigns, and in intelligence operations.[41]

Both the guerrillas and the paramilitaries have kidnapped women and children for the sole purpose of sexual abuse. Girls recruited by armed groups—in addition to being systematically raped—are subjected to sterilization, abortion, and forced birth control. They are victims of various forms of prostitution, slavery, and forced work, and they are frequently forced to fight in the line of fire.[42] According to Human Rights Watch, between a quarter and a half of guerrilla combatants are women, most of whom are minors. The number of women who have died in combat has increased by 114% since 2000.

ABEJORRAL, ANTIOQUIA. NOVEMBER 22, 2005

The first thing that Ángela López noticed after the blast was the terrified running of the horse that she had been leading by the reins. Like in one of those sleights of hand in which a person disappears behind a curtain of smoke, her mother, 65-year-old Gilma Rosa Cardona, who was walking only a few steps behind her, disappeared out of sight in the middle of the smoke rising from the explosion of an anti-personnel land mine. [. . .] She had to watch carefully for a few seconds before she could identify the body below the mass of black earth and shrapnel that was in the crater left by the artifact. The two women had left at 10:30 a.m. on the path to San Vicente, in Abejorral (Antioquia), to stock up on corn where Gilma Rosa's brother lived. They took turns riding by horse. A few minutes before the tragedy, Ángela dismounted and took the reins.[43]

Among the countries that have experienced armed conflicts in the last decade, only Cambodia and Afghanistan have more victims from antipersonnel mines and explosive remnants of war (ERW) than does Colombia. Since 1990, explosive land mines and other improvised explosive devices have increasingly been used, making the country one of the world's most critical cases for mine explosions and victims. According to official figures from the system of information of the Antipersonnel Land Mine Observatory supervised by the vice president,[44] there were 5,152 victims from mine accidents between January 1, 1990, and June 1, 2006. Among these victims, 1,845 were civilians, 184 were women, and 554 were minors. While the average of mine victims was 2 per day in 2004, this figure tripled in 2005. According to Humans Right Watch, the number of land mines and ERW has increased since 2001 by 1,000%, and the percentage of civilian casualties has risen to 30%.[45] Land mines have been reported throughout the entire national territory, except in the San Andrés archipelago.

Given that Colombia is one of the signatories of the Geneva Convention, the public armed forces has committed to refrain from using land mines, and it has destroyed all mines in its arsenal (around twenty thousand) in the past few years. The illegal armed groups—the guerrillas and the self-defense groups—are the parties responsible for planting mines in 627 municipalities. The FARC is considered to be responsible for approximately half of all incidents involving mines and explosive remnants. Their improvised land mines receive names such as "leg-breakers," "Chinese hats," "post-breakers," "Chinese fan," "surprise box," and "rosary."[46]

De-mining in the middle of the conflict is difficult and expensive. According to the Anti-Personnel Land Mine Observatory, for each dollar spent in planting a mine, a thousand must be invested to unearth and disarm it. In 2001, when there were about seventy thousand mines in Colombia, the National Department of Planning estimated that disarming them would take between ten and twenty years and would cost between 22 million and 53 million dollars. This terrible war artifact, which is so cheap to those who utilize them (planting a land mine costs about a dollar), is extremely costly not only for the victims but also for the entire country, given that the rehabilitation of survivors costs approximately $90,000 USD per person. Furthermore, "when a civilian falls, three people are hurt: the person that falls, the person that cares for the victim, and the person who has got to work to support the other two."[47]

Serranía de la Lindosa, Guaviare. July 26, 2006

In December of last year our Committee for Communal Action pro-
posed a program of voluntary eradication of coca plants in exchange
for the construction of a new road, a public health facility, a school, as
well as the establishment of a credit program for obtaining seeds and
livestock. Since this is a national park, we were told that such things were
not allowed; and for this reason even fumigating coca plants by plane
was forbidden. The government decided on a program of forced manual
eradication. We heard that the eradicators were going to be farmers, so
we hoped to find work, but they did not hire anyone from around here.
When the eradicators came with the army, dressed up in their blue uni-
forms, people here recognized many of them: they were "demobilized"
paramilitaries. They eradicated all that they came across; not only the
coca plants, but all the crops. They trampled on and abused the people
they found; they sacked homes; they stole all the animals and valuables
they could find. They treated us all as if we were guerrilla sympathizers
or "chichipatos" (coca merchants). They tortured several men to get
information about the guerrillas' hideouts, and they raped the women and
little girls. One woman was raped by a whole group of eradicators and
they nearly killed her. Here, we took her for dead. They not only got rid
of the coca, they got rid of the people too. I had to leave for Tomachipán,
one of over 200 people. We lost everything. It would have been better if
they had just fumigated us all with airplanes.[48]

Ironically, even though in November 2005 the Supreme Court of Justice ordered the suspension of fumigation until they could clearly determine its effects on human health, only fifteen days later the government
heeded the request of this community leader and decided to "fumigate
with airplanes" in Macarena National Park. This decision was made not
to protect the tenant farmers from the abuses of the manual eradicators
but rather in response to the death of six eradicators due to a land mine
that had been placed underneath a coca plant by guerrillas.[49] In this manner, the government of Colombia lived up to its stated goal—officially
announced in October 2000—of diminishing in the course of six years
50% of the 170,000 hectares of coca that were estimated to exist in the
country at that time. The strategy that was adopted to eradicate the "illicit crops" is called "Plan Colombia," an intervention scheme inscribed
within the parameters of the two main global wars of our time: the war
on drugs and the war on terror. Developed in the United States in the
year 2000 and adopted by three successive Colombian governments, the

explicit goals of Plan Colombia are to cut off production and exportation of illicit drugs and strengthen the war against the guerrillas (in particular against the Revolutionary Armed Forces of Colombia—FARC). "Between 2000 and 2005 Washington paid out nearly $4 billion to Colombia with approximately 75 percent of the total going to the military and the police, and increased its presence in the country with 800 soldiers and 600 security contractors. Indeed, Colombia is now fifth largest recipient of U.S. military aid."[50]

On both fronts—the war on drugs and the war on terror—the results of Plan Colombia have been less than optimal. Even though "there are record-breaking areas of land being fumigated," new areas have been cultivated so that attempts at reduction have been neither effective nor significant. In fact, the report from the United Nations Office of Drugs and Crime (UNODC) shows a 7% increase in hectares of cultivated coca, as well as an increase in tons of cocaine produced in Colombia. "The necessary comparison in this analysis is between the 300 metric tons that were produced in the country in 1996 [. . .] and the actual annual production record of 640 metric tons [produced today], which is to say more than twice of that of ten years ago. This represents twice the amount of drugs in half the amount of cultivated land."[51] Even though the cartels have been dismantled and most of their members extradited to the United States (304 Colombians and 11 foreigners), activities related to the production and traffic of cocaine continue to be rampant and are now organized by small and flexible cartels—the so-called *boutique cartels*.[52] In fact, according to the UNODC report, "the availability of cocaine in the world markets of New York, Los Angeles, Chicago, London and Madrid has not been reduced by even one iota."

The results of the fight against the insurgency are not very convincing either. With the help of Plan Colombia, the military, the police, and Colombian security organizations have undoubtedly become stronger, augmenting their force, their law enforcement capacity, and their geographic spread. Even though they have produced desired results on some fronts, such as kidnapping, there is evidence of corruption and complicity with drug trafficking, the paramilitaries, disappearances, human rights violations, and even kidnappings, too.[53] At the same time, the illegal armed groups continue to control vast areas of the national territory: the FARC—who, despite having their sphere of influence reduced, are still capable of waging war—as well as the paramilitaries—who, in spite of participating in peace negotiations with the government (negotiations that many see as little more than a farce),[54] still maintain control over the areas of the national territory that they have conquered in recent years.[55]

In contrast to the dubious results of these policies' intended impact, their social and environmental "side-effects" are striking. Their costs and "externalities" have been assumed, almost entirely, by the inhabitants of these godforsaken territories. In addition to damaging peoples' health and destroying the considerable biodiversity of fauna and flora in these regions (around 14 million liters of Roundup Ultra enriched with Cosmoflux 411F have been sprayed in open air fumigation over the past decade),[56] this practice has placed unprecedented pressures on the social fabric of aboriginal groups and campesino communities alike. One of the biggest consequences of air dispersal of the herbicides is their direct effect on food safety, which is an important factor in the displacement of villagers. In fact, the farmers firmly denounce the destruction of their personal orchards and of crops such as bananas, yucca, beans, corn, tomatoes, and other fruits and vegetables, as well as the drying of grazing pastures and the poisoning of water wells and streams.

Another social impact is that the credibility of the state and its institutions has been undermined. The inhabitants of these regions come into contact with the state only by means of its corruption and repression. For years, these people have been subject to the conditions of any economic enclave: the large-scale cultivation of coca, poppy, and marijuana is based on the exploitation of labor through coercion and debt peonage. Today, these people see not only how their families have been criminalized, persecuted, and "sprinkled with poison" but also how their own sources of livelihood, their animals and crops, are callously put to death.

It is almost impossible to conclude that the program of fumigation put into practice by Plan Colombia has in any way presented a solution to the main problem of drug processing and trafficking in the territorial conflict of Colombia. To repress this illegal economy in this violent manner has only succeeded in multiplying the enormous revenue that it generates and that serves, in the end, to maintain and increase the size and power of the guerrillas, the self-defense militias, the paramilitaries, and a vast array of other smaller private armies.

Resguardo de Barrancón, Guaviare. July 26, 2006

Two indigenous women and a group of children set out on foot along the road to San José del Guaviare. Surely, the neighbors tell me, they're going to town to beg or perhaps to go fight over the viscera discarded at the market. I have with me a basket of fruits and approach them to offer it. I realize they speak little Spanish. When I extend the fruits to the woman who seems older and whose face is etched by scars, the other woman moves forward and accepts the fruits for her: she can't receive them herself, she has no arms. The older woman tells me that she lost both arms to the explosion of a land mine: it seems that a military base was set up recently near the resguardo. There are several hundred Guayabero Indians located in seven settlements. They have been arriving continuously over the past four years. They have been the victims of an ongoing series of displacements which, because they have not culminated in big city slums, have been rendered completely invisible. The Guayabero are savanna dwellers who lived in seminomadic bands in the higher parts of the Guaviare. With the arrival of the rural settlers who came to occupy this region after the Violence [of the 1940s], it was only a matter of years before they found themselves living among the thickets and shores of the Guaviare River. The coca boom corralled them even more. Presently they have been displaced from the lands they had recognized as resguardo in the 80s and they've all come to Barrancón fleeing the threats of the guerrillas and the paramilitaries alike. The situation here is critical. Apart from the fact that they are disdained by society in general, they have serious problems of nutritional safety and basic health issues. Intense internal conflicts have also begun to arise as a result of the fact that the different clans have to live together now in such close quarters.

The indigenous and Afro-descendent communities who live in collectively owned territories recognized by the state are nevertheless being systematically threatened and driven from their land. They have been made subject to "murders and tortures, massive displacements, forced disappearances, involuntary recruitments of young people to combating units, rape, and the occupation of their territories by guerrilla groups, paramilitaries and other illicit armed actors."[57] As their lands are being increasingly militarized,[58] the intervention of all the armed parties is principally directed at dismantling the system of collective ownership on which the Indians and Afro-descendants base their political claims. At stake is the control over geopolitical or economically strategic corridors (such as the roads that connect the various regions of the Amazonia or the Darién) and to "open up" these lands to intensive extractive economic activities such as timber exploitation, oil extraction, mining (gold, carbon, minerals), the construction of hydroelectric dams, and tourism.

Since the middle of the 1990s the state, paramilitaries, and guerrillas have been systematically invading the indigenous territories, displacing entire populations, and persecuting indigenous leaders. For the state/local power groups who are backed by the army and paramilitary groups as well as for the guerrillas, the Indians represent an obstacle to development. All parties to the territorial conflict consider them to be traditionalists and incapable of "making their lands productive." There is a generalized opinion in Colombia that an error of historic proportions was committed when the government handed over 25% of the nation's territory in the form of *resguardos* to these communities, in effect placing these lands beyond the scope of the market and of all possibility of investment and development. Evidently, the corrective to this has been to put into practice a covert program of extermination, hidden behind the veil of the country's armed conflict. The rate of violence in indigenous zones is 100% greater than the national mean.

The United Nations High Commissioner for Refugees (UNHCR) has repeatedly warned that the indigenous groups in Colombia are increasingly being exposed to violence, and even to the risk of disappearing, as a result of the current conflict.[59] The impact on several ethnic groups has been devastating. The account given by the UN Special Rapporteur points out that

> at least twelve small indigenous groups in the Amazon are at the point of extinction brought on by such diverse processes (armed conflict, illicit harvests, destruction of the environment, economic mega-projects) and their effects upon the living conditions of the population (forced displacements, selective murder of leaders, destruction of the subsistence economy, deterioration of health, and disintegration of the community's social fabric). Forty percent of the indigenous groups of the Amazon are at high or very high levels of risk.

Today, practically all of the members of the *Awa, Kofán, Siona, Co-reguaje, Carijona, Guayabero, Muinane-bora, Chimila, Kankuamo,* and *Witoto* nations are under attack. At issue is a humanitarian emergency of grave proportions.

In 1998 the systematic murder of more than 120 indigenous leaders was denounced for the first time, underscoring one of the principal strategies of the territorial conflict: the systematic attack on the leaders and traditional authorities of both Indians and Afro-descendants. A recent communiqué addressed to the Indigenous Organization of Colombia (ONIC) by the supposedly demobilized United Self-Defense Forces of Colombia—a group that is made up of the principal paramilitary chieftains of the country—expresses this strategy in the bluntest terms:

> Here, we do not tolerate social leaders who work under the
> supposed protection of international humanitarian law [. . .]
> What such people do is favor the interests of the insurgency,
> disguising themselves as leaders and defenders of human rights
> [. . .] This is an invitation to join our crusade against terrorism
> or be prepared to suffer the full weight of our presence. We are
> backed by the armed forces of the state who, in an expression of
> sovereignty, always support us [. . .] If they refuse, they should
> leave and take their humanitarian ideas with them to someplace
> other than our *sacred Colombian territory*.[60]

Between 2003 and 2006, 265 indigenous leaders were murdered.[61]
In various regions of the country, Indians have denounced the fact that
they are being submitted to forced labor, disappearances, and military
persecutions, resulting in an unprecedented wave of suicides among
the youths of these communities.[62] Thirty-nine percent of the displaced
people in Colombia are ethnic minorities. Many indigenous groups have
been displaced to the cities; others have resolved to isolate themselves
in inaccessible places from which they have nevertheless slowly been
run out by the war. Such is the case of the *Nukak-Makú*. These nomadic
people have historically avoided contact but, scared by the presence of the
FARC, they have come out to seek refuge in San José del Guaviare.

It is precisely in the indigenous territories, in the "last bastions" of
Colombia's natural resources, where the military and paramilitary have
intruded most forcefully, reshaping both the system of property ownership
and the landscape itself. The jungles of the Sierra Nevada, the Chocó,
the Catatumbo, the Sarare, the Pacific, and the Amazon are being transformed by the establishment of economic enclaves. These plantations
and lumber yards, oil rigs and gold mines, trample the ownership rights
of the ethnic territories and violate the environmental laws designed to
protect these areas.

Río Mulatos, Serranía de Abibe. February 24, 2005

*In the river illuminated by the moonlight, the commission stopped
a moment to wait for another group. Several leaders informed us that
five bodies were found. "There were signs of shots in the kitchen, words
written in charcoal, blood stains on the floor, and a hand that had slid
over the wood. There we found Alfonso Bolívar, his wife Sandra Milena
Muñoz, and their children: 20-month-old Santiago and 6-year-old Na-
talia Andrea. We also found the body of Alejandro Pérez, who worked*

harvesting coca with Alfonso . . . they chopped the adults into pieces and left only their torsos. They opened up the bowels of the six-year-old girl, same with the 20-month-old boy." Minutes afterwards the other commission appeared with the news that they had found the site of the other bodies: Luis Eduardo, Deiner, and Beyanira. "They were left in open air, in the river, just beyond the school, and alongside the trail that leads to the old Mulatos health center. We saw the child's head on the banks of the river near the corpses." One of the women of the community told us that, "until a decade ago, some 200 families lived in the entire Mulatos canyon. There had been community stores, a school, a health center, and all that is left of all of this is ruins. Armed raids and the deaths of peasant farmers have been pushing us off our lands. A year ago there had been close to ninety families still living here; with one raid, the paramilitaries reduced that number to approximately sixteen. Now who knows how many families will stay."[63]

Perhaps one of the paradigmatic episodes of the war for territorial control in Colombia is the case of the San José de Apartadó Community of Peace. This village, located in the north of Colombia in the Urabá region, arose due to the settlement by campesino farmers who had been displaced by the violence of the middle of the twentieth century. These people founded their communities in this region and lived here in relative calm until the thrust of development introduced large banana plantations and, with them, private armies and paramilitary groups. The fact that unions—traditionally associated in Colombia with subversion—arose in these plantations and that the campesino-settler population was considered "prone to guerrilla warfare" caused the people of San José to become a privileged target of the paramilitary groups.[64] It was in response to this systematic violence that in March 1998 the community declared itself neutral in the conflict and established itself as a Community of Peace.

On February 21, 2005, members of an armed group killed and dismembered eight members of this Community of Peace, among them Luís Eduardo Guerra, his eleven-year-old son Deiner, his companion, seventeen-year-old Beyanira Areiza, and two other children, whose bodies were found in the Río Mulatos canyon. Several witnesses from the region and the community accused the army's 17th Brigade of being the perpetrators of this massacre.[65] For his part, "President Uribe expressed that some leaders of the San José de Apartadó Community of Peace as well as some members of non-governmental organizations that work with the community were obstructing justice; the Chief of State also maintained that there were indications that some leaders of this community had collaborated with the FARC."[66] The office of the United Nations High Commission for Human Rights (which has been contemplating leaving Colombia due to scarce government support) asked for prudence in comments about the massacre.[67] The community of San José regretted that the president had not denounced the killing and had instead made accusations. The inhabitants recalled that the previous year they had proposed to the government that it create a commission that could live with the community for at least a month and thus learn how they lived and what they truly hoped for. "They are upset with us, even the state seems to be furious with us. And it is all because we refuse to take sides in the armed conflict or collaborate with anyone who uses arms. All of the armed groups want to use us."[68]

Both the banana elites in the region and the Andean urban groups, who in this case represent the state, have a specific interpretation of the history of San José de Apartadó, "a village lost on the borders of the jungle in lower Atrato":

> [Since] the Urabá zone has immense strategic value [. . .] one good day the guerrillas took Urabá. And with Urabá, they took over the banana-growing zone. Through force, and not through conviction, the unions became centers of the guerrillas' doctrine and the base of their destabilizing power [. . .] and one of the enclaves of the FARC in this vast territory was precisely San José de Apartadó [. . .] This ceased to be the case once the young governor of Antioquia, Álvaro Uribe Vélez undertook the task of re-conquest, which although it was hard and bloody for the military forces, was also glorious as a quest for liberation [. . .] It was then that San José de Apartadó was born. The creature baptized itself as Community of Peace and presented itself as a movement of supposedly humble people who were armed with nothing but their moral fortitude and the resolve to dismiss all of the armed groups in the conflict [. . .] This Community of Peace served the purpose for which it was created [. . .] It became a destination of choice for tired guerrilla soldiers in need of a vacation, a strategic place to stock provisions, and a center for the preparation of a new assault on Urabá.[69]

Notwithstanding the disdain and ignorance that this version of the history of San José expresses, it also contains the central elements of the geopolitical vision that has historically guided Colombia's territorial appropriation. According to this vision, what is at issue here is the nation's sovereignty over a territory that an illegal army has taken and declared its own. This vision reduces the problem of the Communities of Peace to a question of collaboration: since the Communities of Peace exist in territories that have been taken over by illicit armed groups, it is assumed that the Communities of Peace also tacitly participate in the armed conflict and do so against the national interest. According to this overtly paternalistic vision, these communities are fundamentally lacking (they consist of "humble and naïve people"); thus, or so the argument goes, they are being cynically used by the FARC (the communities became unionized "through force, not through conviction"), and they do not even have a clear sense of whose interests they truly serve. They are, in short, "misguided," and their attempts at declaring themselves neutral are, consequently, "misplaced." No doubt, it is reasoning such as this that explains why the government does in fact recognize the right of banana companies to create their own security enclaves but will not recognize the right to reject weapons for the humanitarian zones created by the Communities of Peace: the government brands these would-be enclaves of peace as "independent republics" and "war zones." In no uncertain terms, the problem is construed in terms of the perceived absence of the state; at issue is how to impose the common good, the national interest, over all of Colombia's national territory. Evidently, the "national interest" that this vision enables is that of the state, in this case embodied by the banana elites in Urabá and by the Andean urban groups in general. It is an interest that is articulated with modern forms of production and corporate development tied to transnational capital.

Although, in Colombia, the foundation of the nation—a New Colombia—and the defense of the national territory are presented as inherently peaceful and beneficial enterprises, these are set into motion through tactics that brutalize historical populations and destroy their landscapes, both of which are considered to be expendable. This was made clear in the text of the "Acuerdo de Ralito," which was signed by a group of congressmen, governors, mayors, and public officials—some of whom are very close with the current president—with the major paramilitary bosses. In this pact, signed "in the name of peace, peaceful coexistence, and just order," the signatories declare that they will undertake "a promise to guarantee the ends of the State." This pact gave de facto legitimacy to homicides, massacres, disappearances, rapes, torture, disembowelments, looting, and displacements.[70]

If we recognize that the capacity of control of the official armed forces is the result of a cultural and social process and not an inherent attribute of the state, it is interesting to note how in Colombia the state/local power groups have historically favored the strengthening of private militias—which escape complete control—over the public force, which theoretically should be held accountable for its actions, formally maintain its codes of honor, and pledge itself to follow the rules of war. Perhaps it is for this reason that the Colombian conflict is no longer considered to be an "internal armed conflict" and has come to be seen as a "frontal war against drugs and terrorism." This shift in focus helps to disguise the fact that one of the main purposes of the conflict's actors is to continue the strategy by means of which the state/local power groups have historically pursued their ideal of territorial pacification. Building the nation geographically has meant the transformation of the historical landscape of social groups—Indians, Afro-descendants, *campesinos*, which are trivialized behind simplistic stereotypes—into a military "theater of operations," with the consequential disciplining of everyday life, the social and political disarticulation of communities, and the "peripheralization" of their localities. Although this strategy of territorial pacification has been resisted historically, the zero tolerance policy addressed to these stigmatized populations has succeeded in transforming them into dispossessed—though not submissive—cheap labour.

Paradoxically, all of the armed actors involved in Colombia's ongoing territorial conflict—those who locally determine which groups may become the incarnation of the state and define the nation—share the same geopolitical vision. By means of initiatives similar to the current government's campaign for "territorial re-conquest," they share the notion that these territories should be "incorporated" into the modern world. In one form or another, all of these groups suggest that they "carry weapons in front of them because they are pulling tractors behind them."[71] With varied nuances, all of the parties in the armed conflict assert the need to implant the modern mode of production and its rational forms of everyday life. And, above all, they assert a similar geopolitical aesthetic—a utopian vision of discrete and geometric spaces. For all parties concerned, the social and environmental costs of this civilizing quest ultimately constitute mere "externalities." These collateral effects, which define life in the no man's lands, make clear what it means in practice to belong to the nation and the tutelage of the state. The "re-founding the Nation"—in the righteous terms of the Ralito pact—covers up—just like the innocent image of the nation as the virgin-mother—the imperviousness of a development project that bleeds its peoples dry and tears up its landscapes, crushing them like the entrails of an iron maiden.

***

During the past eight years, the members of the San José de Apartadó Community of Peace have been building a Monument to Memory. The memorial is constructed with rocks they have brought up from the river. Each rock bears the name of a victim of assassination. At the beginning of 2005, the memorial had 152 names. On March 22, 2005, the eighth anniversary of the declaration of the Community of Peace was commemorated with a "ritual of memory." With candles and testimonies they added to the monument eight new rocks brought from the river, on which they inscribed the names of the victims of Mulatos Canyon.[72]

Our resistance is against the state. But let us be clear on this point; ours is an un-armed resistance, a civil resistance. We want to defend our Constitution and tell the state: it is you who is violating the Constitution. What we are doing is legitimizing the state, not attacking it.[73]

NOTES

I thank Christopher Britt and Erna von der Walde for their comments and suggestions.

1. Unless otherwise indicated, the entries in *italics* are pulled from my fieldwork journals or from testimonies that I have collected (names, when used, have been changed).

2. In the words of Luis Fernando Lodoño, former minister of justice and minister of the interior of the current government, in his column in *El Tiempo*, 14 May 2005.

3. In the words of Santiago Montenegro, former director of the National Planning Department of the current government, in "Geografía y Modelo Político," Lecturas Fin de Semana, *El Tiempo*, Bogotá, 24 June 2006.

4. Documented in an enormous body of ethnographic and archeological research. See, e.g., Van der Hammen 1992; Descola 1986; and Rival 1998.

5. This group of territories has historically been the same: Guajira, Sierra Nevada de Santa Marta, Serranía de Perijá, Catatumbo, the middle valley of the Magdalena River, Serranía de San Lucas, Alto Sinú and San Jorge, Darién, the Pacific coast, the Eastern piedmont, and most of the Amazon and the Orinoco—more than half of the national territory. For a historic, panoramic, and critical analysis of their constitution as liminal social spaces, see Serje 2005.

6. "One in which the government does not have effective control of its territory, is not perceived as legitimate by a significant portion of its population, does not provide domestic security or basic public services to its citizens, and lacks a monopoly on the use of force. A failing state may experience active violence or simply be vulnerable to violence." Available at www.fundforpeace.org/fsi/fsindex.php (visited 23 June 2006).

7. Not unlike local elites (who in many instances maintain private armies), drug traffic cartels and the illegally armed groups act and are perceived by the population as the state, since they control the institutions and the resources and make decisions of state at various levels.

8. *Human Rights Watch*, 2002 Colombia Report. Available at http://hrw.org/wr2k6/pdf/colombia.pdf (visited 23 July 2007).

9. "Van 23 masacres," *El Tiempo*, 24 Jan. 2001.

10. Since very soon after conquest, these regions have become the scene of various forms of slavery that subjected not only the African populations but numerous indigenous peoples as well, who were the objects of an extractive exploitation and converted into a commodity—treated as any other natural resource. Slavery continues to exist in its direct form and under the systems of debt peonage (*endeude* or *enganche*), based on the idea that work is conducted as payment for a debt whose terms are established by the lender, which grows indefinitely, involves the entire family or social group, and is hereditary: a debt that never will be paid off.

11. The technique of "clean and hold" is described by General Carlos Alberto Ospina of the Colombian Army. See the Special Report on Plan Patriota, *El Tiempo*, 5 July 2006.

12. Colombia is one of the seven mega-diverse countries of the world. It has the highest density of biodiversity for unit of land. Evidently, it is considered that "biodiversity should be exploited in a productive manner" and its natural capital "put at the service of development" through "recollection or production activities, processing, and commercialization of goods and services derived from the local biodiversity." J. P. Ruiz, natural resource management specialist of the World Bank in Colombia. "Observatorio de Biocomercio," *El Espectador*, Bogotá, 25 June 2006.

13. Cf. "Mucha Tierra, Pocos Dueños." In *Revista Semana*, Bogotá, March 2004.

14. Although the history of the exploitation of Colombia's abundant natural resources has been presented as a crusade to justify their technification (González 2001), the current state of natural resources shows that their increased depletion parallels the advance of such technification (Marquez 2001). The zones that continue to have high levels of biodiversity are those that have escaped modernization: the historical landscapes of indigenous and Afro-descendant peoples, which the state is now trying to conquer.

15. Figures are taken from the Observatorio de Derechos Humanos de la Vicepresidencia de la República. Bogotá. Available at www.derechoshumanos.gov.co/ (visited 23 June 2006).

16. According to the National Department of Planning, 26,097 homicides were reported annually between 1996 and 2002, which amounts to 63 homicides per 100,000 inhabitants per year. See www.dnp.gov.co/archivos/documentos/DJS_Documentos_ Publicaciones/DJS_Cifras1.pdf (visited 23 June 2006). This is one of the highest rates of homicide in the world and is particularly telling given that Latin America in general has a rate of 30 homicides per 100,000 inhabitants, which in itself is the highest rate of any region in the world (the Middle East and Africa, which follow Latin America, have a rate of 10 for every 100,000). Colombia's rate is 2.5 times higher than that of the rest of Latin America as a whole (Observatorio de Derechos Humanos 2002).

17. Statistics from 1996 and 2002: Bulletin with statistics about violence 1996–2002, DNP (cited website), statistics 2003–2006, Human Rights Observation (cited website). The average of homicides has dropped from 26,097 annually—the average between 1996 and 2002—to 18,111 in 2005. However, the decrease in the homicide statistics is directly related to the improvement of security conditions in large cities (Bogotá, Medellín, Barranquilla, and Cali) and does not reflect the current state of the territorial conflict.

18. According to unofficial statistics from the Departamento Administrativo de Seguiridad (DAS), in the central Bogotá region alone the "amount of disappearances rose to 9,000 people between 1998 and 2003." *El Tiempo*, 3 July 2006. However, there are no statistics about the number of disappeared persons each year in the entire country.

19. Doctors without Borders Report, published in *El Tiempo*, 28 April 2006.

20. In the words of Saskia Loockhartt, UNHCR official in Bogotá.

21. People from the Colombian Andean region use this term to refer to inhabitants of the "hot" lands *(tierra caliente):* the lowlands of the inter-Andean valleys and the coastal regions of the Pacific, the Caribbean, the Amazon, and the Orinoco.

22. The residents of this zone are part of the 2% of Colombians with the highest income and the 7% who hold 40% of the income in Bogotá. Cf. "La ciudad de las desigualdades," *El Tiempo*, Bogotá, 18 June 2006.

23. There have been several scandals regarding this practice in Colombia in the past decade, involving various corporations. For example, in May 2004 Chiquita Brands admitted payments of 1.7 million USD to the AUC, the largest paramilitary organization in Colombia responsible for several massacres in the banana enclave region of Urabá. (Bananera de E.U. negoció 'vacuna' con Carlos Castaño, *El Tiempo*, 16 March 2007: 1–4). According to the World Bank, European multinational companies in Colombia have paid 1 billion US dollars to the guerrillas. Cf. Statements of Paul Collier, group director for Development Research by the World Bank (Multinacionales Europeas han pagado en extorsiones 1000 millones, *El Tiempo*, 6 March 2003: 1–3).

24. The *resguardo* is a colonial institution that recognizes the communal ownership of a portion of land. It is ruled by a *cabildo*, a council with several members and a governor, elected periodically by the communities. Displacement and forced seizure of indigenous territories has been checked in part by a policy of creating and expanding *resguardos*, as a response to the growing importance of the indigenous as political actors and the rise of the indigenous sector in the state's administration. After the approval of the 1992 Constitution, which recognized that Colombia was not Hispanic but rather a pluriethnic and multicultural nation, Ley 70 was promulgated, which recognized Afro-Colombian territories along the same lines as the policy of indigenous *resguardos*. Around 25% of the national territory has today the status of *resguardo* in Colombia.

25. There are literally millions, yet no one knows exactly how many: according to the government, 1.7 million people have been displaced since 1995; according to the UN, between 2 million and 3 million since 1985; according to COHDES, a Colombian NGO, 3.7 million since 1985; and according to the University of the Andes, 2.5 million. "Despojo a desplazados supera el billón de pesos." *El Tiempo*, Bogotá, 5 May 2006. The problem of internal displacement in the world has alarming proportions. In 1999, when the United Nations published its "Governing Principles for Displaced Populations," they calculated that there were 25 million displaced persons, compared to between 8 million and 10 million refugees.

26. Of the displaced population, 63% live in inadequate housing, 49% do not have adequate public services, 23% of children under the age of six suffer from malnutrition, and 25% of children and youth between the ages of ten and twenty-five do not have access to any type of education. These statistics are from the Colombian Constitutional Court's Report, Sentencia T-025, 2004.

27. "We want to be treated like the demobilized combatants" (in other words, that the state should provide them with the same conditions it offers to demobilized combatants and deserters from the guerrillas and the paramilitaries, through an economic and productive support program) was the demand of the nearly five hundred displaced persons who occupied the Bosa park in Bogotá as a protest and as an option of solidarity to survive the precarious conditions that they face.

28.   According to a study conducted by the University of the Andes, "Hacía una política proactiva para la población desplazada," the calculated loss of assets of displaced homes—without taking into account the loss of lands—has risen to 5.3 billion pesos. "Los costos del desplazamiento en Colombia." *Nota Uniandina* 19 (August 2006).

29.   According to the Colombian Institute for Territorial Development (INCODER), it is 4 million hectares, the National Comptroller General affirms that it is 2.6 million, and according to a consultancy contracted by the Social Action of the Presidency of the Republic, it would be 6.8 million hectares. The cited study by the University of the Andes states that the displaced homes have left behind a little more than 4 million hectares (extrapolated figure), which corresponds to 6.7 times the lands gained from the Agrarian Reform between 1993 and 2000; also see "Despojo a desplazados supera el billon de pesos," *El Tiempo*, 5 May 2006, and "Desplazados habrían perdido en a Guerra 6.8 millones de hectáreas," *El Tiempo*, 16 June 2006.

30.   There are several examples of ecotourism programs managed and controlled by—as a friend of mine calls them—"the ecological paramilitary," such as Tairona Park, the "Lost City" in the Sierra Nevada of Santa Marta, and the ecological resorts on the Pacific Coast, in Urabá, or in Córdoba and Sucre on the Caribbean.

31.   Cf. "El portafolio paramilitar," Editorial, *El Tiempo*, 5 July 2005.

32.   See note 24.

33.   Testimony of an employee of the *Programa Indígena* (Red de Solidaridad and World Food Program).

34.   "70 pueblos sitiados por el hambre," *El Tiempo*, 19 Sept. 2004.

35.   CODHES (report cited) affirms that more than one in three displaced families has a female head of household. Approximately 53% of displaced persons are women.

36.   Cf. United Nations Commission on Human Rights, Report of the Special Rapporteur on Violence against Women, Ms. Radhika Coomaraswamy, Integration of the Human Rights of Women and the Gender Perspective, E/CN.4/2002/83/ADD.3, March 11, 2002; and UNHCR, "Violence against Women in Colombia" available at www. peacewomen.org/resources/Colombia/UNHCRVAW04.html (visited 6 June 2006).

37.   Cf. the National Department of Planning and the Human Rights Observatory (*op. cit)*. In fact a recent report about the situation of displaced women, "Salud sexual y reprodutiva en zonas marginales: situación de mujeres desplazadas," conducted by Profamilia, an official organization, emphasizes the conditions of poverty, juvenile pregnancy, domestic abuse, and family violence, but they don't mention the systematic sexual violence to which women and girls are subjected.

38.   Amnesty International 2004.

39.   Interview with a forensic MD (who prefers to keep her anonymity) working with the National Forensic Medicine Institute.

40.   During the last four years, paramilitary groups have assassinated thirty-three female leaders of the National Association of Black, Peasant, and Indigenous Women of Colombia (ANUMCIC), and the guerrillas have assassinated two. The leaders of several partner organizations, among them the Association of Displaced Women of Apartadó and the Corporación Casa de la Mujer, have also been victims of assassination (UNHCR, report cited).

41.   Human Rights Watch, 2003.

42.   See the report, "Infamia: Las niñas de la FARC," *Revista Semana*, 1 July 2006.

43. "Una campesina antioqueña, la última víctima de las minas," *El Tiempo*, 24 Nov. 2005.

44. Available at www.derechoshumanos.gov.co/minas/ (visited 23 July 2007).

45. Human Rights Watch, 2007, Maiming the people. Guerrilla use of antipersonnel landmines and other indiscriminate weapons in Colombia. Available at http://hrw.org/reports/2007/colombia0707/ (visited 27 July 2007).

46. "Colombia: Campo minado." Editorial. *El Tiempo*, 10 Feb. 2006.

47. Declaration of the Director of the Antipersonnel Mines Observatory, "Tres colombianos caen en las trampas cada día." *El Tiempo*, 24 Nov. 2005.

48. Interview which I conducted with a woman displaced by the eradication. The same type of accusation was made public in another region (San José del Fragua) where another manual eradication program was implemented. cf. "Cocaleros del Caquetá denuncian saqueos," *El Tiempo*, 05-08-06.

49. "Glifosato en 2 mil hectáreas de La Macarena." *El Tiempo*, 8 April 2006.

50. Juan Gabriel Tokatlian, "Militarising the Andes," *Daily Times*, Lahore, Pakistan, 16 May 2006, available at www.dailytimes.com.pk/default.asp?=2006\05\16\story_16-5-2006_pg3_5 (visited 8 Dec. 2006).

51. Alberto Rueda, "Menos coca, más cocaína. Report of the SIMCI on drugs," *El Tiempo*, 28 June 2006.

52. Tokatlian, article cited.

53. See Ministerio de Defensa Nacional, "Cumplimiento de la Sentencia ordenada por la Corte Interamericana de Derechos Humanos en el Caso de la masacre de Mapiripán" or "Condena al país por masacre de Mancuso." *El Tiempo*, 28 July 2006, or, for cases in Jamundí, Machado y Pitayó, *El Tiempo*, 5 June 2006.

54. See, for instance, "Ahora ex 'paras' portan armas con salvoconducto." *El Tiempo*, 9 May 2006; "Y si el fallo no convence a 'paras'?" *El Tiempo*, 21 June 2006; "Ex 'paras' solo entregarían el 35% de bienes ofrecidos." *El Tiempo*, 24 July 2006.

55. See María Jimena Duzán, "El paramilitarismo, vivito y coleando," *El Tiempo*, 23 July 2007: 1–19); "Hay grupos emergentes en la mitad del país," *El Tiempo*, 16 July 2007: 1; see the map published by the same newspaper that shows the municipalities that were subject to paramilitary pressures during the last election. "100 municipios en alto riesgo." *El Tiempo*, 5 Mar. 2006.

56. Due to the spraying of the herbicide glyphosate, communities in the area are reportedly 17 times more likely to develop cancer and children are being born with genetic deformities. Each time the crop-spraying planes pass overhead, children develop symptoms of pesticide exposure including vomiting, head and stomach pain, and diarrhea. "*What's your poison? Health threats posed by pesticides in developing countries. A report by the Environmental Justice Foundation*," 2003. Available at www.ejfoundation.org/pdf/whats_your_poison.pdf (visited 23 July 2007).

57. Report of the Special Rapporteur of the United Nations on the situation of human rights and fundamental liberties of indigenous peoples in Colombia, Rodolfo Stavenhagen, 2004. Available at http://daccessdds.un.org/doc/UNDOC/GEN/G07/110/99/PDF/G0711099.pdf?OpenElement (visited 23 July 2007). Henceforth, this will be cited in the text as UN Report.

58. Such is the case, for instance, with the establishment of a High Mountain Batallion in the Sierra Nevada of Santa Marta, located in the midst of some of the most important indigenous settlements.

59. "In the Sierra Nevada 44 forced disappearances, 166 extra-judiciary executions, 92 cases de torture and 52 cases of kidnapping were reported between 1998 and 2002, and massacres were denounced in 2002, where 12 Wiwa women were assassinated, causing the displacement of 1,300 indigenous people" (UN Report).

60. A missive sent out by the Autodefensas Unidas de Colombia on May 8, 2006, to the Organización Nacional Indígena de Colombia (ONIC), the Colectivo de Abogados José Alvear Restrepo (CAJAR), the Instituto Latinoamericano de Servicios Alternativos (ILSA), Unitaria Central de Trabajadores (CUT), the Plataforma Colombiana de Derechos Humanos, and Democracia y Desarrollo. The italics are my own.

61. "In the Amazonía the highest percentage of homicides of Indians is attributed to the AUC (36.7%), the FARC (34.3%), and the military (4.8%)" (UN Report).

62. See, for example, "Sitiados 14 grupos indígenas del Putumayo," *El Tiempo*, 26 Mar. 2003.

63. Jesús Abad Colorado, "El camposanto de San José de Apartadó," *El Tiempo*, 27 Mar. 2005.

64. In 1997, the mayor of the municipality of Apartadó, Gloria Cuartas, denounced the joint action of the 17th Brigade of the Army and paramilitary groups who persecuted communal leaders.

65. The direct participation of the military was proved two years later. According to the newspaper *El Tiempo*, 26 April 2007, "the paramilitary soldier Adriano José Cano, alias 'Melaza' acknowledged Wednesday facing the Minister of Justice and Peace that he served as a guide to the 17th Brigade of the Army, just as testimony from the community claimed." See "Para que reconoció ser guía del Ejército sería clave para aclarar masacre de San José de Apartadó," available at www.eltiempo.com/justicia/juicio_paras/paramilitares/ARTICULO-WEB-NOTA_INTERIOR-3532611.html (visited 15 June 2007). Also see "Contradicciones por masacre en Apartadó," *El Tiempo*, 13 Mar. 2005, and "El Camposanto de San José de Apartadó," *El Tiempo*, 27 June 2006.

66. "En 20 días la fuerza pública tendrá que llegar a San José de Apartadó." *El Tiempo*, 21 Mar. 2005.

67. "Se acaba la oficina de derechos humanos de la ONU en el país?" *El Tiempo*, 27 June 2006.

68. Don Alberto, member of the Community of Peace of San José de Apartadó. "El camposanto de San José de Apartadó." *El Tiempo*, 27 Mar. 2005.

69. "San José de Apartadó," column written by Fernando Londoño, ex–minister for justice and of the interior for President Álvaro Uribe Vélez's government, *El Tiempo*, 14 May 2005.

70. Signed on July 23, 2001, this document set off the "parapolitics scandal" (known in the United States as "paragate") and provided juridical proof of what had been a mouth-to-mouth truth in Colombia for decades. See the text of the accord at http://es.wikipedia.org/wiki/Pacto_de_Ralito (visited 15 June 2007).

71. In the words of the legendary paramilitary leader Carlos Castaño. For his part, President Uribe has said that his policy of "democratic security" is meant to prepare the ground for "productive projects." And for the FARC, the military confrontation is but a first step toward modernization and development.

72. In July 2007, with the death of another Peace Community member, Darío Torres, the number of names on the memorial rose to 170.

73. These are the words of Luís Eduardo Guerra, leader of the Community of Peace of San José de Apartado, assassinated in the massacre of Río Mulatos, February 21, 2005.

Interview for Televisión Valenciana (Spain) on January 15, 2005, reproduced by Revista Número, no. 44 (March 2005), available at www.revistanumero.com/44/hoy.htm (visited 23 July 2007).

BIBLIOGRAPHY

Bakan, Joel. 2004. *The Corporation: The Pathological Pursuit of Money and Power.* Toronto: Penguin.

Chernick, Mark. 2003. "Colombia: La injusticia causa violencia? Las políticas de la democracia, la guerra y el desplazamiento forzado." *Destierros y Desarraigos. Memorias del II seminario internacional Desplazamiento.* Bogotá: Cohdes-OIM. 123–58.

Descola, Philippe. 1986. *La Nature Domestique.* Paris: MSH.

Gonzalez, Fernán. 1994. *"Poblamiento y Conflicto Social en la Historia de Colombia." Territorios, Regiones, Sociedades.* Ed. R. Silva. Bogotá: Universidad del Valle-Cerec. 13–33.

González, Juan Manuel. 2001. "Una aproximación al estudio de la transformación ecológica del paisaje rural colombiano: 1850–1990." *Naturaleza en Disputa. Ensayos de Historia Ambiental de Colombia, 1850–1995.* Ed. G. Palacio. Bogotá: Universidad Nacional de Colombia–ICANH. 75–116.

Legrand, Catherine. 1988. *Colonización y Protesta Campesina en Colombia (1850–1950).* Bogotá: Ediciones Universidad Nacional de Colombia.

Márquez, Germán. 2001. "De la abundancia a la escasez: La transformación de los ecosistemas en Colombia." *Naturaleza en Disputa. Ensayos de Historia Ambiental de Colombia, 1850–1995.* Ed. G. Palacio. Bogotá: Universidad Nacional de Colombia–ICANH. 321–452.

Obregón, Liliana, and Maria Stavropoulou. 1998. "In Search of Hope: The Plight of Displaced Colombians." *The Forsaken People: Case Studies of the Internally Displaced.* Ed. R. Cohen and F. Deng. Washington, DC: Brookings Institution Press.

Parker, Andrew, Mary Russo, Doris Sommer, and Patricia Yeager (eds.) 1992. "Introduction." *Nationalisms and Sexuality.* London: Routledge. 1–20.

Rival, Laura. 1998. "Domestication as an Historical and Symbolic Process: Wild Gardens and Cultivated Forests in the Ecuadoran Amazon." *Advances in Historical Ecology.* Ed. W. Balée. New York: Columbia University Press. 232–52.

Serje, Margarita. 2005. *El Revés de la Nación: Territorios salvajes, fronteras y tierras de nadie.* Bogotá: Ediciones Uniandes–CESO.

Van der Hammen, María Clara. 1992. *El Manejo del Mundo: Naturaleza y sociedad entre los Yukuna de la Amazonia colombiana.* Bogotá: Tropenbos y Tercer Mundo Editores.

5

Torture, Tongues, and Treason

Christopher Britt Arredondo

1

YOU AWAKEN FROM A PAIN-INDUCED STUPOR to discover that you have been strapped to a chair. Unable to move your arms or legs, you feel them shaking anyhow with renewed fear. Your head is tilted back, your mouth held wide open by metal brackets, and your tongue has begun to dry up. You try to swallow. But you can produce no saliva. How long have you been in this position? You do not know. You only feel the air burning its way down your throat as you breathe. And you hear the heavy breathing of the men and women who are standing around you, too, pressing their sweaty bodies against your own. Your eyes dart back and forth now from one face to another, trying to read in them some hint of what your torturers propose to do to you next to get you to speak. But you won't speak, you promise yourself, no matter what they do or threaten to do.

They have been trying to get you to divulge information, to confess your guilt, to betray your ideals now for hours. You have refused to become the traitor they want you to become, and resisted their every attempt to make you speak in a language that is not your own, in a language that contradicts—and quite literally speaks against—your own language: the language of your own people, the language that expresses your loyalty to them, and the trust that they have placed in you. Your enemies want to break down the structures of this communal language of yours; they want to gain control over your tongue; they want to make it speak as if it were not your own tongue. But your tongue is still yours; you are still in command of it; and you will not use it to speak the language of your enemies.

You see a plump hairy hand with a pair of pliers approaching your mouth now. The cold metal of the pliers takes hold of your tongue and squeezes, twisting your tongue into a position you had never guessed was possible. You scream a guttural scream. The pain shoots from your tongue into your brain and races from there throughout your entire body. "Speak, you fucking son of a bitch, speak!" You hear the command and you hear yourself screaming, but you don't speak. The pliers twist your tongue into still another unnatural position, and again you hear the command: "Speak!" You try to say something along the lines of "Go to Hell" but only manage a gargling sound. The pliers twist your tongue again and again, forcing it to take on the unnatural positions it must adopt if it is ever going to produce the sort of speech they want it to produce, the sort of speech that will betray all that you hold dearest, the kind of speech, in the end, that will turn your future into a relentlessly repeating echo of your treason.

The pliers release your tongue now, and the burly hand that has been doing the twisting and turning removes them from your mouth. "Maybe now," you hear a voice say to you, "maybe now that your tongue has taken on a new shape, you will be able to speak to us in our language." You hope this means the torture of your tongue is over. You begin to think your wish will come true as you feel the brackets that have been forcing your mouth open begin to loosen. Your enemies are giving you your mouth back, it seems. They want you to speak. "Speak!" The command falls on you from all sides. So you close your mouth; you swallow in pain; you push air up from your lungs; you snap your tongue into place behind your teeth; and you manage to say "No." "Tighten the brackets again," you hear a voice command. And your mouth is forced open once more. The pliers take hold of your tongue and the torture resumes. And it stops and begins again like this until your tongue is thoroughly mangled. The pain is so severe now that it has reduced you to wanting nothing in life except that this terrible pain should cease. "If you don't speak," a voice threatens you, "we will simply cut your tongue out. You understand?" With your eyes crying, you signal to your torturers that you do understand. "You will speak," a voice commands. And again you signal with your pleading eyes that you will. The pain is too severe. And you don't want to lose your tongue. The pliers let go of your tongue; the clamps that are holding open your mouth come off; you swallow the blood that has been gathering in pools at the back of your throat. And you speak. You say everything that they want you to say. All of it lies.

Exhausted and humiliated, you wait for your torturers to remove the straps that immobilize your body. They have broken you down; they have shattered your loyalties to your loved ones and to yourself. You are now one of them. You speak their language now. But at least they will cure your tongue now too; take care of your tongue and take care of you as well. You have become valuable to them: a source of information, a traitor. They will give you something to ease your pain any time now. You are sure of it. But your torturers only place the clamps back inside your mouth, forcing it open. They take hold of your tongue once more with the pliers. Screaming with horror now, you shoot an accusatory look at your torturers. You get only this as a reply: "Since your tongue speaks as if it were another tongue, it simply cannot be trusted." The pliers violently pull on your tongue, almost ripping it from its base. You see a long curved knife being inserted into your mouth; and then you feel the knife saw its way across the base of your tongue. Before the pain pushes you to the other side of consciousness, you see how the pliers extract your mutilated tongue from your mouth. Everything begins to go a light, hazy gray. You are about to pass out, maybe about to pass away. You can't tell which, but hope you will survive. As you fade away your final thoughts are for your tongue. What will become of it? Now that it is in the possession of your enemies, you think, they can do with it as they please: place it in a laboratory jar; feed it to their dogs for dinner; or send it in a perfumed box home to your family as a symbolic gesture and final threat to them. Your tongue, which is now the tongue of your enemies, will command your family, your friends, all of your loved ones to speak as they are expected to or not speak at all.

2

The Bush administration first sought to deny the charges when reports surfaced that US forces in Afghanistan, Iraq, and Cuba were torturing prisoners. With studied cynicism, administration officials suggested that these reports were enemy propaganda, and dismissed them as attempts to undermine America's resolve in the War on Terror. Then, when pictures from Abu Ghraib emerged in which American servicemen and women were depicted inflicting cruel and unusual punishments on their prisoners, the administration sought to misrepresent the systematic nature of the abuse, and claimed that it was a matter only of a few isolated incidents. With professions of sincere dedication to human rights, administration officials assured the public that the misguided men and women who were responsible for these heinous crimes would be brought to justice. The heads of a few military underlings were made to roll; the damage to America's image at home and abroad was thus controlled, or so the officials hoped; and Americans everywhere could once again hold their heads up high with pride, reassured in their conviction that they were just the sort of people who would never stoop so low as to torture other people, not even their own worst enemies. But then, much to the chagrin of the Bush administration and its Jurassic-conservative electoral base in the American heartland, the real scandal blew open, putting on display (yet again) the administration's true contempt for human rights, for international law, and for democratic freedoms everywhere—whether in America or abroad.

Troubling reports emerged concerning a series of memos that had been written by the President's legal advisors in 2002, when the invasion of Iraq was still only in the planning stages. In these memos—the Bybee and Gonzales memos—Bush administration officials sought to circumvent the language of international treaties against torture. Originally, the administration refused to share these memos publicly, arguing that this would limit the ability of the President's legal advisors to express their opinions freely. But the right of Bush administration officials to conduct secretive debates could not trump the right of Americans to know how their elected leaders were in fact proposing to use the awesome power of the US military to secure their democratic way of life. And so the memos were, in due course, leaked to the public. As a result of this publication, both the systematic nature of the torture in question and the Bush administration's responsibility for it came to light. Public awareness of the real scope of the scandal increased: at issue was not only that US troops had tortured prisoners of war but that the administration had elaborated a new language that permitted the troops to do so with apparent impunity. What was to prove more scandalous still, the administration actually expected to be able to get away with this roguish display of contempt for human rights and the international system of law that protects these rights. At stake, reasoned administration officials, was the security of the so-called American homeland; surely all patriotic Americans would understand that in the face of the unconventional threats posed by international terrorist organizations, the government had no recourse but to follow unconventional strategies of war. Failure to accept this as a fact of *realpolitik* on the part of any American citizen was taken by the administration as evidence of that citizen's apparent lack of patriotism. And any American who dared to exercise his or her freedom of speech and publicly criticize the administration for its woeful war-time strategies and tactics was likewise summarily dismissed as anti-American.

There is nothing, however, that could be more anti-American and more contemptuous of democracy than this underhanded effort by the administration to malign or otherwise silence those who are opposed to its abusive methods of governance. The freedom to speak is one of the basic foundations on which America's ongoing experiment with democracy is based. Any and all attempts by the government to control speech—whether the sort of control to which torturers aspire or the sort that censors hope to achieve—is noxious to democratic culture and undermines the public debates that help sustain that culture and enable it to progress. It is for this reason that American society remains largely unwilling to tolerate torture, censorship, or any other unusual government control over the right to speak freely; it is for this reason too that American society has been disgraced by its government's most recent policies concerning torture. These policies have not only served to undermine the ideals of liberty and solidarity of American democratic culture, they have openly betrayed that culture and its liberal utopian idealism.

3

Not pain, but shame is what torture is ultimately about. Torturers inflict severe pain on their victims in an attempt to humiliate them. For their part, victims of torture withstand such intense pain in order to avoid becoming completely humiliated. This struggle between torturers and their victims is centered on language; torturers inflict pain on their victims in an effort to force them to speak, to divulge information, and to confess, whereas victims resist the pain in an effort to keep their silence and not speak. In this manner, torturers and their victims struggle for control over how the victims of torture are to use their tongues. In other words, torturers inflict severe pain to force their victims to speak *in other words*. These other words do not merely constitute a new vocabulary for the victims, nor do they simply amount to a foreign language which the victims must learn to speak; they are words that are directly opposed to the victim's own preferred language. When a victim of torture speaks this other language, he betrays his own language as well as the community of speakers who share that language with him.

In this sense, torture is akin to censorship. Censors, like torturers, seek to control how their victims use language. Censors are unlike torturers, however, in that they seek to impose silence, rather than force speech. But this difference is not fundamental; it is only secondary. For at heart, censors impose silence in order to achieve the same result that torturers seek to achieve by forcing speech: they aim to make their victims betray their communities.

Torturers and censors work in tandem to create involuntary traitors. That is, they use violent force or threats of violence to transform their victims and compel them to convert to a new set of loyalties, a new credo, a new culture. Involuntary traitors are, in this sense, people who are violently re-socialized and made to become like their enemies. This violent process of re-socialization forces the victims of torture not only to speak the language of their enemies, but to keep the silences of their enemies too. Involuntary traitors are people who, in the final analysis, have been compelled by severe pain and suffering to collaborate in their own humiliating re-socialization.

Of all the cruel and unusual punishments that make up the torturer's repertoire, there is one that demonstrates to perfection this ability of torturers and censors to work together in order to gain total control over how their victims use language. This punishment is elinguation, or the removal of the tongue. This form of punitive discipline has been used throughout the ages as a punishment for slander, for false accusation, for heresy, and other forms of apparently wicked speech. In effect, elinguation identifies the nexus where torture and censorship meet, join forces, and complement each other's secondary goals of forcing speech and forcing silence. That nexus is the tongue, the principle organ of speech. But elinguation represents more than a literal removal of the tongue. It should not be forgotten that in many languages across the world the word for tongue is the same as, or very similar to, the word for language. As such, elinguation signifies also a metaphorical removal of language from the self, a kind of exile of the victim of torture and censorship from his or her preferred community of speech.

It is easy to understand why this form of torture so completely satisfies the desires of the censor: it achieves in dramatic and explicit terms what censorship normally achieves only in metaphorical and implicit terms. Elinguation silences the victims of censorship completely. It is less obvious, however, why this punishment should satisfy the torturer. Torturers want to force their victims to speak, and if the victims have no tongues left in their mouths with which to speak they cannot very well satisfy this desire of the torturer. But elinguation fundamentally satisfies the torturer too. A torturer who decides to practice elinguation effectively gains total control over his victims' tongues; he literally takes possession of them. From the point of view of the victims, this is tantamount to saying that their tongues have become the enemy's tongues. Stolen from their original owners, these repossessed tongues will henceforth betray their own native languages, betray their own original communities of speech, and betray also the cultural values held by these communities of speech. From the point of view of the torturer, nothing could be more satisfying. For, by means of elinguation, the speech of his victims has been transformed into the silence of censorship: a kind of forced silence which, because it can never again be broken, is forever made complicit with the language that the torturer wants his victims to speak.

Betrayal is the end toward which both torture and censorship aim. Each, in its own right, is a method of speech control. Each seeks, on the basis of commands that are backed by violent threats, to break down loyalties and build up new ones in their place. When these two methods are put to work in tandem, they effectively break trust apart; they render meaningless the promises on which trust is built; and they undermine loyalty. By removing their victim's tongues—whether literally, as in the case of elinguation, or metaphorically, as in most other cases of cruel and unusual punishment—torturers and censors exile their victims from their original communities of trust; they remove their victims from their native circles of solidarity; and they force their victims to remake themselves in the image of those who torture them. Cut off in this way from communication with their own communities, displaced from their preferred circles of identification, the victims of torture and censorship become insurmountably isolated.

This isolating breakdown of the communal and cultural structures of language, of trust, and of loyalty is a punishment that is uniquely painful to humans. For insofar as humans are users of tools, they are distinguished from other animals that also use tools by reason of their ability to use the most powerful tool of all: language. To be stripped of language, of culture, of identity and then violently, forcefully, mercilessly re-socialized is the most painful punishment that a human being can be forced to bear. It is therefore also the cruelest and most humiliating punishment imaginable.

4

It used to be that in official circles in Washington, DC, torture was spoken of in the language of the Geneva Conventions as well as the United Nations Convention against Torture and Other Cruel, Inhuman or Degrading Treatment or Punishment. According to this language, which is the language of international law, torture is defined as:

> any act by which severe pain or suffering, whether physical or mental, is intentionally inflicted on a person for such purposes as obtaining from him or a third person information or a confession, punishing him for an act he or a third person has committed or is suspected of having committed, or intimidating or coercing him or a third person, or for any reason based on discrimination of any kind, when such pain or suffering is inflicted by or at the instigation of or with the consent or acquiescence of a public official or other person acting in an official capacity.[1]

The Bybee and Gonzales memos of 2002, however, effectively laid the groundwork for a new way of talking about torture in Washington. These memos reworked the traditional language as follows: "For an act to constitute torture, it must inflict pain that is difficult to endure. Physical pain amounting to torture must be equivalent to the pain accompanying serious physical injury, such as organ failure, impairment of bodily function, or even death." Or again: "For purely mental pain or suffering to amount to torture, it must result in significant psychological harm of significant duration, e.g., lasting for months or even years."[2]

Comparison of these two ways of speaking about torture reveals that the Bush administration has sought to legitimize cruel and humiliating treatment of prisoners of war by splitting hairs over what qualifies as "severe" pain. In practice, these memos suggest, so long as one does not cause permanent organ failure, brain damage, or death, one has not committed an act of torture. This opens up a very broad window of opportunity for practices that are cruel and intended to humiliate people. Indeed, as far as critics of the Bush administration in both the international community and at home have argued and continue to argue, this window of opportunity has been opened far too wide for the good of all concerned, as much for the captives who have been tortured as for the soldiers, CIA operatives, or mercenaries and other proxies under contract with the US government who have been committing acts of torture.

The memos in question, however, do not stop here, with this torturous twist on the definition of torture. They go on to consider how, on the basis of such a re-description of torture, US forces and their proxies might avoid being held legally accountable for what even the Bush administration understands to be cruel and humiliating conduct. "[A] defendant is guilty of torture only if he acts with the express purpose of inflicting severe pain or suffering on a person within his custody or physical control."[3] So those who do treat their prisoners cruelly, these memos argue, may enjoy immunity from both national and international law so long as they meet one of two requirements: 1) the pain they inflict is not severe enough to amount to what the Bush administration says constitutes torture; or 2) they have not acted with the express purpose of inflicting such severe pain. Finally, the rationale for this defense of torture is that "Under the current circumstances [viz., the War on Terror], necessity or self-defense may justify interrogation methods that [are cruel and humiliating but do not *amount* to torture]."[4] It is with this new and highly ambiguous language that the Bush administration has sought to justify acts of cruelty which by all international standards of law do amount to torture.

Generally speaking, efforts to create new languages or to use old languages in new ways and give them a renewed set of meanings, is something to be celebrated as an expression of freedom. Poets and other artists who work with words have done this sort of thing for centuries, and with admirable results. Scientists have done so too, and the outcomes at times have been revolutionary. It is in no small measure thanks to these new artistic and scientific languages that cultures throughout the modern world have progressed. As much in the realm of the humanities as in that of the sciences, such progress has required the participation of extensive communities of inquiry and the freedom of artists and scientists every-where to speak these new languages, to reproduce the new outlooks these languages make possible, to explore the limits of the new perspectives, and to reaffirm the cultural value of an exchange of ideas that is free of all coercion. Cultural progress of this sort has, in short, required freedom of inquiry, of thought, and of speech as well as agreement concerning the proper uses to which the new languages may be put.

The trouble with the kind of new language for torture that the Bush administration has proposed is that it is not based in such a free exchange of ideas and dialogue but in an attempt by a few secretive abusers of language to thwart the language that Americans, in combination with the international community, already do use to speak about torture. In no uncertain terms, the new Bush-speak on torture was born from a secretive discussion among the President and his advisors; it has been backed by a concerted effort to silence those who would doubt the usefulness of this new language to the continuing progress of democratic culture in the world; and it has demonstrated, as perhaps no other form of institutional double-speak to emerge recently from inside the Washington beltway, the hypocrisy of an administration that wants it both ways: to be able to say, together with the rest of the so-called free world, that they are the sort of people who would never torture others, but then go ahead and torture them anyway.

This Janus-faced approach to torture by Americans and their govern-ment is, of course, nothing new. The Bush administration has not invented torture in America; nor have the administration's attempts to provide a justifying discourse for torture been the first to be used by Americans at war. During the conquest and colonization of North America, the colonists from England and elsewhere in Europe effectively tortured, humiliated, and exterminated many Native American tribes. This was all done, naturally enough, in the name of those good pilgrims' prog-ress. For religious reasons too, puritanical communities around Salem, Massachusetts, tortured women as part of these communities' purifying witch-hunts. Throughout much of the national history of America, the imagined burden of the white man to civilize the so-called primitive people under his protection has served as a justification for the torture and lynching of African-American slaves and their descendants. And during the latter half of the twentieth century—a century commonly referred to by apologists for American imperialism as "the American Century"—the School of the Americas trained innumerable right-wing militias from Central and South America in the finer arts of torture. The scandalous torture of prisoners of war in Abu Ghraib and Guantánamo Bay today is but the latest chapter in this long and drawn out history of acts of systematic cruelty by Americans.

And still, in spite of this record of horrors committed by Americans in the name of the civilizing power of American democratic culture, it is not as though Americans have grown accustomed to thinking of themselves as the kind of people who either condone or commit acts of torture. Reasons for this apparent rift between the historical record and the conception that Americans have of themselves and of their government have largely to do with the national language by means of which Americans are socialized. This national language is the language of enlightened liberalism. Americans have been socialized to speak this language; in schools, in history books, in political debate, and at the movies, they use this language to describe themselves, to narrate their past, and to give expression to their belief that they are part of a unique political tradition of increasing individual freedoms and expanding social hopes. It is by no means an exaggeration to say that their ability, as a democratic people, to continue using this language candidly has been compromised by the new Bush-speak on torture. The officials of the Bush administration may want Americans to believe that this tongue-twisting abuse of the language of international law provides American patriots with a justification to treat their perceived enemies with unrestrained cruelty, but in practice it serves to undermine, rather than advance, the liberal ideals and political convictions on which America and other democracies throughout the world are based.

If Americans were not participants in a democratic experiment, and were subject only to the whims of some despotic and tyrannical governing elite, the fact that Americans do torture (and have been torturing for centuries) would not contradict their national language. There would be no scandal, moral, political, or historical. As a people, Americans would not be disgraced by the cruelty of their leaders and guardians. For such a polity would be governed by fear, cruelty, and humiliation. Under such circumstances, Americans would not speak the language of freedom and solidarity that they have traditionally spoken, but a language of obedience and discipline. The contempt that the Bush administration has displayed for human rights, for international law, and for democracy both at home and abroad has brought this language of obedience and discipline danger-ously close to every American citizen's heart. Those who still harbor hope for a future where personal freedoms will increase and social equality will expand must refuse this new language and the authoritarian values of discipline and obedience it so freely expresses.

Americans today face a very real problem when it comes to describ-ing who they are. They have been socialized as liberals, as a people who believe that humiliating others is the worst thing that they can do, but their current government systematically tortures, humiliates, and ma-ligns others—both those it perceives as its anti-American enemies from abroad and those it perceives as its anti-American enemies at home. Such systematic humiliation of others contradicts the principles of American socialization. So, either the American people cease to use their traditional national language and begin to speak of themselves as the sort of people who do condone torture; or they speak out against the attempts by the Bush administration to generate a new language of tyranny for America. That is, either they hold their silence and timidly cave in to the threats with which the Bush administration has been attempting to govern them and the world, or they boldly uphold their ever-weakening freedom to speak against the administration's coercive political tactics and speak out in defense of their liberal, albeit utopian, hope for a government that will do all that is within its power to assure that the freedoms Americans enjoy and the circles of solidarity that they construct do not require the systematic humiliation of other people, including (or even especially) their perceived enemies.

5

When it comes to torture, it may seem a bit out of place to focus so much attention on language, be it the traditional language used by the international community to prohibit torture or the new language proposed by the Bush administration to kind-of-sort-of-but-not-really condone the practice of torture. After all, as both these languages attest, torture involves inflicting severe pain on human bodies and minds; it does not involve the destruction of dictionaries, the violation of grammatical rules, or the breach of linguistic codes. Still, as both the international community and the Bush administration point out, the issue concerning the bodily and mental pain caused by torture is its severity. Perhaps better than any other tool available to us, language can measure this severity. This is the case insofar as language is able to describe pain and provide us with an indication of how severe the pain in question is. This descriptive faculty of language does have its limits, however. Those who have been tortured can attest to the fact that there is pain that is ineffable, indescribable, and beyond the scope of language altogether. Such pain is the most severe. Not surprisingly, it is precisely this kind of pain that torture seeks to cause.

Torture uses severe bodily and mental pain to get its victims to say, think, believe, or do things that will violate who they have become in life. If the torture is successful, the victims will prove unable to talk about what they were forced to say, believe, or do in any fashion that coheres with who they used to be before they were tortured. Thus torture introduces a fundamental split, an aporia, a gap and resounding silence in the narrative structure of the lives of its victims. The things that victims of torture are forced to say, believe, or do are literally beyond linguistic recall. They cannot be woven into the fabric of the victim's life narrative because the language that the victim once used to tell that story is unable either to name or describe these things. Lying beyond the strictures of language, these "things" which the victims of torture say, believe, or do are also, consequently, beyond translation. There is no language capable of describing the ineffable pain of torture.[5]

What makes torture so perverse is that it tricks its victims into believing that such a language might just exist. This trick is fairly elaborate and works in stages. First, torture uses severe, indescribable, and un-narratable pain in order to push its victims into a realm that lies beyond the reach of language. In this realm where silence reigns, the victim suffers a new kind of pain. This is the pain of censorship, of excommunication, and homelessness. The victim's pain is made more unbearable still by this silence that conditions it and recontextualizes it in the solitude of exile. Alone with this terrible pain, and unable either to describe or narrate it, the exiled victim of torture longs desperately for a way to place his pain back within the system of meanings that only language and culture can provide. Second, torture holds out the promise of such a return to the realm of language and civilization to its victims. This is, however, a false promise, which offers only a false return "home," as it were, to the realm of culture and its cooperative systems of shared values and appropriated meanings. The severe pain of torture pushes its victims from their own community and invites them "back" to another, different community, with a language all its own. This other language cannot, however, provide the victims of torture with the meaning they hope to give to their ineffable suffering: for it is the language of the torturer and of the torturer's community that would now provide the victims with a safe passage and return "home" to civilization. Third, the return to language, to meaning, and to culture that torture provides its victims serves to perpetuate the displacement originally caused by the severity of the pain the victims have been made to suffer. The language that torture offers its victims is, in the end, the language of betrayal.

Treason is the language victims of torture are tricked into speaking, for they are led to believe that this language will put an end to their terrible pain-induced exile and allow them to re-enter the world of language and communication. Treason is also the language they must learn to speak if they mean to make the severity of their pain meaningful. This means, in so many words, that victims of torture are tricked into speaking the one language that will forever separate their tongues from their own community's preferred structures of language, trust, and loyalty. The language of treason that torture forces on its victims perpetuates their pain and suffering. It does so by ensuring that the victims cooperate in their own humiliation. Thus, torture stigmatizes their tongues, fills their mouths with filth, and shames them.

6

The torture that the Bush administration has recently instructed American servicemen and women to commit has created two sorts of involuntary traitors. The first kind is to be found among the victims of this torture. They are the ones who, in the hope that they will be able to return from the realm of ineffable pain to the realm of community and language, have learned to speak in tongues. Their betrayal is involuntary in the sense that they are duped into speaking this other language which, rather than return them to their preferred community of language, displaces them in the community of their enemies. The second kind of involuntary traitor is to be found among the torturers themselves and those who, out of complicity with their cruelty, practice censorship. These are the traitors who, because they are overly eager to uphold the trust that American society has placed in them as public servants, have overstepped the limits of that trust and broken it. Their treason is involuntary inasmuch as they have been tricked into confusing torture with freedom and cruelty with patriotism.

There is, of course, a sense in which this confusion provides a unique clarity of purpose and mind. For torturers, acts of torture do constitute freedom. This freedom is limitless. Because they are in total control of their victims, torturers are free to do with the bodies and minds of their victims as they damned well please. In this sense, the limitless nature of the freedom of torturers correlates with the severity of the pain suffered by the victims of torture. Just as torturers inflict pain on their victims in order to humiliate them and exile them to a realm of treasonous silence, they also use their unbounded power to humiliate their victims as a means to step beyond the normative limits that comprise the moral and political life of most human communities. By denying their victims any protection under the law, torturers in effect place themselves above the law. Their freedom to satisfy their every whim is, to all intents and purposes, the only law of torture.

The unbridled freedom of torturers to do as they wish recognizes none of the limits traditionally placed on freedom by the liberal democratic tradition. Indeed, nothing could be more foreign to the torturer's sense of liberty than the liberal idea that his freedom *to* do as he pleases should be limited by his victim's freedom *from* coercion. The relationship between the torturer and his victim is characterized by the most radical inequality imaginable; it is designed with the specific intent of permitting the torturer to violate the freedom of his victims: as much their freedom to speak as they will as their freedom from being forced to speak as they will not to speak. Within the context of torture, the torturer is completely free, and the victim completely denied of freedom.

Extreme positive liberties, of the sort that torturers take with their victims, are the radical freedoms that authoritarian cultures typically oppose to the more moderate negative and positive freedoms of democratic cultures. Liberty, in authoritarian cultures, is wild; it pushes positive freedom beyond any limits that negative freedom might place on it. The liberty of liberalism is, by comparison, rather tame; the liberal's freedom *to* is limited by other liberals' freedom *from* and vice-versa. Thus, it is within the realm of authoritarian cultures (including democratic cultures with authoritarian tendencies) that the confusion of freedom with torture will lead to the corresponding confusion of patriotism with cruelty. Systematic acts of cruelty will seem patriotic to those who commit these acts only when their ability to inflict such humiliating abuses on others is linked to a culture of extreme positive liberties. These are, precisely, the sorts of liberties that the Bush administration has claimed for itself vis-à-vis those so-called enemy combatants it has held captive and tortured in jails throughout Afghanistan, Iraq, Cuba and elsewhere in the violently civilized world.

To claim the positive freedom to torture, as the Bush administration has, constitutes a betrayal of the liberal ideals and social hopes that have traditionally inspired Americans to take pride in their country's democratic freedoms. The Bush administration has sought to replace the language of balanced negative and positive liberties—the language in which the Bill of Rights is written—with the language of a radical, extreme, and forceful positive liberty. The recent and ongoing torture of prisoners by American soldiers demonstrates the extent to which American democratic culture is now grounded, not in the moderate positive and negative freedoms of the liberal tradition that once gave rise to the American Revolution, but in the unrestrained positive freedoms of an authoritarian culture.

That the cruelty of extreme positive freedoms can be justified in terms of a civilizing mission, of which "Securing the Homeland" is only the most recent example, is something that has been proven time and again throughout American history as well as the history of enlightened democratic cultures most everywhere in the modern world. That such justification has served in many instances to silence those who would voice their critiques of this kind of putatively civilizing violence is another unfortunate truism of modern history. Still, insofar as these cruel practices and cynical justifications have not managed to completely undermine ongoing experiments with democracy in America or elsewhere in the world, those who do participate actively in these experiments should feel free to speak about such abuses in the language that describes them best. That is, of course, the language of betrayal, the language that twists tongues and twists meanings such that torture can be confused with freedom and cruelty with patriotism.

7

"Open wide," you urge with cunning kindness. Your victim has been lying unconscious, strapped to the dentist's chair in the center of the room, for over two minutes now. You refuse to proceed with the operation at hand unless he is wide awake and completely aware of the total power you still have over him. You break some smelling stones beneath his nose and he responds as you hoped he would. He opens his eyes. "Open wide," you command again, this time with growing impatience. He seems to think your command was in reference to his eyes only, which he quickly shuts and opens again in an evident and desperate attempt to please you. "Your mouth, you fool; open your filthy mouth. Wider!" You resent having to explain your commands in such detail to this sad excuse for human dignity that lies before you, strapped in the dentist's chair. So you grab hold of his mouth with both hands and pull it open violently. You can see from the way his eyes begin to water and from the sudden, uncontrollable shake of his body that his jaw has finally snapped at the joints and locked into the wide open position you desire and require. "That is much better," you say to him with loving encouragement.

You take hold of your favorite set of pliers again and show them to his crying, pleading, horrified eyes. You adjust the overhanging light so it reveals the depths of your victim's throat. Skillfully, you insert the pliers into his mouth. You watch as the blood-stained metal takes hold of the bit of tongue which still remains and must be cut out in order for your victim's elinguation to be completed to your utter satisfaction. "Pass me the knife," you command one of your dutiful, patriotic, freedom-loving assistants. You take hold of the knife from its handle and slip it down your victim's throat, being careful to lacerate as many vocal chords as possible on the way. Once the knife has reached the depths of your victim's throat, you begin to saw away at what is left of the tongue. And with a final pull of the pliers, you extract the one remaining piece of mangled, meaty tongue.

The pain that now washes over your victim is synchronized with the wave of sheer, powerful delight that washes over your entire being. His pain is your gain. He is drowning in that pain now. He is drowning in it with sorrow and shame: with sorrow because, at your bidding, he did at long last use his tongue to speak to you in your own language; with shame because the silence that you have now imposed on him will forever make him complicit with your unbridled cruelty, your limitless power to humiliate, your unbending dedication to the exercise of such awesome freedom. He is drowning in the pain and may pass out any moment now. So you must work quickly now. Before he passes into a state of unconsciousness, you lean down and whisper your good-bye wishes in his ear: "I trust that you now understand, my friend, what it is we mean when we say that there is no greater love in life than the love of freedom." As you step away from your victim and look him over one last time with hatred, you cannot help but feel proud about how you have contributed, in your own little way, to defending the freedom of your own people from those who profess to hate you, above all, for your enduring freedom.

NOTES

1. UN Convention Against Torture, www.hrweb.org/legal/cat.html.

2. Bybee and Gonzales Memos, www.humanrightsfirst.org/us_law/etn/gonzales/memos.dir.

3. Bybee and Gonzales Memos.

4. Bybee and Gonzales Memos.

5. I owe some of these insights into how the severe pain of torture and its resulting humiliations make it impossible for the victims of torture to reconstitute themselves and their world through language to Richard Rorty's essay, "The last intellectual in Europe: Orwell on cruelty" in *Contingency, Irony, and Solidarity* (Cambridge: Cambridge University Press, 1999), 176–179.

6

The Terrorist We Torture: The Tale of Abdul Hakim Murad

Stephanie Athey

IN HIS CONTROVERSIAL RESPONSE TO THE 9/11 ATTACKS, Alan Dershowitz argued that to limit torture, we must authorize it in special cases. In 2002's *Why Terrorism Works*, he confronts the reader with this undeniable "empirical reality":

> The tragic reality is that torture sometimes works, much though many people wish it did not. There are numerous instances in which torture has produced self-proving thoughtful information that was necessary to prevent harm to civilians.[1]

Instead of "numerous instances," however, Dershowitz gives us only one, the case of Pakistani terrorist Abdul Hakim Murad.

Tortured in the Philippines in 1995, Murad was tried in the US and is now serving time for a terrorist conspiracy that many now view as a precursor to the attacks in the US in September 2001, "a plot to knock down 11 or 12 commercial airliners flying over the Pacific and a plot to kill the Pope," according to Dershowitz in one interview.[2]

Dershowitz's reliance on Murad was hardly novel; following the 9/11 attacks a score of journalists rediscovered in Murad the very embodiment of the ticking time bomb terrorist. For years after, his case has received virtually uncontested repetition in news and arguments by influential legal voices on "torture," such as Dershowitz—who cites Murad frequently in television appearances and in print—and Richard Posner, Sanford Levinson and David Luban. In all but the last, Murad is made to answer the question "Does torture work?"[3]

In the idiom of these arguments on torture, the question is not in truth about torture but a question that situates the writer amongst his or her peers. "Does torture work?" separates the sturdy thinker who has done his real world homework from the willowy idealist lost in a daydream. This half-formed rhetorical prop is designed to be answered with an anecdote. And Murad's case has been designed to be that anecdote.[4]

This essay weighs the recent writing on Murad against its conflicting source material to offer a case study in the speed and power of torture myth-making. Like the breathtakingly ungrounded claims borne on the back of the Battle of Algiers, the tale of Murad functions to deflect complex thinking on torture and to support the practice. Remarkable here is the agility with which the US "war on terror" produced a homespun mythic equivalent from material so ill-suited to demonstrate its claims.

But Murad's story is also index to something more. The writing on Murad is embedded in a wider group of news stories that first emerged in mid-September 2001 when dozens of news features and commentaries began to debate the utility of torture in the war on terror in major media outlets. Speculation on torture gathered momentum in the weeks *before* the November 2001 Executive Order on military tribunals signaled the scope of the administration's intentions toward captives, and it gained critical mass years before the 2004 photos from Abu Ghraib. Hypothetical torture became a big news story during years when actual torture was not getting reported.[5]

In other words, the speculative press was defining torture and imagining its uses both in advance of and alongside the torture memos and interrogation protocols quietly being drawn up inside the Executive Branch. Broadly influential, the news writing struck narrative postures, anointed experts, and lent terminology, propositions and anecdotal evidence that were taken up and repeated in other arenas.

In this sense, the myth-making of Murad and the "torture debate" in which he plays his part should be read as a critical discourse of empire unfolding in the present. This is true not only because the stories debate the proper role and function of violence, a key tool in securing and defining the "new" American empire so vigorously proclaimed in a plethora of recent books on the subject. It is true also because the *language of violence* will be a more flexible and pervasive instrument of empire, accomplishing things that violence alone cannot.

For instance, once one's attention is drawn to it, it is obvious that such speculation on torture would do the work of imagining the terrorist we torture. But the writing is about much more than this. One chief product of this discourse is the palpable sense of moral community it deliberately crafts and wields. The speculation imagines and defines "torture" surely, but also the community that will authorize it and benefit from it or end it. What is true of writing on Murad, then, is true of the larger "debate." In elaborating a concept of the "terrorist we torture," what is at stake in that debate is the imaginative constitution of three deeply interdependent notions: the terrorist, torture, and ourselves.[6]

TRACKING MURAD

When Abdul Hakim Murad was arrested in the Philippines in 1995, he was already a licensed commercial pilot who had received his flight training at a number of US schools. He was also one member of a three-man cell that was methodically working out logistical difficulties associated with a plan to plant bombs on at least two flights originating in Asia and heading to the US. Accounts of Murad's plot alternately claim he was targeting two, ten, eleven or twelve planes at one time. However, for many reasons, Murad's intentions and the conflicting claims made about them are an important part of the story.

According to the plan, Murad was to assemble a liquid bomb beneath his passenger seat and set its timer during the first leg of a flight; he would deplane on layover and repeat the process on a second aircraft. The bombs would be timed to explode together, during the trans-Pacific segment of each flight. The process could be repeated on multiple planes and the timers could be set hours and days ahead. This scheme was referred to as *Bojinka* or "loud bang" by Ramzi Yousef, Murad's notorious accomplice.

Ramzi Yousef, well-known in the US for his role in a 1993 World Trade Center attack, had made a "dry run" at Bojinka in late December 1994, exploding a device on a Philippines Airlines flight, killing one passenger. In January 1995, Murad and his two accomplices were arrested and the plot foiled by Philippine officials. The FBI mounted a case that convicted Yousef, Murad, and their financial officer, Walid Khan Amin Shah, in New York in 1996.

In the immediate wake of the attacks in 2001, the Philippine National Police made sure the press knew the FBI had bungled. Since 1995, the FBI had known that terrorists with a connection to a notorious bin Laden associate, Khalid Sheik Mohammad (Yousef's uncle), were developing a vision of attack by passenger airline.

While more than a few voices in the US and international press now insisted Murad's case was a warning that went unheeded and an unconscionable intelligence failure, other reporting hailed him as an intelligence success. This is because Murad experienced prolonged and systematic torture in the custody of the Philippine National Police (PNP) and intelligence service. Arrested on January 7, 1995, five days before Pope John Paul II paid a high security visit to Manila, Murad was held until mid-April. During months of "tactical interrogation," he confessed to several plots.

Murad's allegations of violent torture were carried in the news of his 1996 trial. Judge Kevin Thomas Duffy made a finding of "no torture" despite medical testimony backing Murad's claims and an audio tape of his first interrogation. The sounds on the tape, according to the judge, were indeed suspect, but they may or may not indicate a drowning procedure. The judge further stated that Murad's hands would not have been shackled *and* pinned down in the manner he claimed in one instance, nor would torture and treatment of his wounds have proceeded simultaneously as Murad claimed. (In these assertions, at least, the judge divulged a limited understanding of torture practice.) Finally, he held that even if Murad's confession had been assembled under uncertain conditions overseas, it was repeated "freely" once Philippine intelligence handed him into FBI custody. It was therefore admissible in court. FBI agent Frank Pellegrino had worked closely with the PNP and visited Manila many times during Murad's ordeal, and it was Agent Pellegrino who took Murad's statement during a five hour in-flight interview from Manila to New York.[7]

Though Judge Duffy flatly dismissed the notion, the Philippine authorities acknowledged the torture. In 1995 as well as today, they claim their work on Murad as a great success. Two Filipina reporters verified the torture with the PNP for *Under the Crescent Moon: Rebellion in Mindanao*, published in 2000. In their book, Marites Vitug and Glenda Gloria draw on declassified Philippine National Police and FBI intelligence reports, as well as courtroom testimony from the 1996 trial. Reference to the book is important because *Under the Crescent Moon* is cited repeatedly in 2001 and after by commentaries that showcase Murad's torture. Even so, those same commentaries uniformly ignore or suppress important elements of the complete story Vitug and Gloria try to tell, elements later confirmed by other sources.[8] Yet, from those commentaries, Murad's story takes wing. The very ubiquity of his story becomes self-confirming.

RECOUNTING MURAD

Reading the current stories together, one can see exact or nearly exact repetitions, the kind that arise when papers and lawyers crib from each other. However, what is remarkable is the amount of variation and conflict in the writing on Murad. Puzzling contradictions of fact are allowed to stand without question, including the number and kind of targets under attack, how and even whether the Pope was a target, and whether suicide attack by air was ever planned.[9] Even more bizarrely, several reports portray obviously disparate plots as a single unified scheme.[10]

Which portions of which plots were under way, exactly; which were "foiled" by torture? The claims made for Murad's torture are specific, namely, his torture "produced self-proving thoughtful information that was necessary to prevent harm to civilians."[11] Given the well-known correlations between false confession and duress, let alone false confession and torture, it is surprising that none of this reporting registers the discrepancies. The point is not to say no plots were under way, but to ask at what point this proliferation of conflicting accounts would in itself merit attention, raising a shade of doubt concerning the validity of the confessions, the utility of torture, or, at the least, the reliability of the reporting?

But there are greater problems than clarity at stake. Rather than a tale that grows suspect through error or fixed through repetition, there seems to be a more dynamic echo and distortion at work. From story to story, aspects of Murad's physical ordeal, his arrest, and his plans are amplified and embroidered; other details are recast or removed.

What emerges is a purpose-driven parable, one that reinforces favorite premises and comes packaged with all the suspense, horror, and didactic zeal of a good story. Instead of flat affect and passive construction, we routinely get an action vignette steeped in the language of noir-nostalgia. Doug Struck introduces the story of Murad's torture into the post-9/11 news stream in a September 23, 2001, *Washington Post* report.

> Murad would not talk. Handed over to intelligence agents, he taunted them. That didn't last. "For weeks, agents hit him with a chair and a long piece of wood, forced water into his mouth and crushed lighted cigarettes into his private parts," wrote journalists Marites Vitug and Glenda Gloria in "Under the Crescent Moon," an acclaimed book on Abu Sayyaf. "His ribs were almost totally broken and his captors were surprised he survived."
>
> An investigator intimately knowledgeable of the investigation confirmed the torture, but gloated that it was Murad's fears of Jews that finally broke him. "We impersonated the Mossad," he said referring to the Israeli intelligence service. "He thought we were going to take him to Israel."
>
> Murad told all. One of his two roommates in Apt. 603 was a young Kuwaiti chemical engineer named Ramzi Ahmed Yousef, who had helped him plan the 1993 explosions at the World Trade Center, he said. They were in Manila to make a bomb to kill the Pope. One of them would hide it under a priest's robes, and try to get close enough to kiss the pontiff as the bomb went off.
>
> The next part of the plan was to bomb American airliners. The device on the Philippine airliner was a dry run, he said. Murad

had earned a commercial pilot's license, and told investigators
he had planned to fly a plane into the CIA headquarters.[12]

Murad's plans are harrowing, and the terse phrasing that opens and closes
the scene of violence confirms the power of torture: "Murad would not
talk," "Murad told all."

Struck supplements *Under the Crescent Moon* with a new anonymous
source. Deemed credible despite his "gloating" delivery, he introduces
a detail not found elsewhere: impersonating the Mossad. This anecdote
takes flight. It is reprised in Jay Winik's *Wall Street Journal* piece, "Security Comes Before Liberty":

> In 1995, a little-known operative, Abdul Hakim Murad,
> was arrested in the Philippines on a policeman's hunch. Inside
> Murad's apartment were passports and a homemade bomb fac-
> tory—beakers, filters, fuses and funnel; gallons of sulfuric acid
> and nitric acid, large cooking kettles.
>
> Handed over to intelligence agents, Murad was violently
> tortured. For weeks, according to the book "Under the Crescent
> Moon," agents struck him with a chair and pounded him with a
> heavy piece of wood, breaking nearly every rib. Even then, he
> remained silent. In the end, they broke him through a psycho-
> logical trick. A few Philippine agents posed as members of the
> Mossad and told Murad they were taking him to Israel. Terrified
> of being turned over to the Israelis, he finally told all. Then and
> only then.
>
> And what a treasure trove of information it was. . . .
>
> One wonders of course, what would have happened if Murad
> had been in American custody.[13]

Winik kicks up the drama and insinuates the moral: US squeamishness
about torture would have sacrificed information and lives. Other stories
will be more forthright in saying it is time for Americans to take a page
from the Philippines' playbook.

The contrast between US and Filipino methods becomes the first of
several recurring motifs in the coverage. As Peter Maas writes in "Torture
Tough or Lite: If a Terror Suspect Won't Talk, Should He Be Made To?"
"In many countries, terrorism suspects like Mr. Murad rarely receive the
local equivalent of the Miranda rights; instead, they are tortured."[14]

Second, most stories can't resist publishing the details of torture, but
these are selected and showcased differently in each account. The effect
is that we seem to look right at the act of torture with all its repugnance
and horror. Routinely omitted are electroshock and rape, perhaps because

these are aspects of the Philippine playbook less appealing to emulate. According to Murad's motion to suppress, he was kept blindfolded and subjected to rape, threats of rape, dragging of his body back and forth across his cell, cigarette burns on his genitals, hands and feet, electric shock, drowning, force-feeding with liquid, bone-breaking beatings, and the "denial of proper sustenance." To this list Vitug and Gloria add the application of ice to his body.[15]

Third, the Mossad anecdote serves the explicit function of distinguishing physical torture from "psychological methods." In *Newsweek*'s widely read "Time to Think About Torture," of November 5, 2001, Jonathan Alter states the lesson plainly: "Some torture clearly works." Yet he suppresses details of Murad's extreme physical assault entirely. "Philippine police reportedly helped crack the 1993 World Trade Center bombings (plus a plot to crash 11 US airliners and kill the Pope) by convincing a suspect that they were about to turn him over to the Israelis."[16]

In keeping with Alter's proposal that the US permit "psychological" torture, including immersion in high-decibel sound, he ignores the burnt genitals and broken ribs. (Notably he also collapses his own distinction between torture to prevent future terror and torture to "crack" a past case.) Peter Maas, too, takes up the Mossad lesson: "Mr. Murad, who feared Jews as much as he hated them, quickly spilled the beans." He quotes "a prominent terrorism expert": "You've got to engage in this psychological game. Not just pain but wearing him down physically and spiritually." Here is the odd but common suggestion that "wearing him down physically" is not truly *physical* but more properly psychological in nature. In fact, "psychological" techniques deliberately distress the body to affect the mind and personality. The sensory deprivation and high-decibel auditory assaults that intrigue Alter (and have been practiced on detainees in Bagram and Guantánamo and Iraq) are good examples of this. So too is the alternate version of the Mossad story told in a different context by one of Murad's interrogators. Here, extreme hunger seems a more powerful motivation to "talk" than the "fear and hatred of Jews." Denied food for a long period, Murad is taunted with a Big Mac and fries. Unmoved by a choice between extradition to the Americans or the Mossad, he speaks up when the interrogators begin to walk out with the food.[17]

Despite the fact that "psychological" tactics take place under conditions already set by ongoing physical and mental suffering and violence, the Mossad anecdote becomes charged with a talismanic quality, marking out a magic line that is merely a wishful distinction. Matus' *Daily Standard* piece asserts the distinction between US and Philippine methods and contrasts psychological and physical torture in a single headline:

"Making Terrorists Talk: America Doesn't Use Torture to Get Information Out of Terrorists. Perhaps We Just Need to Use the Magic Word: 'Mossad.'"[18]

Finally, no one has done more to peddle the parable of Murad than Alan Dershowitz. In writing, he offers the story in nearly the same ubiquitous stylized form seen so far and concludes "there can be no doubt" that torture sometimes works. In Dershowitz or Richard Posner or Sanford Levinson, Murad's case is positioned as a foothold in the "real," a point of sturdy leverage from which one quickly pushes off into gross generalization or pure speculation. Hence the increasing weight borne by Murad builds to Dershowitz' colossally uninformed assertion:

> It is precisely because torture sometimes does work and can sometimes prevent major disasters that it still exists in many parts of the world and has been totally eliminated from none.[19]

Moreover, as a stand-in for real world knowledge of torture, the brief exhibition of Murad initiates the reader into the community of the "morally serious," to use Levinson's terms. "Whether lawyers or simply citizens," when "we" see Murad's ordeal, we know that torture is repugnant and also pragmatic, provided we look no further into its conditions of possibility and its effects.[20]

ASSESSING MURAD

Were Murad not so satisfying in his narrative incarnation as ticking time bomb terrorist, his case might have motivated writers to a more thorough and responsible use of original sources and the back file of their own newspapers, where reporting on Murad's trial appeared in 1996. These sources confound the favorite premises of the Murad parable.

Timing and Torture. The claim that torture was an urgent, race-against-the-clock affair, is belied by the circumstances and duration. Philippine authorities explained, "What was at stake was the life of the Pope."[21] Yet the Pope came and went within the first nine days of his ordeal. Murad was tortured systematically and continuously over three months' time.[22] The January 7 interrogation tape that suggests a drowning procedure indicates torture was a first approach on the day of his capture, not a last resort.[23] Nor is torture a means to an end, a practice that stops when the talking begins. January and February transcripts and intelligence reports suggest Murad was "cooperating" *and* being tortured for a long period.[24] As a ritual of detention, torture and talking proceeded in tandem until his April release to the FBI.

Investigation and Torture. An additional problem for the claim that this torture prevented imminent terror lies in the fact that the terror plots, whatever they were in actuality, were routed at the moment Murad was arrested. At that time, the Manila apartment that served as the cell's bomb-making laboratory was shut down, and information at the site tracked the two accomplices. Indeed, Shah was arrested five days later, and Yousef was arrested February 7.[25] Though plotters and weapons were quickly in hand, torture continued in grossly ingenious ways for two months more.

Of course, officials could not have known that the plots were scuttled completely on the first day. But stories that attributed the "break" in the case to torture flatly ignore the evidence said to be found in Murad's apartment. In addition to bomb-making equipment and evidence that tracked co-conspirators, a computer there was said to hold photos and aliases, airline names, flight numbers, and timer detonation settings. With this wealth of detail, airline security could have "foiled" the Bojinka plot promptly, even if accomplices and bombs were not already in hand. If the evidence at the scene was what the police said it was, swift use of routine tools of investigation could have or did deliver more useful intelligence more quickly than the tools of torture.[26]

Blame the Mossad: Police Credibility I. It is against this mass of physical evidence that Murad's torturers are asked to evaluate the relative "efficacy of torture" they perpetrated for several months. This is not unique to Murad's case. Again and again it is the torture team which is allowed to attest to its own success, individuals who have the most at stake in asserting the value of their methods. That one admits to torture poses no problem of credibility.

In this light, we ought to reconsider the "gloating" anecdote of the Mossad that becomes a stock element of the story: "We impersonated the Mossad . . . He thought we were going to take him to Israel." The claim combines braggadocio and self-justification, and torturers are known to indulge in both, depending on the audience. Jacobo Timerman writes of his own torturers' tendency to exaggerate when recounting the very procedures he had just endured. John Conroy's excellent comparative look at torture by Israelis, English, and the US police demonstrates that torturers routinely blame others for worse behavior; that is, they contrast their "humane" techniques with more extreme methods used elsewhere. In the terms of the torturer's boast, the listener is meant to understand that, in comparison to the Mossad, the gross violence of the Filipino perpetrators was nothing.[27]

Police Credibility II: Planted Evidence. As with the conflicting confessions, there are conflicting reports of materials found at Murad's apartment. Unconscionably, all recent accounts of Murad omit the fact that the Philippine police invented evidence, falsified reports, and memorized testimony concerning evidence on the scene. This fact is available in press coverage of the 1996 trial and in *Under the Crescent Moon*. During that trial, two Philippine officers unexpectedly testified that they had manipulated evidence under orders. They surprised the defense, who were already planning to argue that the files in the laptop computer had been "altered and changed consequentially" by the PNP.[28] The episode highlights what reporters might have pursued but did not, just as it throws into question the reliability of the police sources on the matter of the torture, on the confessions, and the links between torture and myriad other forms of corruption. If torture is permitted under professional pressure to "make a case," what is not?

U.S. Collaboration in Torture. Vitug and Gloria remind their readers that torture was systematized in the Philippines under Ferdinand Marcos as a means to force criminal suspects to incriminate themselves, and torture has remained a tool of the judicial system. What they find unique about Murad's case was that he was not Filipino. The potential for international repercussions had previously spared foreigners such severe assault.

But the international implications of Murad's capture were clear from the outset and would have weighed in favor of aggressive treatment, not against it. The US shared information on potential plots in advance of the Pope's visit. At the time of Murad's capture, the Philippine police were aware the US was offering a $2 million dollar reward for tips on Ramzi Yousef, Murad's accomplice. Within a week of Murad's capture, the CIA and the FBI were informed, and "a team of intelligence agents flew in from Washington."[29] The FBI received transcripts of ongoing "tactical interrogation," and Murad's interrogators received frequent visits from FBI agent Pellegrino.[30] The PNP understood the working relationship: "The US realized . . . it was in their best interest to have all information extracted from Murad by all means possible—in the Philippines. 'They preferred we did the dirty job for them,' says a Camp Crame official."[31]

Though the 1996 reporting raised the issue of collaboration in torture, the current writing on Murad obscures the FBI's role in order to contrast US methods favorably with those in the Philippines. To suggest the US was *not* aware of the torture seems deliberately naïve. Moreover, it is a position staked out in a historical vacuum.

The PNP of the 1990s had earned a considerable reputation for violence, a reputation of which the FBI would have been aware. According to Amnesty International's 2003 report, "Philippines: Torture Persists," the government's 1992 amnesty deal for right-wing military torturers and death squads extended to the PNP and furthered the rise of corrupt officials in that organization.[32]

The drowning and stomach pumping Murad endured were infamous features of America's first years in the Philippines. Water torture and other military atrocities were discussed heatedly early in the 1900s and were admitted to be US policy in some cases.[33] Since that time, the Philippines has served as a laboratory and training ground for development of US counterinsurgency relationships and tactics. During the 1950s, Colonel Edward Lansdale "rehearsed" techniques in the Philippines that were deemed atrocities when associated with Vietnam's Operation Phoenix, a program Lansdale helped devise. So too, during the late 1970s and 1980s—throughout the Marcos dictatorship—the CIA and Joint US Military Advisory Group worked with the Philippines intelligence service and military on counterinsurgency efforts.[34]

Murad's torture and the longer story of US counterinsurgency collaboration in the Philippines should remind us that the current practice of extraordinary rendition has a long foreground. Across the twentieth century US intelligence services have developed and nurtured relationships with their counterparts abroad, relationships built on the exchange of intelligence, techniques and equipment, and on routines of deniability which maintain the US in an "advisory" role while allowing the US to benefit from the terror, suppressive power, and self-incriminations that torture generates. The notion has gained currency of late that while the CIA's so-called "psychological paradigm" for torture has been responsible for torture relationships in the past and present, the FBI's hands are clean.[35] However, as Murad's case shows, the FBI cannot be so easily exonerated.

Indeed, we needn't go so far back as Murad's 1995 experience in the Philippines to discover that intelligence agencies including the FBI have preferred the advisor-to-torture role when dealing with al-Qaeda suspects. Allegations of torture posed problems in criminal cases in 2000, when three of the four defendants brought to trial for the 1998 embassy bombings in Kenya and Tanzania argued that they had signed confessions only after physical coercion in Pakistan and Kenya under the supervision of the FBI. These cases follow a pattern similar to that of Murad.[36]

THE TERRORIST, TORTURE, AND OURSELVES

Given the PNP reputation, the intensive FBI collaboration, the visits, and the shared interrogation transcripts, the more patent and tenable conclusion is that the Philippine authorities tortured Murad over an extended period with US knowledge and did so in order to build a case for US courts.

Though his story has been circulated to argue for a torture "exception" to US law, Murad's capture, torture and trial offer a potent demonstration of how the US legal system has progressively and effectively accommodated or integrated the use of torture—not banned it.

Of course, such conclusions and the links to the historical dimensions of US torture practice have all been scrubbed from Murad's case. Reinvented as parable, Murad offers instead a set of false premises and distinctions: that psychological techniques are separable from physical pain and that there is a clear distinction between psychological and physical torture; likewise, that there is a clear distinction between torture for "prevention" of future terror and torture for "confession" of past crimes; that torture "works" better than investigation and that torturers are reliable sources when it comes to evaluating their own methods; and above all, that torture is something alien to the contemporary US, not something thoroughly integrated into police work, domestic systems of punishment, or international security relationships.[37]

These contentions are so powerfully encoded in the parable of Murad, indeed in the "torture debate" in general, that even those who argue forcefully *against* the use of torture find themselves repeating and reinforcing these premises. For instance, both opponents and advocates for the torture of terrorists present torture as a "new" temptation, one the country must either consider or continue to reject. This is an effort of amnesia, certainly, but above all an assertion of identity that enlists readers into a compelling fantasy. In this fantasy, state violence is an extra measure, not a core feature of the state; "we" have banned torture from our midst, not simply relegated it to certain spaces and client states, certain agencies or prisons, certain theaters of operation, certain populations. To recruit readers into such a fantasy, the writing presumes and projects a community unmarked by torture, excluding many of "us" who have been victims or witnesses to police violence, who are immigrants or refugees from torture regimes, who were witnesses or targets of COINTELPRO activity, who are subjects of government suspicion now, and on.

Myths like those spun from Murad facilitate such communal fantasy, and they are key to the community-building function of torture. They exhibit the body of the terrorist in prose in such a way as to stymie objections and, seemingly, consolidate a (limited) community of morally judicious but vigilant citizens who are supportive of state violence because they trust they will be protected by it, not subject to it.

So too, although it appears to exhibit "torture" in all its dreadful "empirical reality," the story is designed to distract us from the institutional, logistical and contextual features of torture practice. The story of Abdul Hakim Murad therefore is an example of a classic torture myth that is also a sleight of hand.

In my view, getting to "what really happened" in the Murad case is by now impossible. What demands attention, rather, is the revision and recycling of the story itself, the unreliable narratives that emerge from torture and the fantasies that surround it. Here, the thicket of misinformation generated by torture, police corruption, and carefully crafted routines of deniability is made only denser by the disparate motives and mixed agendas that marked the interplay between US agencies and Philippine officials.

Finally, the amplification and distortion of Murad's story raises questions concerning the mixed agendas of the journalists or jurists who, since 9/11, aim to "debate" torture with a measure of "moral seriousness" but nonetheless misuse sources, ignore conflicting information, and borrow the anecdotes of others without a second glance.

At bottom, the failure to be thoughtfully informed by their own "real" examples is but a symptom of the striking *disinterest* in torture that characterizes the debate, disinterest in the communal as well as political meanings and functions of torture, its social history (as opposed to legal history), its technology and supply chain and profits, its professional routines, its conditions of possibility, and its many other human dimensions, including its impact on survivors and families, and its consequences for police, security contractors, corrections personnel, military units, and societies.

NOTES

I thank Lisa Lynch, Andy Nathan, Darius Rejali and Tom Hilde for sharing their thoughts on this essay. I also gratefully acknowledge Paul Martin and the Center for the Study of Human Rights at Columbia University for supporting this research.

1. Alan Dershowitz, *Why Terrorism Works: Understanding the Threat, Responding to the Challenge* (New Haven: Yale University Press, 2002), 137.

2. "Dershowitz: U.S. Needs Improved Torture Tactics." Newsmax.com, May 22, 2004, http://email.newsmax.com/archives/ic/2004/5/22/132018.shtml (accessed July 19, 2006).

3. One 2004 news story quotes an objection to the suggestion that Murad's case is a ticking bomb scenario: Michael Slackman, "What's Wrong With Torturing A Qaeda Higher-Up?" *New York Times*, May 16, 2004. In the legal writing, only David Luban calls attention to the conflicted wording in one description of Murad's torture. His 2005 *Virginia Law Review* essay offers a detailed rebuttal of the "time bomb" hypothetical. Reprinted as "Liberalism, Torture and the Ticking Bomb," *The Torture Debate in America*, ed. Karen J. Greenberg (New York: Cambridge University Press, 2006), 35–83.

4. One sees this when confronted with a relevant question, as reformulated by Darius Rejali: Does torture work *better than* something else, e.g. better than other modes of investigation? Such a question can promote thought about institutional practices and players, requiring historical and comparative depth beyond the anecdotal.

5. One survey counted as few as six investigative pieces from 2001–April 2004 that looked at brutal and illegal measures used in handling US prisoners. Sherry Ricchiardi, "Missed Signals," *American Journalism Review*, August–September 2004. See also, Eric Umansky, "Failures of Imagination," *Columbia Journalism Review*, September 2006.

6. For development of this notion and analysis of the representation of "torture" in the speculative press writing on the practice, see Stephanie Athey, "Torture: Alibi and Archetype in US News and Law Since 2001," *Culture and Conflict: Cultural Studies Perspectives on War*, ed. Nico Carpentier (Cambridge Scholars Press, forthcoming).

7. For Judge Kevin Thomas Duffy's opinion on the motion to suppress, see *US v. Yousef, Murad and Shah*. 925 F. Supp. 1063, 1065 (S.D.N.Y. 1996). At Murad's trial in 1996, two medical experts testified that his medical record and behavior were consistent with his allegations of torture. One expert stated the evidence indicated torture conclusively. Christopher Wren, "Experts Say Plot Suspect Showed Signs of Torture," *New York Times*, August 23, 1996. In court, Murad contended the FBI would have turned back for the Philippines if he recanted what he had said under torture.

8. Marites Danguilan Vitug and Glenda M. Gloria, *Under the Crescent Moon: Rebellion in Mindanao* (Quezon City, Manila: Ateneo Center for Social Policy & Public Affairs/ Institute for Popular Democracy, 2000). Murad's case is taken up by Rohan Gunaratna, *Inside Al Qaeda: Global Network of Terror* (New York: Berkley Books, 2003), and Peter Lance, *1000 Years For Revenge: International Terrorism and the FBI, The Untold Story* (New York: Regan Books, 2003). See also Christopher Wren's coverage of the 1996 trial in the *New York Times*.

9. Such conflicts appear when reading across several sources (cited in full below), including depiction of a plan to explode two US passenger planes (Vitug and Gloria) or, to explode ten planes simultaneously or eleven (Winik, Fainaru) or twelve planes (Wren). Stories suggest that Murad had planned to assassinate the Pope by disguising himself as a priest, kissing the Pope and detonating explosives hidden under his cassock (Winik). Indeed, in one version, police found a cassock in his apartment (Francia), or, in another, police found a phone message from a tailor working on a cassock (Brzezinski). However, the FBI FD-302 interrogation report and Vitug and Gloria both note Murad objected to assassination; the plan was to detonate three bombs along the parade route, hoping to incite "world wide panic" and kill onlookers. The Joint Congressional Inquiry into intelligence failures prior to 9/11 found that the plan to assassinate the Pope and to dive a plane into the CIA headquarters were "only at the 'discussion' stage and therefore not included" in the indictment for conspiracy. The 9/11 Commission reinforced this view, finding talk of a kamikaze mission to have been "casual conversation" with "no specific plan for execution." Even so, this plot to crash a plane was widely reported, albeit in conflicting versions: Murad planned to fly a private Cessna into the CIA headquarters (Brzezinski, Fainaru, Dershowitz). Or he would use a large commercial jet (Borger). The plane would be filled with explosives (Brzezinski, Dershowitz), or nerve gas (Winik), or it would dive into the Pentagon, not the CIA, or into a nuclear plant (Wren). Jay Winik, "Security Comes Before Liberty," *Wall Street Journal*, October 23, 2001; Christopher Wren, "Terror Case Hinges on Laptop Computer," *New York Times*, July 18, 1996; Christopher Wren, "Terror Suspect Spoke Freely of Plot, Agent Says," *New York*

Times, August 6, 1996; Luis H. Francia, "Local is Global," *Village Voice*, September 26, 2001; Matthew Brzezinski, "Bust and Boom": "Six years before the September 11 attacks, Philippine police took down an al Qaeda cell that had been plotting among other things, to fly explosives-laden planes into the Pentagon—and possibly some skyscrapers," *Washington Post*, December, 30, 2001; "Appendix I: FBI 302 Re: Interrogation of Abdul Hakim Murad, May 11, 1995," in Lance, *1000 Years For Revenge*, 509; Staff Director Eleanor Hill, "HPSCI-SSCI Joint Inquiry Staff Statement. Part I," September 18, 2002, www.fas.org/irp/congress/2002_hr/ 091802hill.html (accessed September 11, 2006). *The 9/11 Commission Report* (New York: Norton, 2004), 491n.33; Steve Fainaru, "Clues Pointed to Changed Terrorist Tactics," *Washington Post*, May 19, 2002; Julian Borger, "Unheeded Warnings," *The Guardian*, December 19, 2003.

10.   The unified scheme is nonetheless attributed to a cell of only three men, featuring numerous synchronized elements and a variety of targets and methods. For example, "More ominously, Murad recounted a horrific plot to assassinate Pope John Paul II in Manila, simultaneously blow up 11 U.S. airplanes in the Pacific, and fly another plane, loaded with nerve gas into the Central Intelligence Agency" (Winik). Yet details in the same stories often indicate this would have been impossible since Murad would need to commit suicide twice (suicide-bombing the Pope and then flying into the CIA headquarters, for instance). See also Steve Fainaru, "Clues Pointed to Changed Terrorist Tactics," *Washington Post*, May 19, 2002: "The clues included a 1995 plot to blow up 11 American jetliners over the Pacific Ocean, then crash a light plane into CIA headquarters—a suicide mission to have been carried out by a Pakistani pilot who had trained at flight schools in North Carolina, Texas and New York."

11.   Dershowitz, *Why Terrorism Works*, 137.

12.   Doug Struck, et. al., "Borderless Network of Terror, Bin Laden Followers Reach Across the Globe," *Washington Post*, September 23, 2001.

13.   Winik, "Security Comes Before Liberty."

14.   Peter Maas, "Torture, Tough or Lite: If a Terror Suspect Won't Talk, Should He Be Made To?" *The New York Times*, March 9, 2003.

15.   "Pakistani Claims Torture At Hands of Filipino Men," *Hobart Mercury* (Australia) May 11, 1996, reported that Murad testified to being raped. The report adds other details not printed in the US press, including electroshock: "Murad said his captors put an electric device on his genitals, burned him with cigarettes, threw urine on him, repeatedly dunked his head in water, kicked and beat him." One US article says that Murad feared the "possibility of being raped to death," but again adds he feared the Mossad more, so he confessed. Victorino Matus, "Making Terrorists Talk: America Doesn't Use Torture to Get Information Out of Terrorists. Perhaps We Just Need to use the Magic Word: Mossad," *Daily Standard*, January 29, 2002, Lexis-Nexis, http://web.lexis-nexis .com/universe (accessed March 9, 2006).

16.   Jonathan Alter, "Time to Think About Torture," *Newsweek*, November 5, 2001, 45.

17.   Peter Lance interviewed Colonel Rodolfo Mendoza in April 2002. Lance writes that Mendoza and Major Alberto Ferro confront Murad after he has been denied food for a long period. He is told the only thing left for the Philippine authorities to decide is whether to turn Murad over to the "Americans or Mossad": "'You are a bomber. Tell me something now or I will call Tel Aviv.' Murad eyed him defiantly. Then Mendoza nodded to Major Ferro, who grabbed the burger and fries. Both of them started to leave the room when Murad blurted out, 'The Trade Center . . . I . . .' 'What?' said the colonel,

turning on his heel. 'I'm involved in it,' said Murad." Lance, *1000 Years For Revenge*, 275–77.

18.   Matus, "Making Terrorists Talk," *Daily Standard*.

19.   Dershowitz, *Why Terrorism Works*, 138.

20.   Sanford Levinson, "The Debate on Torture: War Against Virtual States," *Dissent* 50.3 (2003): 79. Levinson replays most elements of this argument in his "Precommitment and Postcommitment: The Ban On Torture In The Wake of September 11," *Texas Law Review* 81 (June 2003), and "Contemplating Torture: An Introduction," *Torture: A Collection* (New York: Oxford University Press, 2004), 23–43. Richard A. Posner borrows the Murad anecdote in "Torture, Terrorism, and Interrogation," *Torture: A Collection*, 291–298. Inventing a "moral community" and enumerating its characteristics are core elements of this writing on torture in my view, so it is worth noting that Elaine Scarry leans heavily on Dershowitz's presumptions about the American people as she traces errors in his reasoning. Scarry, "Five Errors in the Reasoning of Alan Dershowitz," *Torture: A Collection*, 281– 290.

21.   Vitug and Gloria, *Under the Crescent Moon*, 223.

22.   Pope John Paul II's visit to the Philippines, January 12–16, 1995. Murad was captured on January 7.

23.   Vitug and Gloria and many post-2001 news reports suggest the police resorted to torture after two days of silence, but an audio tape entered into evidence at trial suggests Murad's torture began the day of his capture. Even Judge Kevin Duffy, who dismissed expert testimony and Murad's own allegations of torture, wrote that the sounds on the tape were suspicious: "the only objective evidence that remotely supports Murad's allegations of torture is a taped interrogation session dated January 7, 1995, the day the Philippines authorities state that Murad was arrested." "Certain portions of that tape were played during the hearing, which Murad claims reflect his condition immediately following an episode of the drowning procedure which he allegedly suffered." *Yousef*, 925 F. Supp. Journalist Peter Lance reinforces the disturbing nature of these recorded interrogations: "transcripts of Murad's interrogation suggest that he was denied water and force-fed liquids." Lance, *1000 Years For Revenge*, 274.

24.   Lance and Gunaratna cite substantive information drawn from January 7 and January 20 interrogation transcripts, and Vitug and Gloria cite February PNP intelligence debriefing reports throughout. Lance, *1000 Years For Revenge*, 311, 342; Gunaratna, *Inside Al Qaeda*, 240.

25.   Wali Khan Amin Shah was arrested January 12, 1995 in Manila. Lance, *1000 Years For Revenge*, 311. He later escaped from PNP custody and was re-apprehended in Malaysia on December 11. *Yousef*, 925 F. Supp.

26.   Only one 2005 mention of Murad discusses the so-called success of his torture yet also suggests investigative work with the laptop evidence might have been of equal value in the case. Joseph Lelyveld, "Interrogating Ourselves," *New York Times Magazine*, June 12, 2005, 12. Darius Rejali argues that reliance on torture "deskills" the intelligence or police service that uses it. Torture saps energy and resources from modes of investigation that collect, follow and develop information. He discusses Murad's case as it was carried by Brzezinski and Maas to underscore this point in *Torture and Democracy* (Princeton University Press, forthcoming).

27.   Jacobo Timerman, *Prisoner Without a Name, Cell Without a Number*, trans. Toby Talbot (New York: Vintage, 1981). John Conroy, *Unspeakable Acts, Ordinary People: The Dynamics of Torture* (New York: Alfred A. Knopf, 2000).

28. Christopher S. Wren, "Terror Case Hinges on Laptop Computer," *New York Times*, July 18, 1996. See also Vitug and Gloria on Officer Orlando Ramilo, who claimed he alerted the FBI to the falsified evidence, a fact the FBI did not disclose to the defense.

29. Brzezinski, "Bust and Boom." See also *Yousef*, 925. F. Supp.

30. The FBI admittedly received transcripts of interrogations, but said they did not receive the January 7, 1995 tape that lent some credence to the allegations of "drowning torture." *Yousef*, 925 F. Supp. FBI agent Pellegrino "met frequently with police officials in the Philippines during the three months that they detained Mr. Murad." Christopher S. Wren, "Case Accusing Three of Plotting to Bomb Jets Shows a Flaw," *New York Times*, August 8, 1996.

31. Vitug and Gloria, *Under the Crescent Moon*, 2; Christopher Wren, "Computer Expert Testifies in Terror Trial," *New York Times*, July 24, 1996.

32. Amnesty International, "Philippines—Torture Persists." 24 January 2003, http://web.amnesty.org/library/index/engasa350012003.

33. Of course, drowning or "waterboarding" has been publicly supported by Bush administration officials, e.g. in 2005 by Porter Goss, then director of the CIA. Officials do not deny waterboarding is one of the "alternative" techniques permissible under the Military Commissions Act of 2006. Darius Rejali notes that Americans reintroduced ancient water tortures into the twentieth century. "In 1902 . . . US soldiers put funnels in the mouths of Filipinos to force water into their organs. William Howard Taft, governor of the Philippines, carelessly conceded to the Senate that pumping was the policy in some cases . . . President Theodore Roosevelt privately called pumping a mild torture." In "Of Human Bondage," Salon.com, June 18 2004. Secretary of War Elihu Root, pressured by Senate hearings in 1902, called publicly for courts-martial over the use of the "water cure." "More Courts-Martial in the Philippines," *New York Times*, April 16, 1902.

34. E. San Juan, Jr., "Imperialist War Against Terrorism and Revolution in the Philippines," *Left Curve* 28 (January 31, 2004): 40.

35. Alfred McCoy has written a timely and important book on the development of the CIA's torture methodology. In outlining the CIA's "psychological paradigm," his terminology unwittingly supports the rhetoric of euphemism that disguises deliberate attempts to stress the body as simply psychological. He makes no mention of the motions to suppress when he argues the embassy bombing cases (in Kenya and Tanzania) were models of "careful investigation and noncoercive interrogation." He contrasts the FBI's "by the book" restraint with CIA methodology. In drawing this conclusion he cites Jane Mayer's reporting on CIA torture renditions, in which FBI agent Daniel Coleman speaks for the bureau's work in this investigation. McCoy, *A Question of Torture: CIA Interrogation From the Cold War to the War on Terror* (New York: Metropolitan Books, 2006), 203. Mayer, "Outsourcing Torture: Annals of Justice," *New Yorker*, February 14, 2005, 116–18.

36. That pattern bears investigation. Americans acknowledged control over interrogations of suspects in Kenya, where defendants alleged the US and Kenyans worked in tag-team fashion to ensure defendants relinquished rights to lawyers. Mohammed Saddiq Odeh said he was held by the Pakistanis for seven days and then transferred to Nairobi for twelve. Pakistanis subjected him to "violence, threats of torture, psychological coercion, sleep deprivation and other inhumane conditions." Mr. Odeh alleged the Kenyans threatened him with worse than Pakistan. See Benjamin Weiser, "Asserting Coercion, Embassy Bombing Suspect Tries to Suppress Statements," *New York Times*, July 13, 2000; Weiser, "US Faces Tough Challenge to Statements in Terrorism Case,"

New York Times, January 25, 2001. According to attorney Jack Sachs, initially assigned to Odeh's case, "Three days and three nights without food and without water, under bright lights, no sleep—what would anybody say?" Weiser, "Bombing Defendant Said to Claim Coercion," *New York Times*, September 5, 1998. Judge Leonard Sands initially suppressed statements by Mohamed al-'Owhali, interrogated in Kenya. His defense "cited the presence of F.B.I. agents and a senior prosecutor from New York during much of the interrogation and argued that the questioning was effectively controlled by the American government." Judge Sands allowed the prosecution to reargue the motion in closed court. Weiser, "Terror Trial Judge to Again Weigh Suppression," *New York Times*, January 19, 2001.

37. On electric shock technology in policing, see Human Rights Clinic, *In the Shadows of the War on Terror: Persistent Police Brutality and Abuse in the United States.* A Report Prepared for the United Nations Human Rights Committee on the Occasion of its Review of the United States of America's Second and Third Periodic Report to the Human Rights Committee, Columbia Law School, May 2006. Darius Rejali, "Modern Torture as a Civic Marker: Solving a Global Anxiety with a New Political Technology," *Journal of Human Rights* 2.2 (June 2003): 153–171.

7

The Torturers and Their Public

Alphonso Lingis

1945, PICTURES OF AUSCHWITZ. Photographs of naked bodies piled up on top one another. During the war, the conflict was defined as a conflict of ideologies—Nazi, Fascist, Democratic, and Socialist. After the publication of these pictures, Germany, land of Kant, Hegel, Schelling, Heisenberg, Bach, Beethoven, and Brahms, became the land of death camps.

1972, Vietnam. Photograph of a nine-year-old girl running naked, screaming, burning with napalm. This picture is what remains of the war. The strategic importance of the Indochinese peninsula, of containing the spread of Soviet and Chinese Communism, the domino theory—this discourse has been forgotten.

2004, Abu Ghraib. Photographs of naked bodies piled up on top of one another. Derisive laughter of the torturers. Laughter of Spc. Sabrina Harman, her head bent next to the crushed head of a captive bludgeoned to death in Abu Ghraib prison. For Muslims from Morocco to Mindanao, from South Africa to Uzbekistan, the rhetoric of liberation collapses before these pictures. For the judgment of public opinion across the world, the reality of the American occupation of Iraq is defined by these pictures.

Governments that practiced torture of prisoners—Czarist Russia, Chile, Argentina, France in Algeria—do not make public the practice of state torture; people are just "disappeared." When the German public, after the war, came to know, their representatives acted to institutionally ban torture, and capital punishment too.

No pictures have more insistently been propagated by the media than the pictures of Abu Ghraib; every American saw them—and saw the subsequent revelations from Guantánamo, Bagram, Camps Bucca, Mercury, and Tiger and read reports from the far-flung Gulag of secret American prison camps. But for the American public they in the end provoked no question affecting national policy. In the presidential elections John Kerry made no allusion to them, and the public reelected, with a significant majority, George W. Bush, who promptly elevated Alberto Gonzales, who had defined the policy of state torture of captives, to the post of Attorney General. In 2004, a group of the nation's top legal experts—Alan Dershowitz of Harvard, Jean Elshtain of the University of

Chicago, Oren Gross of Minnesota, Sanford Levinson of the University of Texas, and Richard Posner of the University of Chicago Law School, in a collective volume entitled *Torture*, sought for ways to institutionalize torture in the "war on terror."

From earliest times, war has been a prime topic of art—depicted in epics such as the Mahabharata, the Iliad, the Jewish Bible, and in architectural monuments such as Angkor Wat, Chichen-Itzá, and the cathedral of Santiago de Campostela celebrating the defeat of the Moors in Spain and the Spanish conquest of South America. This art depicted the ruler as sublime in himself, absorbing into his destiny the lives of nameless multitudes. It depicted the slaughter of armies and populations turning into golden radiance about the victorious ruler.

High art worked to justify the slaughter of war, even when the campaign was not victorious, by depicting these deaths as redeemed in the heaven above by the anointed lord. Such are martyrs immediately received into the arms of God, such is the Christian Son of God who laid down his life for the salvation of men, and such are those fallen in battle. After the French Revolution, it is the nation that assumes the functions of God; the blood of those who die in war pulses through the nation and they live on in its immortality and glory.

Francisco de Goya's set of 80 etchings, *Disasters of War*, finished in 1808 but not published until 1863, 49 years after the end of the Napoleonic occupation of Spain, is the first great work of contemporary art. They depict close-up men cornered and disarmed and then castrated and dismembered, the butchering of the infirm and aged unable to fight or flee, the mutilation and slaughter of children. The great causes of the war—the Napoleonic armies heralding the Enlightenment advancing into the darkness and superstition of rural Spain, the resistance of the indigenous people and its loyalties, traditions, and values—are invisible; soldiers, peasants, women, children tear at one another like so many rabid dogs. Goya depicts mutilated corpses covered with flies and picked at by vultures under dark skies, where there is no god above to witness, pity, and redeem so much agony, so many deaths.

The classical art of wars and battlefields depicted, in and through the spectacle of mass slaughter, a transcendent sphere of the good—they invoked the victorious Alexander, Charlemagne, or Joan of Arc absorbing into himself or herself the agony and death of the brave and redeeming them with his or her glory, or else invoked a transcendent God pitying, honoring, and redeeming those fallen in battle. With Goya, both the glorious Napoleon and the glorious King of Spain have disappeared; God has disappeared. Their place is taken by the viewer, who in his horror and disgust, feels rising from his depths his own core moral instincts, an immanent sphere of the good. Thus, after having been first suppressed and not published until thirty-five years after his death, Goya's *Disasters of War*, depicting nothing but rabid and pointless slaughter, now rose to displace classical art to be proclaimed the great and essential humanist art of our time.

Although Goya's pictures of war have been recognized as truthful to the point that they have virtually put an end to the classical art that glorified and redeemed agony and death in war, they had no effect on the forces that drive Europeans to war, to the wars in which they were to twice embroil most of the world. Does this make us think that humanist art has no power to affect the course of human conduct—or does it make us think that the humanist sentiments it provokes—the conviction of a core moral integrity in us—actually functions to serve the war industry in our times?

Jake and Dinos Chapman spoke of the secret pleasure Goya barely concealed in his set of etchings of the horrors of war drawn with such artistic perfection. In the year 2000 they purchased for 50,000 pounds sterling a set of Goya's etchings and painted grinning clown and puppy-dog faces over the faces Goya had depicted stricken with heart-wrenching pathos. By desecrating Goya's work, the art desperately called humanist in our barbarous age, the Chapmans denounce the public's conviction of their own core moral instincts as the principle obstacle to the lucid analysis of the state and the military juggernaut. Ethics henceforth would have to undertake an extensive analysis of the aims of nation-states and of the internal dialectics of military technology.

The media had itself suppressed the Abu Ghraib torture photographs for two weeks after they received them; now every news hour projected them again and again—the media and the public could not have enough of them. These photographs do not depict the victorious United States War President as absorbing into his destiny the glorious deeds of his troops. What dominates in the photographs taken at Abu Ghraib and the recent FBI report of practices at Guantánamo was the bizarre sexual degradation of the captives. The photographs feature men forced into homosexual acts and piled up naked penis upon buttocks in a grotesque forced homosexual orgy before the gleeful smirks of young American women. In these photographs there is no sign of the proclaimed cause of the war—the liberation and democratization of Iraq, and, although the picture of the hooded captive with arms outstretched invokes the Spanish Inquisition, there is here no evidence of a transcendent God guiding the hands of the torturers. His place is taken by the viewer. Viewers outside of the United States judged the acts depicted: they took them to exhibit the causes of liberation and democratization as lies, following upon the lies that Iraq possessed weapons of mass destruction capable of destroying Great Britain within 45 minutes. But viewers in the United States felt repugnance and disgust, felt rising from their depths their own core moral instincts, an immanent sphere of the good.

The insistent projection of the photographs to the American public was contrived to provoke intense feelings of revulsion. President Bush gave the watchword: Americans view these images with disgust and repugnance. The intensity of disgust and repugnance across the land functioned as evidence, in each viewer, of his or her own core decency, his or her instinctual moral integrity. The aroused feeling of their own core moral integrity convinced them that, apart from these few perverts, the 150,000 National Guardsmen and enlisted servicemen and women there are brave, generous, idealistic liberators—Senator Lieberman even insisted: "kind."

The now approved media broadcast of the photographs would serve the American invasion. In his first public statement after the release of the photographs, Secretary of State Colin Powell declared: "Now the world will see American Justice." The army itself was charged with the investigation and with punishing these few of its troops for violation of its own code of conduct. The public was reassured of the irreproachable integrity of the army, whose procedures would now be installed in the interim Iraq government for the public trial of Saddam Hussein, immediately arraigned. The photographs had functioned to convince the American public of their intrinsic righteousness, and the intrinsic righteousness of a collective action taken in their name by citizens like themselves.

Immediately after the attack of 9/11 on the control centers of American military and economic power, the American War President had identified the attackers as irrationally motivated by pure evil and, by contrast, the American population as good. But launching, from Florida, long-range high-altitude bombers to reduce Afghanistan to rubble was too obviously a massive outburst of revenge to convince the Americans of their intrinsic goodness. It was the photographs, the disgust and revulsion they aroused, that made their intrinsic goodness evident to them. They returned President Bush to office by a majority, seeing in him one like themselves.

8

Are there times when we have to accept torture?

Ariel Dorfman, Originally an Op-Ed in The Guardian
(Saturday May 8, 2004)

IS TORTURE EVER JUSTIFIED? That is the dirty question left out of the universal protestations of disgust, revulsion, and shame that have greeted the release of photos showing British and American soldiers tormenting prisoners in Iraq.

It is a question that was most unforgettably put forward over 130 years ago by Fyodor Dostoevsky in *The Brothers Karamazov*. In that novel, the saintly Alyosha Karamazov is tempted by his brother Ivan, confronted with an unbearable choice. Let us suppose, Ivan says, that in order to bring men eternal happiness, it was essential and inevitable to torture to death one tiny creature, only one small child. Would you consent?

Ivan has preceded his question with stories about suffering children—a seven-year-old girl beaten senseless by her parents and enclosed in a freezing wooden outhouse and made to eat her own excrement; an eight-year-old serf boy torn to pieces by hounds in front of his mother for the edification of a landowner. True cases plucked from newspapers by Dostoevsky that merely hint at the almost unimaginable cruelty that awaited humanity in the years to come.

How would Ivan react to the ways in which the 20th century ended up refining pain, industrialising pain, producing pain on a massive, rational, technological scale; a century that would produce manuals on pain and how to inflict it, training courses on how to increase it, and catalogues that explained where to acquire the instruments that ensured that pain would be unlimited; a century that handed out medals for those who had written the manuals and commended those who designed the courses and rewarded and enriched those who had produced the instruments in those catalogues of death? Ivan Karamazov's question—would you consent?—is just as dreadfully relevant now, in a world where 132 countries routinely practice that sort of humiliation and damage on detainees, because it takes us into the impossible heart of the matter regarding torture; it demands that we confront the real and inexorable dilemma that the existence and persistence of torture poses, particularly after the terrorist attacks of September 11, 2001. Ivan's words remind us that torture is justified by those who apply and perform it: this is the price, it is implied, that needs to be paid by the suffering few in order to guarantee happiness for the rest of society, the enormous majority given security and wellbeing by those horrors inflicted in some dark cellar, some faraway pit, some abominable police station.

Make no mistake: every regime that tortures does so in the name of salvation, some superior goal, some promise of paradise. Call it communism, call it the free market, call it the free world, call it the national interest, call it fascism, call it the leader, call it civilisation, call it the service of God, call it the need for information; call it what you will, the cost of paradise, the promise of some sort of paradise, Ivan Karamazov continues to whisper to us, will always be hell for at least one person somewhere, sometime.

An uncomfortable truth: the American and British soldiers in Iraq, like torturers everywhere, do not think of themselves as evil, but rather as guardians of the common good, dedicated patriots who get their hands soiled and endure perhaps some sleepless nights in order to deliver the blind ignorant majority from violence and anxiety. Nor are the motives of the demonised enemy significant, not even the fact that they are naked and under the boot because they dared to resist a foreign power occupying their land.

And if it turns out—a statistical certainty—that at least one of the victims is innocent of what he is accused, as blameless as the children mentioned by Ivan Karamazov, that does not matter either. He must suffer the fate of the supposedly guilty: everything justified in the name of a higher mission, state stability in the time of Saddam, and now, in the post-Saddam era, making the same country and the whole region stable for democracy. So those who support the present operations in Iraq are no different from citizens in all those other lands where torture is a tedious fact of life, all of them needing to face Ivan's question, whether they would consciously be able to accept that their dreams of heaven depend on an eternal inferno of distress for one innocent human being; or whether, like Alyosha, they would softly reply: "No, I do not consent."

What Alyosha is telling Ivan, in the name of humanity, is that he will not accept responsibility for someone else torturing in his name. He is telling us that torture is not a crime committed only against a body, but also a crime committed against the imagination. It presupposes, it requires, it craves the abrogation of our capacity to imagine someone else's suffering, to dehumanise him or her so much that their pain is not our pain. It demands this of the torturer, placing the victim outside and beyond any form of compassion or empathy, but also demands of everyone else the same distancing, the same numbness, those who know and close their eyes, those who do not want to know and close their eyes, those who close their eyes and ears and hearts.

Alyosha knows, as we should, that torture does not, therefore, only corrupt those directly involved in the terrible contact between two bodies, one that has all the power and the other that has all the pain, one that can do what it wants and the other that cannot do anything except wait and pray and resist. Torture also corrupts the whole social fabric because it prescribes a silencing of what has been happening between those two bodies; it forces people to make believe that nothing, in fact, has been happening; it necessitates that we lie to ourselves about what is being done not that far, after all, from where we talk, while we munch chocolate, smile at a lover, read a book, listen to a concerto, exercise in the morning. Torture obliges us to be deaf and blind and mute—and that is what Alyosha cannot consent to.

There is, however, a further question, even more troubling, that Ivan does not ask his brother or us: what if the person being endlessly tortured for our wellbeing is guilty?

What if we could erect a future of love and harmony on the everlasting pain of someone who had himself committed mass murder, who had tortured those children; what if we were invited to enjoy Eden all over again while one despicable human being was incessantly receiving the horrors he imposed upon others? And more urgently: what if the person whose genitals are being crushed and skin is being burnt knows the whereabouts of a bomb that is about to explode and kill millions?

Would we answer: yes, I do consent? That under certain very limited circumstances, torture is acceptable?

That is the real question to humanity thrown up by the photos of those suffering bodies in the stark rooms of Iraq, an agony—let us not forget—about to be perpetrated again today and tomorrow in so many prisons everywhere else on our sad, anonymous planet as one man with the power of life and death in his godlike hands approaches another who is totally defenseless. Are we that scared? Are we so scared that we are willing to knowingly let others perpetrate, in the dark and in our name, acts of terror that will eternally corrode and corrupt us?

* * *

Are we really so fearful?

Ariel Dorfman, Originally an Op-Ed in The Washington Post
(Sunday, September 24, 2006)

IT STAYS WITH ME, still haunts me, the first time—it was in Chile, in October of 1973—that I met someone who had been tortured. To save my life, I had sought refuge in the Argentine Embassy some weeks after the coup that had toppled the democratically elected government of Salvador Allende.

And then, suddenly, one afternoon, there he was. A large-boned man, gaunt and yet strangely flabby, with eyes like a child, eyes that could not stop blinking and a body that could not stop shivering.

That is what stays with me—that he was cold under the balmy afternoon sun of Santiago de Chile, trembling as though he would never be warm again, as though the electric current was still coursing through him. Still possessed, somehow still inhabited by his captors, still imprisoned in that cell in the National Stadium, his hands disobeying the orders from his brain to quell the shuddering, his body unable to forget what had been done to it just as, nearly 33 years later, I, too, cannot banish that devastated life from my memory.

It was his image, in fact, that swirled up from the past as I pondered the current political debate in the United States about the practicality of torture. Something in me must have needed to resurrect that victim, force my fellow citizens to spend a few minutes with the eternal iciness that had settled into that man's heart and flesh, and demand that they take a good hard look at him before anyone dare maintain that, to save lives, it might be necessary to inflict unbearable pain on a fellow human being. Perhaps the optimist in me hoped that this damaged Argentine man could, all these decades later, help shatter the perverse innocence of contemporary Americans, just as he had burst the bubble of ignorance protecting the young Chilean I used to be, someone who back then had encountered torture mainly through books and movies and newspaper reports.

That is not, however, the only lesson that today's ruthless world can learn from that distant man condemned to shiver forever.

All those years ago, that torture victim kept moving his lips, trying to articulate an explanation, muttering the same words over and over.

"It was a mistake," he repeated incessantly, and in the next few days I pieced together his sad and foolish tale. He was an Argentine revolutionary who had fled his homeland and, as soon as he had crossed the mountains into Chile, had begun to boast about what he would do to the military there if it staged a coup, about his expertise with arms of every sort, about his colossal stash of weapons. Bluster and braggadocio—and every word of it false.

But how could he convince those men who were beating him, hooking his penis to electric wires, waterboarding him? How could he prove to them that he had been lying, prancing in front of his Chilean comrades, just trying to impress the ladies with his fraudulent insurgent persona?

Of course, he couldn't. He confessed to anything and everything they wanted to drag from his hoarse, howling throat; he invented accomplices and addresses and culprits; and then, when it became apparent that all this was imaginary, he was subjected to further ordeals.

There was no escape.

That is the hideous predicament of the torture victim. It was always the same story, what I discovered in the ensuing years, as I became an unwilling expert on all manner of torments and degradations, my life and my writing overflowing with grief from every continent. Each of those mutilated spines and fractured lives—Chinese, Guatemalan, Egyptian, Indonesian, Iranian, Uzbek, need I go on?—all of them, men and women alike, surrendered the same story of essential asymmetry, where one man has all the power in the world and the other has nothing but pain, where one man can decree death at the flick of a wrist and the other can only pray that the wrist will be flicked soon.

It is a story that our species has listened to with mounting revulsion, a horror that has led almost every nation to sign treaties over the past decades declaring these abominations as crimes against humanity, transgressions interdicted all across the earth. That is the wisdom, national and international, that has taken us thousands of years of tribulation and shame to achieve. That is the wisdom we are being asked to throw away when we formulate the question—Does torture work?—when we allow ourselves to ask whether we can afford to outlaw torture if we want to defeat terrorism.

I will leave others to claim that torture, in fact, does not work, that confessions obtained under duress—such as that extracted from the heaving body of that poor Argentine braggart in some Santiago cesspool in 1973—are useless. Or to contend that the United States had better not do that to anyone in our custody lest someday another nation or entity or group decides to treat our prisoners the same way.

I find these arguments—and there are many more—to be irrefutable. But I cannot bring myself to use them, for fear of honoring the debate by participating in it.

Can't the United States see that when we allow someone to be tortured by our agents, it is not only the victim and the perpetrator who are corrupted, not only the "intelligence" that is contaminated, but also everyone who looked away and said they did not know, everyone who consented tacitly to that outrage so they could sleep a little safer at night, all the citizens who did not march in the streets by the millions to demand the resignation of whoever suggested, even whispered, that torture is inevitable in our day and age, that we must embrace its darkness?

Are we so morally sick, so deaf and dumb and blind, that we do not understand this? Are we so fearful, so in love with our own security and steeped in our own pain, that we are really willing to let people be tortured in the name of America? Have we so lost our bearings that we do not realize that each of us could be that hapless Argentine who sat under the Santiago sun, so possessed by the evil done to him that he could not stop shivering?

9

Torture's New Methods and Meanings

Pilar Calveiro
(Translated by William Nichols and Thomas C. Hilde)

As in the past, the most atrocious forms of torture are practiced today through systematic *disappearance*, which runs through the serpentine paths of a vast network of clandestine detention centers. From relatively visible sites, such as the concentration camp at Guantánamo Bay, to others whose existence is denied, such as the so-called "black sites" of the CIA, and including recognized prisons in which undeclared prisoners are kept illegally alongside registered detainees, people deprived of legal protection become part of a universe of exception in which torture is applied without restrictions.

1. THE FLEXIBILIZATION OF THE LAW

The decision by the United States government and its allies to resort to these practices has initiated a series of legalistic discussions, which argue for the compatibility of these practices with established laws. Similarly, Prisoner of War status for the detainees at Guantánamo Bay has been dismissed in favor of designating them as, rather, *illegal combatants*.[1] This designation excludes them from the protections offered by the Geneva Conventions, which involve conditions of detention, transportation, and, above all, the right not to be interrogated. Along with the "redefinition" of the prisoner, *the concept of torture itself is also redefined*, delimiting it in an attempt to open a legal umbrella that excludes some practices of forced interrogation often defined as torture. Lastly, the abduction and illegal transfer of prisoners through a vast network of countries, many of them European, has been "protected" under the rubric of *renditions*. This implies that the issue is a matter of the legal delivery of detainees, similar to extradition, when in reality we are dealing with "transfers" to countries whose legislation and practices permit greater discretion in the application of interrogation methods and guarantee impunity for those responsible. In this way, illegal and dehumanizing practices are transferred, as is their eventual responsibility, to peripheral countries, although such policies remain under the command of the intelligence services of the main countries in question.

2. The superposition of legal and illegal circuits in the disappearance of persons

Within the network of clandestine centers of detention, Guantánamo is a kind of *axis* connecting legal and illegal repression. Recognized as an institution for detention administered by the security forces of the United States, it is not even known who is there, which is to say that in many cases we are dealing with virtual "missing" persons. Guantánamo is nevertheless only the "tip of the iceberg" of the clandestine repressive network, the most visible aspect of this "invisibilized" universe. The existence of "ghost detainees"—that is, *disappeareds* (desaparecidos)—has also been documented within penal institutions recognized as such (AI: 2005), as in the case of Abu Ghraib. Lastly, a *network* of completely clandestine detention centers, known as "black sites," was created and has been operated by the CIA since the beginning of the so-called war on terror. These are scattered across several countries and are probably also located in North American military installations. This all constitutes *a vast, illegal repressive network operating within legal structures*, and endowed with the capacity to alternate between the legal and illegal, black, and otherwise hidden components of the apparatus.

To synthesize, be it 1) via a concentration camp that may be visible but whose population goes missing, "invisible"; 2) via the image of "ghost detainees" in the illegal prisons; or 3) via the abduction of persons to the "black sites," we find ourselves facing a state-sponsored policy of disappearances. This same policy is administered by legal intelligence services that, with the permission of the States, create illegal underground networks, thus establishing a permanent *State of Exception* regarding those sectors of the population defined as "terrorist." With respect to terrorists, the repressive legal/illegal network "excepts" itself from adhering to and fulfilling conventions and accords. It resorts to the "disappearance" of persons as a way of removing them from public scrutiny and in order to do anything at all to them during any length of time. This is the most *radical* form of torture, then, because *it is as unlimited in its form as it is in duration.*

3. The global network

This repressive network of disappeared persons is global. Human rights organizations and journalistic investigations—such as some of those undertaken by the *Washington Post*[2] and by Seymour Hersh—mention the existence of "black sites" in Singapore, Thailand, Pakistan, Afghanistan, Kosovo,[3] Poland, Romania, and other unspecified countries in Eastern Europe. These sites are managed through a network of secret intelligence centers called CTIC. This CIA-affiliated network extends to some 20 countries in Europe, Asia, and the Middle East while also connected with the visible network of local intelligence agencies in the majority of the nations. These visible and invisible networks, though distinctly different, both come together in the passage of information and prisoners, as well as in the kidnapping, disappearance, torture, and execution of prisoners.

It is also widely known that CIA "prison planes" have repeatedly used airports in various countries to transfer prisoners from certain detention centers to others. In "private flights," persons detained illegally are transported to places designed for torture and kidnapping, where they remain for as much time as deemed necessary by the clandestine U.S. intelligence services.

Amnesty International reported that some 800 illegal transfers have taken place to and through at least 8 European countries in what the CIA calls "renditions." They also demonstrated, on the basis of 6 cases,[4] the involvement of seven European nations in these practices: Germany, Bosnia, Herzegovina, Italy, Macedonia, the United Kingdom, and Sweden (AI: 2006).

At issue is a global network, whose reach recognizes no borders or limits other than those of a few "rebel" states. There is no possible exile for the persecuted; there is no "outside." Everything remains under the jurisdiction of this planetary "megapolice" and its intelligence services—exempt from laws that are observed only hypothetically—in which the security and information forces of several countries are involved, though with *differentiated functions*. The direction of these forces lies in the hands of the North American intelligence services, undoubtedly with the participation of its closest allies. The facilitation of key information, the kidnapping of people and their transfer, constitute a larger network with varying levels of involvement of the many lesser "allies." Lastly, the confinement centers where information is obtained through torture seem to be perfectly suited to peripheral countries with long traditions of human rights violations, a sort of artificial extra-territoriality since all of the survivors stress the fact that they were interrogated by North American intelligence personnel and had been in centers staffed by North Americans.

4. THE VISIBILIZATION OF THE CLANDESTINE

This entire disappearing universe, which makes itself disappear by rendering itself invisible, is, nonetheless, quite *visible*. What have we seen of it? Basically two things: a few photos from Guantánamo and others from Abu Ghraib. The former show us prisoners dressed in orange, handcuffed and blindfolded, with their heads lowered and having obvious difficulty walking, or being transferred on stretchers to the "tough interrogations." These are images not only of defeat but also of the most absolute loss, including the loss of the body itself. One can almost smell the fear when viewing these images. The photos, practically the same image repeated in different circumstances with only minor variations, seem to say, "Look at them, this is what happens to the 'terrorists,' those who declare themselves to be our enemies, or perhaps, those *we* declare to be our enemies."

The photos from Abu Ghraib, on the other hand, present us with the very moment of torment: the mountains of bodies or the individual bodies as they suffer. There are virtually no faces, only suffering bodies. These images, which render visible that which is most vehemently denied, have been reproduced around the globe. One could say that this has happened because the curtain of concealment has been withdrawn, but this argument is not terribly convincing. There are indignant voices, true, but no evidence or testimony has been produced by the most important international organizations, nor have any of the "democratic" governments applied pressure, nor have there been any mass movements in the United States or any other part of the world. Quite simply, one sees and one keeps quiet. That is, one knows, the entire world knows, we all know. We know and that knowledge binds us because it makes us, in a sense, a part of the plot of complicity and silence.

Visibilization functions, then, as a show of power, as if to boast of one's own impunity, as a vehicle of fear and submission. Conversely, *invizibilization* and the demand for silence guarantee the limitless perpetuation of disappearances and torture as technique, which binds them in a knot of complicity.

5. THE FORMS OF TORMENT

It is important to determine what types of torture are practiced in this network of concentration camps in order to observe what the imperial power does with the bodies, how it processes them, what marks it leaves and, as a consequence, how it conceives of itself, because the scars it leaves upon the tortured bodies are also the scars inflicted upon the social body as a whole.

If we adhere to the notion of torture defined in the Geneva Conventions[5] as well as elemental common sense, the kidnapping and total isolation themselves constitute forms of torture. The accounts of everyday life in clandestine detention centers offered by Muhammed al-Asad and two other people reveal that they "were confined in absolute isolation, and never talked with anyone except their interrogators. Inside the cells, the loudspeakers emitted white noise, a constant low intensity buzzing. The electric light was kept lit 24 hours a day. During an entire year they did not know what country they were in. None of the men ever saw the other two, nor any other detainee" (AI: AMR 51/177/2005). Likewise, in Guantánamo, the detainees remain isolated in their miniscule cells, constructed with solid windowless walls, which they are barely allowed to leave during the day. Such are the conditions that they have led to hunger strikes as means of protest as well as to several suicide attempts. One of the prisoners, Shaker Aamer, stated to his lawyer, "I am dying little by little here, mentally and physically. And all of us are going through the same thing. . . . I prefer to accelerate the process that will inevitably produce itself. . . . I prefer to die peacefully of my own accord. . . . It is my right" (AI: AMR 51/007/2006).

In turn, the conditions for the transfer of the kidnapped are equally atrocious, as is attested to through the testimony of Khaled al-Masri, who has, since his release, filed a lawsuit against the North American authorities.

Apart from the torment involved in living and transfer conditions, a series of authorized practices are routinely carried out in these places which, while inflicting suffering, are nonetheless not considered torture, in keeping with the "legal" distinctions referred to above. Such techniques as *sleep deprivation*, the use of *military dogs, sensory deprivation* (such as the hooding of prisoners or the use of black masks that hinder sight, earflaps that inhibit hearing, surgical masks that restrict the sense of smell, and thick gloves that dull the sense of touch), exposure to *extreme heat or cold*, and forced *"stress" positions* (such as remaining in a squatting position for several hours) have been included in the list of 50 *irregular techniques of "permitted" interrogations* (Engelhardt), under the justification that they constitute "exceptional" but necessary treatment in view of the "exceptionality" of the enemy terrorist.

Beyond these generalized techniques, presumably "light" because they do not produce any sharp physical pain, survivor testimony recounts the application of other methods, equally commonplace in "tough interrogations," and supposedly (only supposedly) unauthorized. The majority of them are relatively similar—as much for their brutality as for their techniques—to those recorded in other situations of disappeared persons: beatings, cuts, burns, hangings, dry asphyxia or with water, electric shock, bone fractures, rapes, food deprivation, deprivation of water, and dog attacks.

On the other hand, these are the techniques that authorities are attempting to exempt from the rubric of torture, those that appear relatively "new" in and of themselves, or in their modes of application. In the first place, what stands out is extreme isolation as a form of punishment. *Lack of communication* has been a regularly used penalty in the penitentiary system since its inception, but in more recent cases the technique is taken to the most infuriating extremes, as a systematic practice. The long months without any communication with any other human being, as testimony from survivors of Guantánamo black sites confirms, provoke "depression, paranoia, aggression, hallucinations, and induce suicide" (AI: 2005a). That is, this isolation entails deep suffering that seems literally to be maddening.[6] Mamdouh Habib recalls that Muhammad al Madni,[7] confined for years in a cell near his own in Guantánamo, "had gone completely mad" and he heard him say: "Speak to me, please. . . . I am depressed . . . I need to speak with someone" (AI: 2006a).

In addition to this type of isolation, *sensory deprivation*, cutting off the senses (with earflaps, blinders, masks, hoods, gloves), imposes a much more radical inability to communicate. The use of hoods and isolation techniques share certain similarities with the torture regime in Argentina, which can be considered an early version of this same pattern of repression.[8] However, the means and scope of current techniques of solitary confinement are much more severe.

Other practices related to the aforementioned could be considered an entirely new breed. Exposure to *white noise combined with hooding*, mentioned in several accounts, is a form of simultaneous disruption of sight and hearing, adding to the spatial isolation that occurs through sensory deprivation. It is known that this "produces confusion and psychological agitation, and after 40 minutes the majority of the victims begin to hallucinate" (AI: 2005a). Something similar occurs with the constant exposure to loud music and intermittent lights, based on the saturation of the senses as a means of nullifying them.

Certain techniques affect sleep, such as the exposure to monotonous noises in uncomfortable or "stressful" positions. *Deprivation or disruption of sleep patterns* is one of the most common forms of torture and probably the most damaging in this network of clandestine detention centers. This technique affects the nervous system in general and creates a kind of "hollowing" or exhaustion of the mind.

Together, all the techniques described as "stressful" violently strain the senses and bodily functions by disrupting them, altering them, and traumatizing them. They take the subjects to the edge of madness through specific procedures of disorientation, and isolation through the obstruction, alteration or saturation of the senses. They provoke a kind of madness, a state of desperation that incites suicide or leads to a willingness to die of hunger, such as occurred at Guantánamo.[9] Attempting this impossible self-destruction magnifies the desperation and tension.

6. BOYS THAT PLAY?

We can add another catalogue of torture alongside the testimonies of survivors: the photographs from Abu Ghraib. We see the very moment of torture in these photographs from an entirely original angle up to now, an outside view impossible for the hooded victim to capture. It is an outside view that, curiously, situates the one doing the cutting, crushing, and beating on the inside—where he should be.

Some of the images attest to what has already been stated in the testimonies, while adding to them. The viewer's special status provokes, in a way, that unique shudder of the witness to the horror.[10] But the photos also demonstrate what the survivors could not see or say: a) Lynndie England, small and grimacing, leads a naked man by a dog leash through a hallway with papers strewn about the floor and rags and robes hanging on the walls (probably those belonging to the prisoners, nude in their cells); b) behind a pyramid of unclothed bodies,[11] buttocks facing the camera (from another shot we know that these are hooded persons), the jailers pose, a woman and a man[12] with latex gloves, contemplating the prisoners, smiling and showing their raised thumbs in a sign of victory; c) Lynndie England, with a cigarette in her mouth, pointing to the penis of a nude hooded prisoner—whose body is beautiful—as if she were shooting him with a weapon; d) Sabrina Harman, with green latex gloves, giving a wide smile and, raising her thumb, leans next to the face of a dead, bloody prisoner, with a bandaged eye and his body stuffed inside a bag filled with ice.

These photos reveal the types of "permitted" torture that is not thought of as torture: the multifarious humiliation that has come to be called "abuse."[13] But there is *a double humiliation* here: that of the prisoners and that of their jailers, the abuse of an Other as well as of the human condition through the very act of torture.

What is new in these images is not the sexual humiliation. In one way or another, this has always been present. Likewise, it matters very little if such acts are homosexual or heterosexual; any forced sexual practice is an abuse and is, in conditions of incarceration, a form of torture, whether in the Islamic world or the Christian West. The newness is not even the existence of photos that attest to such crude mistreatment, but rather the inclusion of the perpetrators, smiling and victorious within the photographic frame. Alongside the horror, without recognizing it, they themselves are sensorially deprived, anesthetized: they see without seeing and coexist with the horror without feeling it. In principle, they seem proud to be torturers, which would represent an authentic innovation in the self-representation of the repressor.

In previous experiences of torture elsewhere, the torturer never recognized himself as a torturer, but rather used euphemisms to describe his "work," and tended to think of himself as a kind of technician carrying out a disagreeable but necessary function (in which it would be impossible for him to have any pride).[14] By avoiding any reference to and even "concealing" this "dirty job," these torturers appeared to harbor some notion of the existence of an ethical principle transgressed by their practices.

The young torturers of Abu Ghraib appear even to fail to recognize that they might be doing something reprehensible, which would be a form not of boasting of their status as torturers or disavowing the fact, but of not acknowledging it in a much more absolute and intimate way. They smiled for the cameras, they posed because "they didn't feel there was something bad about what the photos show . . . (that's why) they were taken, to circulate them so that so many people might see them" (Sontag, 2004).

Yet, not everything here is the stupor of unawareness or the ignorance of some ethical principle by way of an atrocious "innocence." This might exonerate the individuals in question to some extent. The green latex gloves are also the mark of something else. The thumb raised as a sign of triumph is wrapped in those visible and unmistakable gloves, like those used by surgeons, or perhaps cleaning workers who wear them so as not to dirty their hands. The gloves are a sign that they are carrying out an "operation" that is "dirty" and that gets them dirty. The atrocious unawareness in their smiles is the opposite of cruelty that recognizes itself as such; it senses impunity. This sense of impunity is an inescapable explanation for the very possibility of the photos and their dissemination.

If the forms of torture applied in Abu Ghraib were something habitual, then photographing them was as well. In reality, "the images passed from computer to computer throughout the entire 320th Battalion" (Hersh: 48) and only one person, Specialist Joseph Darby, submitted a letter denouncing them. This open circulation indicates as much the "normalcy" of what the images show as it does its photographic record. The abuses "seemed almost routine" (Hersh: 46), among other things, because they were authorized. The fact that Darby's complaint was anonymous points to, precisely, the involvement of immediate superiors who cannot be denounced openly.

The use of torture or the act of photographing it cannot be considered part of a special "micro-climate," created only in Abu Ghraib. In Afghanistan as well as in Iraq, prisoners were photographed and filmed during interrogations (Hersh: 60–61); the same occurs in the so-called "black sites." Khaled al-Masri, whose testimony was mentioned above, recounts that, as they beat and stripped him, "at all times he heard the sound of cameras taking pictures" (El País: 8-12-2005). Given the active participation of the torturers in the beatings and abuses he describes, it seems more than probable that they would have been included in these photos.

Were the images from Abu Ghraib really emailed home in order to share them with friends? In any case, they are already there, and the best way of "normalizing" them is to render their situation something out of the ordinary, something accounted for by the extreme psychological conditions soldiers must endure. Rush Limbaugh expressed something along these lines in his radio program: "You know, these people are being fired at every day. I'm talking about people having a good time, these people. You ever heard of emotional release?" (Sontag). In other words, emotional releases (due to the stress!) that are discharged at the expense of others.

In effect, as media figures have treated it, this is a case of common, ordinary kids having some fun torturing others; in this case, the others are very different in linguistic, religious, and cultural terms. They are terrorists, which makes it much easier to absolve these "kids." The expression "having fun" is correct, although it might seem excessive to us. Even the protagonists in the images themselves use this language. For example, one of the marines who performed watch duties in Guantánamo recounted that the commanders of his squad urged them to "visit the prisoners" when there were no outside visitors or news media nearby. "We tried to screw with them as much as we could, inflicting small doses of pain . . . we couldn't break their leg or something. . . . One thing we used to do was put hoods on them and take them out in the Humvee, confusing them until they didn't know where they were. . . . We didn't understand what they were saying. It wasn't about getting information from them. We only wanted to have some fun playing with their heads" (Hersh: 35).[15]

Additionally, in Abu Ghraib a pair of dog handlers who had cornered two prisoners against the wall, threatening them with the animals, said that they were not interrogating them but that "they were having a contest to see how many detainees they could make urinate themselves" (Hersh: 59). That is, they were having fun.

Torture becomes a game if there is authorization and a previous anesthetizing process in regard to the Other. This phenomenon occurs not only among soldiers necessarily affected by the brutality of war. The anesthetizing process implicates society beyond the circumstances of war; it precedes war but its force comes through war and it is functional in relation to war. It is principally oriented towards the Arab, Muslim, and terrorist; but it can extend much further beyond.

Torture is authorized, applied, and redefined as something else. It is normalized as a practice and discursively transformed into a "game," thus completely obscuring awareness of its implications with regard to one's other, one's equal, and oneself. It nonetheless distinctly damages the humanity of those who practice it as much as those who endure it. Despite the contrivances of power, the torturer knows deep within exactly what he is doing.

7. THE REASONS FOR TORTURE

The fact that torture is treated as a "game" or "entertainment" doesn't allow us to explain the motives of the torturer as a function of gratuitous, "playful" sadism or psychological pathology. On the contrary, the torturer can be and usually is a "normal" man or woman and their institutionally initiated and developed violence has *specific ends and uses*.

The reasons for torture are to be found in a global machinery that considers torture a political option. This apparatus, this network controlled by the North American state and endorsed by other western and non-western states, validates torture as a systematic state practice in those areas where it seeks control. At the same time, the attempt to redefine torture by expanding its legal application and, above all, applying it to those classified as "terrorists" is not generated by a pathology on the part of its functionaries (without denying that this may play a role in more than one case) but rather through its functionality.

The terrorist—an enemy who can be "disappeared," tortured, or locked away if he doesn't die beforehand—is the member of Al Qaeda or international networks that threaten the Western countries, but it is also the Taliban in Afghanistan, the insurgency in Iraq, Palestinians in Gaza, or the militant wing of Hezbollah in Lebanon. That is, it is whoever confronts the politics of the global empire in those places it attempts to impose itself and is, above all, he who defies its military power. In the face of this, torture is, now as in the past, the most efficient means for the United States to obtain useful information in the service of destroying their enemy. It is particularly efficient when there are no limits to its use.[16]

When the concentration camp at Guantánamo was created, it was explicitly stated from the outset, and without provoking any diplomatic scandal, that they sought useful information about the terrorist networks from the prisoners. Survivors of the "black sites" also mention their interrogators' search for information, as noted in the testimony of Al-Masri (El País: 8-12-2005) and Muhammad al-Assad (AI: 2005a).

But Seymour Hersh has perhaps best reconstructed the relation between torture, interrogation, and information, based on the case of Abu Ghraib. Hersh affirms that the use of interrogations in Guantánamo during the first months was a failure because "more than half of those who were incarcerated there didn't have any reason to be there (and because) there was no rational method for determining who was important and who wasn't" (Hersh: 24). This is to say that the North American services were ignorant of their enemy, and that they couldn't obtain useful information since they weren't even able to distinguish between an ordinary Arab and a terrorist, a confusion that, from the beginning, was very revealing.

In November of 2002, General Geoffrey Miller took over command of the base with authorization to utilize the so-called *special—that is, illegal—methods of interrogation*. It appears that this didn't produce many results, given that the detainees around that time had been "out of circulation" for several months, rendering obsolete any information they might have.

By that time, the US had already established the SAP program whose end was to establish clandestine interrogation centers, outside any legal restriction. By the end of August 2003, "the war in Iraq was going poorly and the information obtained in many of the prisons in the country was barely relevant" (Hersh: 42), for which reason they decided to use harsher methods on the detainees. In that moment, General Miller took a group of experts to Iraq to analyze the prison system there. They concluded that "the detention installations should facilitate the interrogations . . .

[in order to] obtain confidential information quickly" (Hersh: 53). That is, they proposed a "guantanamization" of Iraq's penitentiary system.

Donald Rumsfeld approved the use of illegal techniques (SAP) in Iraq and ordered the 205th Military Intelligence Brigade to assume tactical control over the prison at Abu Ghraib. Between October and December 2003, numerous cases of "flagrant, gratuitous, and even sadistic mistreatment" were recorded according to the Taguba Report,[17] which attributed primary responsibility for the incidents to intelligence personnel and contracted civilians.

The Taguba Report also shows that Military Police (to which the people in the photos belong) "had received orders to modify the penitentiary conditions in order to make the interrogations by military intelligence 'easier.'" The intelligence personnel in addition to the contracted civilians "emphatically requested that the Military Police create physical and mental conditions favorable for interrogating the witnesses." In this same sense, Specialist Sabrina Harman stated that "MI wanted to get them to talk. It is Graner and Frederick's job to do things for MI and OGA to get these people to talk." Military intelligence personnel told the Military Police, "loosen this guy up for us," and "make sure he has a bad night." Then they praised the conduct of Graner and Frederik[18] with phrases like "Good job, they're breaking down real fast. They answer every question. They're giving out good information" (Hersh: 52–53).

Up to this point, what military intelligence considered "preparation" by the "interrogators" was what the young Military Police did as part of the "entertainment" designed to soften up the prisoners. What happened in the "wooden building" and the "metal building" where the important detainees were kept, where civil and intelligence personnel carried out "interrogations," where even the Military Police didn't enter? Certainly, they used the "unauthorized" methods there.

From the accounts above, one comes away with the understanding that the primary intention of torture is to obtain useful information in order to eliminate the clandestine resistance networks—particularly those which are armed—independent of any actual ability to mount a resistance.

The United States and its allies face an Other in the Arab world that is radically different. This, on one hand, facilitates the act of dehumanizing him; but, on the other, it makes it very difficult to know him and, consequently, to control him.

While an interrogator needs a translator, a linguist—as it is noted in the testimony—who serves as his cultural translator? What ability does he have to interpret what is said and what isn't said? How does he scrutinize any information he might receive? Does he really know what to ask and how to do it? It seems quite improbable. We need to add that the more ignorant and blind the repressive mechanism, the more the number increases of accidental victims who are completely "useless" for providing information. Torture tends to be efficient, however, especially when it is unrestricted; this is why it is used. And in general it is successful in extracting some information, however partial and insignificant, that feeds the cycle of disappearances, torture, interrogation, and information.

8. OTHER USES OF TORTURE

Torture does not only pursue information. It is also *a form of punishment*, a "policy of retaliation upon bodies and minds for simply daring to oppose the empire militarily" (Straga: 5) or having defied it in any way. As such, it contains a "pedagogical" message directed at global society: Don't you dare.

It seeks to drive its subjects mad not only to soften them up for the interrogator, but also as a form of *vengeance*. There is no attempt to "reform" or re-educate; the Arab terrorist is an Other so unyielding that he can only be confined, punished, and executed.

Some torture practices, such as forced nudity and hooding (nothing in common with those used in Argentina, but rather in accordance with the "model" of the Ku Klux Klan, more familiar to the North American torturers), accentuate the defenselessness of the prisoner to make him more vulnerable during interrogation. But they also seize his humanity by covering his face and removing his clothes. These practices are part of the process of *dehumanization* that facilitates the destruction of prisoners through the system of concentration camps. This occurs in all forms of humiliation, including sexual ones.

Through the mechanisms of confinement and torture, the system also attains its *self-confirmation*. The men "confess," turning the suspicion that had hung over them into something real, confirming the existence of "terrorists" and the danger they present. They confess both what they have done and what they have not done in order to make the punishment stop, and the difficulty of distinguishing the one from the other is magnified by the cultural distance and military ineptitude.

Moreover, even if the types of techniques used by this system of global disappearance center on the production of psychical imbalances, the prisoners' madness also functions as a "confirmation" of those very traits the imperial power attributes to them: mad, irrational, suicidal, and murderous. In effect, their madness is verified in confinement, as with Muhammad Saad al-Madni and many others.[19] It can be verified likewise that they have, for the interrogators, an incomprehensible form of rationality; indeed, they attempt suicide, which is why "we don't allow them access to drugs or other objects that they could use to hurt themselves with," according to Lieutenant William Costello (El País: 21.8–2002). But they attempt suicide even through hunger strikes, not because they are desperate but because their life doesn't matter to them and they try "to call attention to the media and pressure the United States government," as Lieutenant Colonel Jeremy Martin, spokesperson for Guantánamo, declared (AI: 2006a).

In conclusion, the search for information is the primary objective of torture. However, the punishment of the "offender" and his "pedagogical" function with respect to the rest of society; his destruction and madness, stripping him of his humanity, to which his debased condition testifies; the self-confirmation of the system of disappearances and its "meaning" are all objectives of torture, and are equally important in buttressing the new world order and its repressive mechanisms.

10. CLUES

The forms of organized repression are useful for mapping out the political power that employs and applies them. They reveal practices that, while central, remain concealed behind other, more "presentable" institutions. They clearly indicate what is punished and how and, therefore, show how power behaves and represents itself.

In the case of global reorganization, the tools we need are still too fragmented to do anything resembling cartography. A major part of the repressive system remains in the shadows and only allows us faint glimpses of its existence. Nevertheless, observation of some of its practices and the "innovations" they introduce can provide us with certain very preliminary clues regarding some of the characteristics of the current global power structure and its ongoing transformations.

- The repressive system deals with a global power exercised through an organization of networks with no geographical center, but with a strong *concentration of command in small state and private elites*.
- It acts as a permanent *State of Exception* with relation to a portion of the population, defined as an enemy completely excluded from the *State of Law*.
- It attempts to transform the current State of Law—applicable only to part of the world population—in such a way that the existence of a parallel,

permanent State of Exception is recognized within a system of legality. This implies an attempt to reorganize national and international law to facilitate the coexistence of a State of Law and a State of Exception.

- It deals with a power that, by virtue of this redefined relationship between the State of Law and the State of Exception, claims permanent, *unlimited prerogative.* One can say that, despite the similarity to totalitarianism, it is nonetheless quite different. There is a difference between the total and the unlimited. The first, by attempting to embrace a totality, recognizes its own limits. That which is unlimited, on the other hand, is more open and closer to the idea of "doing anything anywhere," recognizing the impossibility of totalization.

- The "terrorist" is the generic term for those excluded from the law. This category includes a set of political subjects whose common trait is having opposed the current reorganization—which excludes them—and above all those who defy the monopoly of military power. At present, the terms "Arab" and "terrorist" have melded into each other. This adds a *racist component*, a kind of new anti-Semitism, encouraged, paradoxically, by the Jewish State of Israel. However, armed non-Arabic groups have also received this label, and its consequent threat. Given the ambiguity of the term, it may be "flexibilized" and extended as necessary.

- The "terrorist," the radically excluded, is a *disposable or storable excess.* There is no room for him. No attempt is made to neutralize, readapt, or normalize him. Quite simply, he is hunted down and incarcerated. There exists no information about the "termination" process: that is, whether there are methods of elimination and what they might be.

- All acts of repression happen inside the system, given its global character. Therefore, the distinction between military and police action is blurred, such that repression acts as a *planetary mega-police* with information and intelligence activities at the center of the system.

- Consequently, we are dealing with power focused on the control of the flow of information, thus centralizing it. Controlling, altering, and censoring communication in their turn become forms of punishment. In fact, the primary and clearest form of exclusion within this new parallel penitentiary system is the prohibition of all communication through absolute confinement. These elements seem to signal the *centrality of communication in the new forms of organized power.*

- The neutralization of the disposable subjects is sought through so-called "sensory deprivation"; that is, the *obstruction, distortion, or saturation of principally the visual and auditory senses.* This seems to suggest that control of the "captured" uses similar procedures, attempting preferably to control the senses of sight and hearing.

- The characteristics of personnel involved in repression and the normalization of torture both inside and out of the military institutions suggest that part of this *sensorial control— a kind of general anesthesia* which allows neither sight nor sound nor, above all, any feeling—is that the suffering of the radically different Other can come to be seen as part of a game.

- These processes occur both within and external to the repressive system, but in distinct ways. The visibilization of that which takes place in the network's clandestine operations is a way of "marking" all of society in distinct ways. On one hand, it signals the force of power as well as its *impunity*. On the other hand, it spreads a sense of generalized defenselessness and fear, which leads to *immobility*. It also forces us to be "participants" in the atrocity, thus creating a kind of co-responsibility. Lastly, it creates the fictitious sense that the atrocities belong to an entirely *foreign world* when, in truth, the "prosecution" that happens over there is deeply and powerfully connected with the way the *ensemble* of society is treated.

In conclusion, the principal idea behind this review of the current forms of repression, and torture's role therein, is related to the possibility of advancing towards a cartography of a power we have yet to understand completely because it is never fully established. It is a power that continues to mutate, to shed its skin. It thus becomes imperative that we identify how its networks are connected, what designs they sketch, how they organize, how they fragment, and where they fall apart.

NOTES

1. It is worth noting that the figure of "enemy combatants" has also been applied to U.S. citizens who were either expelled from the country or remain incarcerated in military prisons.

2. The investigations by the *Washington Post* published in November 2005 coincide with the testimony of 3 Yemeni prisoners who "appeared" in May of 2005 while remaining detained in legal prisons without charge, and who were interviewed by Amnesty International (AI: AMR 51/177/2005).

3. The European commissioner for Human Rights, Älvaro Gil Robles, recounted having seen in September of 2002, in Kosovo, a sort of replica of the concentration camp in Guantánamo in the interior of the military base at Camp Bondsteel, near Faizaj, south of Pristina. According to Robles, there were small wooden cabins in the base surrounded by tall, barbed-wire fences, in each of which were enclosed 15–20 prisoners dressed in orange uniforms. As in Guantánamo, the prisoners had no contact with lawyers nor were they granted any legal proceedings. (*La Jornada*: 26-11-2005).

4. These 6 cases produced 13 victims, of which 8 were ultimately transferred to Guantánamo, 2 remain missing, 2 were released, and 1 is incarcerated in Egypt.

5. According to this definition, torture basically consists of overall acts that provoke pain or suffering, physical or mental, intentionally inflicted upon a person with the purpose of obtaining information or taking vengeance.

6. This characteristic is shared among some incarceration systems in modern high-security prisons.

7. This is a person detained in Indonesia in 2002, and later transferred to Egypt where he "disappeared." He reappeared in Guantánamo in 2004. There is no written documentation, and information about him has come second-hand from other prisoners who have been released.

8. I refer here to a type of punishment based on a cycle of disappearance-torture-isolation-storage-dumping, different from the conceptualization of concentration camps employed by the Nazis, for example.

9. It is worth pointing out that, even in these conditions, it isn't a peaceful death. Quite the opposite. To be on a hunger strike in Guantánamo implies being force-fed, with probes applied in a way that intentionally produces pain, as well as other types of humiliating or painful treatment.

10. Even Donald Rumsfeld, one of the primary parties responsible for the authorization of these practices, said in reference to the photos that show the "abuses," "to read about them, as I say, is one thing. But to see these photographs seems incredible to me. . . . Not for being three-dimensional. Not for the colors. It was something completely different" (Hersh: 88). Perhaps this is similar to the "internal shudder" that the final solution provoked in Eichmann?

11. The Argentinean case is an antecedent use of human "pyramids" with prisoners (Conadep: 211). Even the act of photographing them isn't new. During the war in Vietnam, "Col. George S. Patton—son of the famous Patton—sent a Christmas card that prayed for 'Peace on Earth' with photographs of mutilated Vietcong combatants meticulously piled one on top of another" (Hersh: 13).

12. Sabrina Harman and Charles Graner.

13. Upon seeing the photos from Abu Ghraib, the Secretary of Defense, Donald Rumsfeld said, "My impression is that the accusation is, for now, one of abuse, which I think is technically different from torture . . . And for that reason I will not use the word torture" (Sontag: 2).

14. I developed this idea in *Poder y desaparición*.

15. Likewise, in the Argentine experience there is some precedent to this practice of "playing" in order to make the prisoners suffer (Actis: 208).

16. The case of Argentina, as of many other Latin American countries, confirms the usefulness of unlimited state torture for obtaining information. Its application was decisive in destroying the clandestine militia networks.

17. General Antonio M. Taguba was commissioned by the North American government to carry out a secret investigation of Abu Ghraib, at the beginning of 2004, after having found out about the existence of photographs documenting the abuses.

18. These are two of the personnel appearing in the photos.

19. The Red Cross said, since September 2002, "that a 'disconcerting deterioration' in the psychological state of a great number of detainees had been observed" (AI: 2004).

BIBLIOGRAPHY

Actis Munú, Cristina Aldini, Liliana Gardella, Miriam Lewin, Elisa Tokar. *Ese infierno*. Buenos Aires, Editorial Sudamericana, 2001.

Amnesty International (AI). "Undermining Security: Violations of Human Dignity, the Rule of Law and the National Security Strategy in 'War on Terror' Detentions." AMR 51/061/2004, 2004.

Amnesty International (AI). "Report 2004: United States." http://web.amnesty.org/web/ web.nsf/print/C460F521958942BAC1256FDB0037EC78, 2005.

Amnesty International (AI). "The Case of Muhammad Abdullah Salah al-Assad." http:// web.amnesty.org/web/web.nsf/print/stoptorture-071105-appeal-esl, 2005a.

Amnesty International (AI). "United States/Yemen, Secret Detention in CIA "Black Sites." AMR 51/177/2005, 2005b.

Amnesty International (AI). "Partners in Crime: Europe's Role in US Renditions." EUR 01/008/2006, 2006.

Amnesty International (AI). "Who are the Guantánamo detainees? Case sheet 15: Yemeni national: Abdulsalam al-Hela." AMR 51/007/2006, 2006a.

Amnesty International (AI). "Ask Amnesty Online Discussion Series: Lives Torn Apart." http://web.amnestyusa.org/askamnesty/live/display.php?topic=51, 21 February, 2006, 2006b.

Barón, Ana. "La investigación del Washington Post. Cómo Estados Unidos armó la red de cárceles clandestinas." Buenos Aires, *El Clarín*, 20 November, 2005.

Buda, Blanca. *Cuerpo I, Zona IV*. Buenos Aires, Contrapunto, 1988.

Conadep. *Nunca más, Informe de la Comisión Nacional sobre la Desaparición de Personas*. Buenos Aires, Eudeba, 1991.

Engelhardt, Tom. "El sistema de tortura aplicado por Estados Unidos en Irak, Afganistán y Guantánamo." *Mother Jones, IAR Noticias*.

Geuna, Graciela. *Testimonio presentado ante CADHU,* mimeo.

Gras, Martín. *Testimonio presentado ante CADHU*, mimeo, 1980.

Hersh, Seymour. "Torture at Abu Ghraib." "Obediencia debida." México, Aguilar, 2004.

Puar, Jasbir. "Abu Ghraib: Arguing Against Exceptionalism." *Feminist Studies*, Summer 2004.

Rodríguez Molas, Ricardo. *Historia de la tortura y el orden represivo en Argentina*. Textos documentales, Buenos Aires, Eudeba, 1984.

Sontag, Susan. "What Have We Done?" *The Guardian*, 24 May, 2004.

Straga, Daniel. "Los prisioneros de Guantánamo a la luz del Convenio III de Ginebra." *Rebelión Internacional*, 2 August, 2002.

Vilariño, Raúl David. "Yo maté secuestré y vi torturar en la Escuela de Mecánica de la Armada." *La Semana*, núm. 370, 5 January, 1984.

Walzer, Michael. *Reflexiones sobre la guerra*. Barcelona, Paidós, 2004.

10

Torture as a Greater Evil

Carlos Castresana

> *I was perfectly frantic—a reckless witness under*
> *the torture—and would have told them anything*
>
> Charles Dickens, *Great Expectations*

THE ABSOLUTE PROHIBITION OF TORTURE has been a basic principle left out of discussion in both domestic and international law during the last 60 years, even if torture has continued to be widely applied around the world. However, after the September 11, 2001 terrorist attacks, the discussion has been renewed. Not only have the cases of torture increased in number and gained visibility, but the law enforcement bodies of supposedly democratic countries where torture was eradicated a long time ago, or happened only exceptionally, are now on the list of those using torture on a regular basis in their fight against terrorism. A new debate seems to arise: prestigious academics are proposing the legalization of torture, even if limited, and they seem to be winning the debate if we judge by the efforts of the US Government in supporting and guaranteeing immunity for those involved in cases constituting torture beyond doubt, or if we listen to Prime Minister Tony Blair, speaking about plans for new measures in Britain's antiterrorism policy, assuring, *"Let no one be in any doubt. The rules of the game are changing."*

THE PROHIBITION

Torture was abolished in Naples in 1738, England in 1762, Austria in 1776, and France in 1780. The prohibition was extended throughout most of the national legal systems during these decades.

The absolute prohibition of torture today is generally grounded in the fundamental value of human dignity. Torture did not begin to be eradicated as a consequence of moral or political principles, however, or because it was considered an evil in itself, but mainly for practical or instrumental reasons when the English model of criminal process began to be imported into continental European law, evolving from the inquisitorial to the accusatorial system. The basic maxim of the accusatorial criminal process was enunciated by Hobbes[1] when he affirmed *"Nemo tenetur se detegere*": nobody can be forced to incriminate himself. The principle had been incorporated into English law by a Statute in 1641.[2] In contrast to the continental monarchies, the British sovereign was entitled to punish his subjects only if the defendant was proven guilty before an impartial tribunal. In order to ensure that the trial was fair, both the prosecution and the defense had to have equal arms before the tribunal and opportunities to argue, present, and refute evidence. To grant this equality, the defendant could not be compelled to cooperate with the accusers[3] and, as a consequence, confession was non-compulsory and torture was prohibited.

Moreover, despite current discussion in the academic world about its effectiveness, torture had already been discredited as a source of evidence almost four centuries ago: "*What is confessed in such a situation tends only to relieve the pain of he who is being tortured, not to provide information to the torturers,*" observed Hobbes[4] in 1651.

Evidence that torture is useless—apart from being immoral—since it does not contribute to discovering truth, but rather perverts the entire process, had been empirically established two decades earlier by Friedrich Spee von Langefeld, a Jesuit priest in charge of administering the last sacraments to women sentenced as witches and then burned at the stake by the German Inquisition.[5]

So, the prohibition was mainly instrumental and pre-revolutionary.

THE POLITICAL AND LEGAL ARGUMENT

The Enlightenment had provided the legal and philosophical grounds; but it was during the American and French Revolutions that torture was linked to human dignity and became a political issue for the first time.

The prohibition of torture is one of the identity traits of democratic societies, since human dignity constitutes the basis of the modern social contract. Political prohibition of torture marks a turning point in human history: before, absolute monarchies and the *ancien régime*; afterwards, Revolution and the modern democratic States. No better expression of this principle is to be found than in the Declaration of Independence of the United States, where it was established as a self-evident truth that every human being is endowed with certain inalienable rights and, more importantly, that government exists to guarantee these rights and its legitimacy depends on its promise to respect and ensure them. From this moment on, the basic value of democracy is human dignity. Government and the rule of law are the instruments for preserving this value, and the specific rights in which this value materializes are principally the rights to life, liberty, and personal integrity. No room has been left for torture.

Revolution considered dignity a universal value, equal for every human being. The ideologists of the new State converted the law of nature—the law of the strongest—into the law of mankind—the law of the weakest.[6] The natural tendency of the stronger to abuse its power has to be balanced by the rule of law, which guarantees equal rights and opportunities for every person. This is the reason why the essence of democracy in the legal construction of the modern State is not only or mainly the periodic democratic renewal of governments through the electoral processes—this is the condition, not the substance—but the rule of law[7]: submission to the legal order, not only by minorities, to whom law is imposed, but by the majority as well. The decision or the interest of the majority can not justify everything. Rights of minorities must also be preserved.[8] The pursuit of happiness, the utilitarian doctrine of the greater good, has some limits. This legal and political structure was later reproduced in every national Constitution during the 19th century and first half of the 20th century.

The model broke down in 1945. In the aftermath of the Second World War, the international community realized that war was no longer an affair of gentlemen killing each other in the battlefields. Most of the victims were not combatants but civilians who didn't lose their lives as a consequence of the hostilities, but in the rearguard under the repression of some of the belligerent States. This was another turning point. A new paradigm was established in the UN Charter and in every Convention approved in the years to come: human rights would no longer be considered a domestic affair submitted to only within the bounds of sovereignty of each State. Basic human rights henceforth provided the founding content of a new universal social contract. The international community adopted the promise of respecting and ensuring human rights at a global level, granting to international bodies—mainly the United Nations—the right of interference in the domestic affairs of any State unwilling or unable to fulfill its duties.

It is obvious that the Cold War provided many safe havens for egregious abuses in the following years, but let us be clear about this: we live today in an extremely dangerous world for the reason that States and the international community have not honored their promises. We live amid insecurity because even though we have the legal instruments, these instruments are not applied. We call this impunity. It is the black hole of our domestic and international justice systems.

TORTURE AND THE RULE OF LAW

> *The heirs of the French, English and American revolutions had partly*
> *believed in their own phrases about the rights of man, freedom of speech,*
> *equality before the law, and the like, and had even allowed their conduct*
> *to be influenced by them to some extent.*

George Orwell, *1984*

States can commit many abuses against human rights. Some of these abuses are even more serious or have worse consequences than torture. Why, then, is it so important that States refrain from using torture? The answer is simple: torture affects the basic pillars of the legal structure of democratic States, its very essence. Even if every brick is important, we can remove some of them without risking the building. This is not the case, however, when addressing the issue of human dignity. Accepting the practice of torture, even the soft modalities of cruel, inhuman or degrading treatment, or removing—even partially—its prohibition, compromises the safety and threatens the collapse of our whole legal system.

Torture is prohibited, and its prohibition is absolute since it implies an outrage against human dignity. This is a non-negotiable value. In contrast to those rights defined by exclusion,[9] physical and mental integrity, the main right representing human dignity, is a right of inclusion,[10] shared by every human being, superior and indivisible: the torturer destroys the victim's dignity, but at the same time destroys his own dignity. This is the rationale used to explain why we legally label torture *inhumane* treatment, proclaiming—though not very successfully—that it is improper conduct for mankind. Unrestricted respect for human dignity draws the boundary between civilization and barbarism.

Torture is important because when its prohibition is not respected, all legal democratic structures become contaminated. The problem neither begins nor ends in the violation of the right to physical or mental integrity of a detainee in order to gather information: the problem begins prior to the violation and continues afterwards. Given the right to personal freedom, when a suspected terrorist is arrested and his captors wish to impose coercive interrogation, the suspect cannot be taken to a conventional detention facility. Secret facilities must be provided in order to prevent the detainee from having contact with other detainees who are not going to be tortured. This transforms the arrest into an *illegal detention*. In such conditions—clandestine and tortured—the detainee cannot be presented before a regular judge in conventional and prompt legal terms. This violation thus transforms the detention into a *kidnapping* or *unlawful confinement*, and renders it necessary to create exceptional or secret military courts not bound by due process standards. Those who still refuse to cooperate even after special coercive interrogation must be secretly surrendered to "partner" authorities in other countries, where they will ultimately be tortured without limit. This is called *forced disappearance*, and in many cases, if death does not follow torture, the detention will end in the clandestine *extrajudicial execution* of the detainee.

The corruption of the legal system does not end with those who propose or justify, who practice, who order or authorize, who know and do not avoid, or those who should have known torture is being committed. Criminal responsibility ends here, but moral complicity inexorably expands its stain throughout all official institutions and society, the people on whose behalf torture is practiced.

WHY SHOULD WE RECONSIDER THE PROHIBITION?

> *Practices which had been long abandoned, in some cases for hundreds of years—imprisonment without trial . . . torture to extract confessions . . . —not only became common again, but were tolerated and even defended by people who considered themselves enlightened and progressive.*

George Orwell, *1984*

The response from utilitarians proposing legalization is the following: the situation is extremely dangerous, our authorities torture in order to protect us and will continue torturing whatever we do: so, let us make legal what is real.

To convince us, and bypass the instinctive repulsion that torture provokes in any normal person, the supporters of legalization present us with the hypothetical and extreme case of the terrorist and the ticking bomb. Let us legalize torture at least in this case, they say. Who could oppose this, if so many lives are at stake?

Well, the first answer is: as a rule, the ticking bomb case does not exist. It is a fraud. Secondly, accepting that improbable and extreme cases may happen sometimes, this still does not justify legalizing torture. Criminal law has provided different solutions for such cases for a long time. We can use the example of the terrorist and the ticking bomb; or the case of the person who finds a ticking bomb inside a theater and, in order to save the majority of lives, must exit through the crowd stabbing those who involuntarily obstruct his way; or the case of the survivors of a sunken ship denying others access to the overcrowded boat. And many others. The answer is not in legalizing torture, injury, or murder, because none of these situations exclude damage to values the law is intended to protect. If such acts are not committed with the intention of causing damage but of preserving an equal or superior value, the results of punishment are excluded because the act qualifies for the defense of necessity.

This legal scheme would not be affected by the judicial warrant that some authors propose as a remedy. The warrant, if the conduct is justified, will add nothing; and if it is not justified, will neither diminish its reproachfulness nor the responsibility of the torturer: it will merely add another element of responsibility for the offense, the authorizing judge.

According to its supporters, legalized torture should be controlled by judicial authorities. Under this condition, they say, slippery slopes would not occur. This is not true. In spite of being considered a crime, the practice has still been widespread in recent years and, with a few exceptions, rarely prosecuted, even in cases with overwhelming evidence. Why should accountability improve through making the practice legal? Judicial *ex ante* supervision would not avoid the abuses, just as judicial *ex post* jurisdiction is not avoiding them right now.

Moreover, some utilitarians argue, legalization would reduce the use of torture to extreme cases. This is also false. For several years now, there has not been a plane flying over Guantánamo, Baghram, or Abu Ghraib with a ticking bomb, and we know what has happened in these places. Utilitarians say we are naïve, but they ignore or prefer to ignore the real situations in which torture is usually committed, which are much more similar than imagined to the hypothetical example they use. In most cases, interrogators desist from conventional investigation techniques and resort to torture because, even without the ticking bomb, time works against them. Anyone having studied torture in the "dirty war" in Latin America during the 70s and 80s knows that torture is a countdown. The information a terrorist can provide is useful for only a few hours after his capture, the time between his arrest being known and the rest of the members of the group hiding arms and documents, destroying evidence, and escaping. The detainee knows that he must resist for only a few hours. The interrogator knows that he needs the information immediately or it will become useless. This is the real scenario, the one which renders naïve the proposal of limited legalization, the one which renders the slippery slopes unavoidable.

Moreover, there is another motive, also taught by experience, because torture, once legalized, would become necessarily widespread: it is useless if not systematic. Hobbes and Von Spee showed us centuries ago that information gathered through torture is not reliable. Given this, the only way to gather accurate information is to detain as many suspicious persons as possible; systematically torture all of them; gather gross information; and later, crossing-checking all the information, a little valuable information may be ready to be exploited.[11]

Even accepting a limited and controlled legalization, where would the limit be? In the proven, probable, or possible terrorist; in the suspected one; in the innocent who nonetheless happens to have the information; in the absolutely innocent, if we can save thousands of lives? Where is the limit of what can be done: restraining in painful conditions, hooding, burning, killing? Where can such a utilitarian ethic, utility, greater good, or general happiness carry us? The further we travel this path, the closer we get to al Qaeda.

Torture is self-evidently beyond moral, legal, and political lines, and must remain there. Any public servant knows he must not cross it, and knows too that if he does, he must have very good reasons to justify the transgression. If we delete or move the line, we will not be legalizing and bringing into our field something that is presently illegal. It will mean displacing ourselves into the field of illegality. The place where torture exists, in fact, does not depend on where we draw the line, but on where the line must be according to our founding values, civilization, and even decency. Law is an instrument for preserving our values, not violating them.

CROSSING THE LINE

Nothing was illegal since there were no longer any laws

George Orwell, *1984*

There is something worse than breaking the law: distorting the law. Breaches have—at least, theoretically—their legal response, but when authorities distort the law, and especially when the distortion is systematic, the problem is much more serious because certitude and legal security disappear. The rule of law becomes useless. Nothing is what it seems to be, and nobody knows what is legal or illegal.

In *1984*, George Orwell defined a totalitarian state. We do not live in a totalitarian regime nor are we moving towards one, because—I hope—we still enjoy some important mechanisms that counteract that tendency. Yet, in some ways, the somber Orwellian prediction seems to have become accurate. Since 2001, governments of democratic states have secretly crossed the lines of domestic and international law. When they have been discovered, mostly by the mass media,[12] these states have tried and continue to try not only to change the law, drawing new utilitarian limits, but to distort the laws in force in order to create an appearance of legality for things that are clearly unlawful, extending at the same time the fear[13] and the stain of complicity to all of society. A full explanation of the situation built around the war on terror exceeds the scope of this work, but let us look at some examples, because torture is in the eye of this hurricane.

The problem began with the definition of the "war on terror" itself. After September 11, 2001, a US Congress Joint Resolution authorized the President "to use all necessary and appropriate force against those nations, organizations or persons he determines planned, authorized, committed or aided" the 9-11 attacks. "Use of force" is the legal term for war. Congress thus authorized the President to wage war against any nation, organization or person deemed responsible. The problem is that international law only recognizes war between sovereign States that have ratified the Conventions, not between States and organizations or individuals.[14] The reason is simple: the Geneva Conventions are written under the assumption that it is useless to attempt to regulate conflict between parties if one of the parties—al Qaeda in this case—is unable or unwilling to respect any regulation. The apparent contradiction can be easily solved through interpretation: war may be waged against Afghanistan or other responsible nations; but against terrorist groups or individuals, only regular (no military) domestic or international law may be used. Instead, the American and several European governments abused the contradiction. The US government declared[15] that an armed conflict existed between the US and Afghanistan in which the Geneva Conventions applied, and that another, different armed conflict with no specific geographical location existed between the US and al Qaeda in which the Conventions did not apply. Since then, governments in the war on terror have used part of the law and customs of war against suspected terrorists where it has been in their interest, mainly entitling Coalition forces to kill terrorists, and have denied the applicability of the remaining part when it has implied submitting the conduct of war to any binding rule.[16]

This fiction has permitted the lawyers of the war on terror to create Guantánamo and other safe havens beyond the reach of any jurisdiction.[17] To fill these facilities, they have invented the new extralegal category—a masterpiece of Orwellian doublethink—of "enemy combatants." Neither combatants nor civilians,[18] enemy combatants are detainees but not prisoners, because they have been arrested in a war that is neither domestic nor international. They are not entitled to kill but are targets to be killed. For them, it is not only the case that "*war is peace, freedom is slavery, and ignorance is strength*,"[19] but forced disappearance is rendition, due process is a secret trial before a military commission, and, most importantly, torture is a coercive interrogation device.

The US government's current stance on torture is the opposite of that of the rest of the democratic international community (in this case, UK included). Torture was banned, supposedly forever, in 1948 with the Universal Declaration of Human Rights. The prohibition was ratified in 1949 in the Geneva Conventions, and in 1966 in the International Covenant of Civil and Political Rights. It was proclaimed universal in the 1984 Convention Against Torture and Other Cruel, Inhumane or Degrading Treatment or Punishment. Finally, the protection was expanded in 1998 in the Rome Statute, already signed by 139 and ratified by 102 sovereign States.[20] For them, torture means the intentional infliction of severe pain or suffering upon a person in custody. No more, no less. Official capacity and motives of the perpetrator are irrelevant.

The Office of Legal Counsel of the US Department of Justice, on the contrary, determined in August 2002 that torture could only be considered such when pain brought death, organ failure, serious impairment of body functions, or post-traumatic stress disorder. Moreover, the OLC Report continued, torture law does not apply to interrogations ordered by the US President in the use of his powers in the war on terror. And anyway, the Report concluded, self-defense or necessity justify torture.

A possible comment to the OLC Report could be the statement addressed by the American Court in Nuremberg[21] to the jurists of the Nazi regime: "*you destroyed law and justice in Germany utilizing the empty forms of legal process*."

Hopefully, there is some good news. The US Supreme Court (*Hamdan v. Rumsfeld*) has recently declared[22] illegal the Guantánamo military commissions created by presidential power. This is a very positive and hopeful step: first, because the Supreme Court accepts its duty of controlling, checking and balancing the executive, and enters for the first time since 9-11 into the field of *arcana imperii*, demonstrating that Locke, Montesquieu, and the separation of powers are not completely dead; second, because it declares the Geneva Conventions enforceable; and third, because the counsel representing the plaintiff—a suspected al Qaeda/Muslim/Arab/terrorist—were American military lawyers, which demonstrates that somebody somewhere still believes in the rules of fair play, and that the Anglo-American legal democratic heritage is alive as well.

Conclusion

> *The unbounded licentiousness of ill-directed*
> *power has produced until now a long and authorised*
> *example of the most unfeeling barbarity*

Beccaria, "On Crimes and Punishments" (1764)

What does the widespread use of torture followed by impunity mean in a democratic society today? The breach of the social contract.

Torture was reserved in Rome for foreigners and slaves. It was no different in Nazi Germany: it was necessary to deprive the German Jewish population of their nationality before deporting, persecuting, and exterminating them.[23] The same was done during the Argentinean dictatorship.[24] In order to work properly and to be effective, torture must consider the victim an alien. This requires the denial of human dignity.

The US Supreme Court declared in 1966 (*Miranda v. Arizona*) that "incommunicado interrogation" was "destructive of human dignity." Today, in the face of an objectively worse situation, the Court has been capable of establishing a humanitarian minimum, but no more.[25]

There is no clash of civilizations. There are many cultures, but only one civilization. By defending torture, and violating and distorting the rule of law, those responsible for the war on terror are not only spreading a stain over the entire society they say they are serving; they are, moreover, alienating the most powerful weapon democratic states have to counteract barbarism: the moral superiority of civilization, the consideration of inalienable human dignity as the fundamental value upon which the political structure of human societies must be built. By doing so, they have taken an opposing path to the one that can solve the problem. Instead of bringing barbarians to this side of the line, instead of inviting them to share the 21st century with us, we are returning with them to the Middle Ages.

It is no accident that the practice of torture was extended from foreigners to Roman citizens for political offences in emergency situations, and became widespread only after the fall of the republic and the arrival of the empire. Did tyranny bring torture, or was it actually torture that brought tyranny?

It is a fact that we face unprecedented dangers. In this context, every reasonable person agrees that some exceptional measures must be taken. Perhaps those who honestly believe that torture is the lesser of evils in confronting the threat we face should consider whether the real challenge we should accept is to be faithful to our values and defend civilization with the tools of democracy, even assuming the costs this decision may represent. To be utilitarians, taking into account that after five years of the war on terror support for al Qaeda continues to grow,[26] perhaps we should conclude that the rule of law is the true lesser evil.

NOTES

1. *On the Citizen* (Cambridge: Cambridge University Press, 1998). Quoted in Luigi Ferrajoli, *Derecho y Razón* (Madrid: Editorial Trotta, 1995). 608.

2. And into the US Constitution through the Fifth Amendment in 1791.

3. Equality of arms before the tribunal comes from the origin of the accusatorial procedural system, when a public prosecution didn't exist, but tribunals were created to put an end to private vengeance by impartially arbitrating conflicts between particulars. When the lawsuit came from the Sovereign, it was treated as any other plaintiff's.

4. Hobbes. *Leviathan*. Quoted in Ferrajoli, *Derecho y Razón*. 676–677.

5. Friedrich Spee Von Langenfeld, *Cautio Criminalis, or a book on witch trials*. (Charlottesville: University of Virginia Press, 2003). Why—asked Spee—are there so many more witches in Germany that in any other place in Europe? Maybe the Devil prefers German women for some reason over other women? He offered his findings in his book. The answer was torture. There were no more witches in Germany than elsewhere. The number of judgments was much higher simply because the German Inquisition used torture systematically, and because Inquisitors did not use it to punish the defendants nor to get their confession, but to gather information: before being convicted and in exchange for stopping the torture, the suspected witch had to reveal the name of another woman, who was then arrested and tortured with the same purpose, and so on. The motive of this endless chain of pain: the salary of the Inquisitors was determined by the number of witches they sent to the bonfire.

6. Luigi Ferrajoli, *Derechos y Garantías* (Madrid: Editorial Trotta, 1999).

7. Luigi Ferrajoli, *Derechos y Garantías*. 23.

8. *Oliver Brown et al. v. Board of Education of Topeka, Kansas*. US Supreme Court 1954.

9. The right to property, for instance. My ownership over some things is characterized by the exclusion of any other ownership over the same thing. See Ferrajoli, *Derechos y Garantías*, 46.

10. Ferrajoli, *Derechos y Garantías*, Page 46.

11. Torture is like gold mining. You need to process tons of mineral before getting a gram of the precious metal. Pinochet or Videla are good examples: 35,000 cases of torture in Chile. 30,000 forced disappearances in Argentina. Can we even imagine the numbers if torture had been legal? Both Argentina and Chile are countries with small populations: can someone imagine the numbers at a worldwide level?

12. We pray with James Joyce in *Ulysses*: "give us this day our daily press."

13. Scaring the public has been another tool used and abused in trying to make torture acceptable. As Aldous Huxley pointed out in the 1946 edition of *Brave New World*, "what's the point of truth, or beauty, or knowledge, when the anthrax bombs are popping around you?"

14. The only exception is armed conflict between a State and insurgent forces in its own territory; i.e. a domestic armed conflict, the Common Article 3 of the four Geneva Conventions.

15. White House Press Statement February 7, 2002.

16. Similarly, in September 2002, knowing that the UN Charter and international customary law only permit the use of force against a sovereign State in the case of self-defence after an attack, or before an imminent threat, the US government changed its National Security Strategy, establishing that force could be used pre-emptively not only before an *imminent* threat but also before a *sufficient* threat. Six months later, the new doctrine was applied to Iraq. Obviously, no country, not even the US, can unilaterally change international law. Moreover, the standard of imminent threat had been established precisely after an incident between the US and the UK in the 19th century, the "Caroline case." It was confirmed as customary international law in 1946 by the Nuremberg Tribunal in the Judgment of the top Nazi leaders. To exonerate themselves, some of them invoked the defense that the German invasion of Norway and the Soviet Union had been preemptive. They were found guilty of aggression, sentenced to death and hanged.

17. Until the US Supreme Court has decided otherwise. See below comment on *Hamdan v. Rumsfeld, 2006.*

18. Geneva tries not to leave empty holes: combatants are those entitled to use force, i.e., to kill and be killed. With the exceptions of spies (undercover combatants) and mercenaries (combatants of fortune) all the rest are non-combatants; thus, civilians. "Enemy combatant" is redundant nonsense because every combatant, if not your own, is an enemy. "Illegal combatant" is a contradiction in terms: every combatant is legal, because if he is not legal, he cannot be a combatant.

19. George Orwell, *1984.*

20. As of August 22, 2006. www.ICCnow.org.

21. US v. Joseph Altstoetter et al. III Trials of war criminals before the Nuremberg Military Tribunals Under Control Council Law no. 10, 1946–1949. 983 (1948).

22. US Supreme Court, No. 05-184, June 29, 2006.

23. See Hannah Arendt, *Eichmann en Jerusalem. Un estudio sobre la banalidad del mal* (Madrid: Editorial Lumen, 1999). 66.

24. Before being exterminated, the guerrilla groups were labeled as apatrids.

25. *Hamdan v. Rumsfeld* is not a full success because the Court has refused to declare the plaintiff entitled to prisoner of war status. The Court declares the Guantánamo military commissions illegal, and uses a minimal portion of the Geneva Conventions necessary for that purpose, but it refuses to discuss the applicability of the full Conventions. The argument: there is a war between the US and Al Qaeda, and Common Article 3 applies. This is not true: Common Article 3 applies only to domestic conflicts. The Supreme Court bypasses this fact in declaring that Article 2 (international conflicts) cannot be applied since Al Qaeda is not a High Contracting Party, forgetting that international conflicts are not only wars in the literal sense, but also cases of armed foreign occupation of territories of one State by another State: precisely the scenario of Hamdan's detention in Afghanistan.

26. In countries such as Jordan or Pakistan, 60 and 51 percent of the population respectively support Al Qaeda. *The Economist.*

11

Legitimacy, Identity, Violence, and the Law

Michael Hatfield

The Shock of American Torture

I was surprised the Americans would do such a thing. It shocked me.

Jamil El Banna, Guantánamo Bay detainee[1]

THE WORLD NOW KNOWS that Americans have been torturing individuals in America's care. These are no mere incidents of war. International law accepts that innocents will be unintentionally maimed and mutilated. But it does not permit those in the care of a nation to be intentionally maimed and mutilated. Nevertheless, intentional maiming and mutilating by Americans has spread from Cuba and Afghanistan to Iraq and, perhaps, elsewhere.

Torture is prohibited by the Universal Declaration of Human Rights, the International Covenant on Civil and Political Rights, the Convention Against Torture and Other Cruel, Inhuman, Degrading Treatment or Punishment, and the Geneva Conventions. However, the prohibition of torture is so fundamental to the international order, it does not need to be contained in one of these agreements in order to have the force of law. In international law, it is a preemptory legal norm no state is free to contravene. It is part of the obligations that every state owes to all other states by virtue of being a legitimate member of the international community.[2]

The United States has enacted its own laws to implement this internationally imposed obligation. Under domestic American law, Americans torturing (or attempting to torture or conspiring to torture) outside of the United States can be punished by imprisonment or, if the victim dies, the death penalty.[3]

Despite the illegality of torture, the United States government's position has been that none of the barbaric acts are "torture" in any legally prohibited sense. It has claimed that what is clearly torture by any moral standard is not torture under American legal standards. The global moral consensus likely would have accepted isolated acts of torture. What cannot be accepted, however, is the claim of legality. By refusing to submit its law to international standards, the United States has established that its only limit on the world stage will be its military power.

CIVILIZATION AND ITS DEFINITIONS

> America's idea of what is torture is not the same as ours and does not appear to coincide with that of most civilised nations.

The Honorable Mr. Justice Lawrence Collins, Her Majesty's High Court of Justice[4]

Before the physical torture, there were lawyers who advised the American government that it could proceed to torture without legal culpability. Lawyers with treatises and statutes and dictionaries piled high on their desks convinced themselves that torture was not "torture." Their reasoning was recorded in the now infamous August 1, 2002, "torture memo,"[5] signed by then Assistant Attorney General Jay S. Bybee.[6] The torture memo provided legal advice regarding standards of conduct for interrogation under American law. Ignoring binding legal authority and all arguments to the contrary, the lawyers concluded that no interrogation technique fits the definition of "torture" unless the victim feels pain akin in severity to death or organ failure but that, even then, the president of the United States could legally order such interrogation techniques as the choice of the lesser evil: harming a single individual in order to prevent further terrorist attacks.

It is difficult to believe that the memorandum was written in a good faith attempt to constrain behavior. After all, legal culpability for torture is quite easily avoided by refusing to intentionally maim and mutilate those in your care. As with laws against rape, battery, arson, and abduction, the international laws against torture were drafted to buttress undeniable moral norms. Unlike laws on wills, trusts, corporations, and tax, the laws were not intended to facilitate planning. And it is difficult to believe a detailed memorandum was necessary to comply with the law. Our moral intuition to avoid intentionally inflicting pain is itself sufficient to avoid criminal liability for torture—just as it is to avoid criminal liability for wife beating, murder, and child molesting.

The legal permission in the torture memorandum seems more likely an attempt to avoid a personal sense of moral responsibility. Those involved in torture have been known to seek out religious permission, religious assurances that they are not moral monsters. Being granted these assurances, individuals who are not usually vicious or sadistic accept their role as torturers.[7] Humans have an immense ability to inflict cruelty.

However, we have a very limited ability to believe ourselves to be cruel. Perhaps this was at the root of seeking legal advice. When the torturer believes that he has been authorized by the larger demands of goodness to torture, he is then no longer personally responsible. He becomes but an agent of a greater, exceptional moral cause.

Through the torture memo, the government lawyers provided the means by which someone (directly or indirectly) guilty of torture could hide it from himself. Under these special circumstances of legal advice, the torturer need not consider himself a moral monster even if he acts monstrously by all other standards he knows. That is, when the lawyer gave the *legal* authority to the actor with *practical* authority, the lawyer made *the law* into the author of the actor's actions. It was the law that became responsible for allowing what it does rather than the torturer being responsible for doing what it is he did. Thus, the torturer does not have to believe he is cruel or immoral. He is a deputized agent of the law's wisdom.

The government lawyers spoke on behalf of a higher authority, the law. It was not their personal endorsement of the morally suspect that was needed but rather the conclusion that the law endorses it. With ample opportunity for American citizens to affect the democratic law-making process, it is no misuse of language to equate the American law with the collective American will. Thus, with the torturer's reliance on the lawyer's advice, his self-understanding is that he is the agent of the American people—entrusted with this power for their protection.

DECREASING LEGITIMACY BY DECREASING SELF-LIMITS

The stories they told were remarkably similar—terrible beatings, hung from the wrists and beaten, removal of clothing, hooding, exposure naked to extreme cold, naked in front of female guards, sexual taunting by both male and female guards/interrogators, some sexual abuse (rectal intrusion), terrible uncomfortable positions for hours.

An American lawyer after meeting with Guantánamo Bay detainees[8]

While not pristine, the United States' relatively good historical deference to moral and legal limits on its power has maintained its political legitimacy. Now, however, the United States' torture of those in its care has made it increasingly difficult for it to leverage moral authority into political power. Even though the law is insufficient to prevent torture, the international legal prohibition of torture is not impractical. As with all *malum in se* crimes,[9] the law's power is not so much a deterrent. More

importantly, this deference to morality is each state's means of identifying its power as moral and not merely actual. It is a state's sacrifice to
a standard other than its actual power—a moral standard. It represents
the state's voluntary will to limit its power in the light of morality. It is
a *sine qua non* of the state's political legitimacy insofar as the state has
to convince others that it accepts normative limits and not just physical
limits.

The fact that America is a relatively functional democracy makes the
matter much worse. Those tortured, their friends and family members,
and all the other members of the international community are entitled
to infer that if American law permits torture, it is because the American people want it this way. From this perspective, it was not only the
United States government at fault but Americans themselves. The same
dynamics that allow the legal advice to comfort an American torturer are
at work here as well. If the American lawyer's advice is that torture is
permissible under American law and can be used because the American
people have entrusted their leaders with this legal power, then it is the
American people—and not just a handful of rogue sadists—whose will
is at work.

The law in a democracy matters because it reflects how the citizens
choose to define themselves and their relationship to history; how it is
they explain themselves to others. The law in a democracy is the citizen's
means of communicating what type of nation they intend theirs to be.
Our laws fix our identity—for ourselves, our children, our friends, and
our enemies.

The laws of a nation are its idealized identity. Political legitimacy
notes the idealized identity but also the distance between the ideal and the
actual. Many nations have idealized identities of democracy and freedom
without any actual realization of either. They have statutes comprised
of written rights actually denied in the workplaces, streets, prisons and
court rooms. In a democracy such as the United States, however, the
people are morally responsible for this idealized vision of themselves.
A claim that the laws permit the morally prohibited is a claim about the
moral identity of Americans, not rogue leadership.

The argument as to whether or not American laws do in fact permit
morally prohibited torture is an argument about America's self-chosen
identity. If the legal interpretations claimed by the United States government are not a reliable construction of American law, then Americans
can blame their leadership for acting illegally. This may do much or little
to help to prevent future torture. However, it is essential in the struggle
between Americans to choose who we shall be as a people, to choose

and defend our identity. A visible struggle among Americans on this issue will play a large part in the international assessment of American legitimacy. This struggle over how to interpret the law is a struggle for national moral identity.

WHO IS FOR TORTURE?

> *Make no mistake: Every regime that tortures does so in the name of salvation, some superior goal, some promise of paradise. Call it communism, call it the free market, call it the free world, call it the national interest, call it fascism, call it the leader, call it civilization, call it the service of God, call it the need for information, call it what you will, the cost of paradise, the promise of some sort of paradise, Ivan Karamazov continues to whisper to us, will always be hell for at least one person somewhere, sometime.*
>
> Ariel Dorfman, Chilean novelist, essayist, playwright, and human rights activist[10]

The belief that maiming and twisting and breaking human minds and bodies are supposed to safeguard our well-being arises from the darkest depths of human confusion. The conclusion that torture is appropriate can be reached only by ignoring not only human dignity but our human inabilities, uncertainties, and untrustworthiness. These all combine to make torture an inherently unmanageable form of violence that ultimately destroys those who use it. Torture is a modern taboo. It is illegal for good reason. So, how could American lawyers convince themselves it is legal?

The first step in arguing torture is legal is to exclude the history and purpose of the relevant legal standards and focus only on specific words in texts. Manipulating the tension between the specific words and the general purpose of a legal rule is a well worn legal reasoning technique. Typically, the more tightly focused on specific definitions, the more technical, legalistic, and aggressive the argument is. This technique allows the lawyer to narrow the definition of torture so as to expand its use.[11] The argument does not authorize "torture," of course, since "torture" is illegal. Rather, the argument authorizes coercive interrogation techniques, sorting into this category various acts of torture that are not "torture." This is lawyering as euphemism-engineering.

A second lawyering technique is used as a back-up in case the line between torture and "torture" is later determined not to be quite where the lawyer drew it. The technique is to appeal to utilitarian moral reasoning. This is why the legal discussions of torture often read like a college freshman's paper in Philosophy 101. Lawyers such as Jay S. Bybee appeal to utilitarianism with a simple "lesser-of-two-evils" argument that invokes the criminal defense of necessity.[12] Other lawyers are sufficiently confident to express an explicitly utilitarian formula complete with symbols such as "L = the number of lives that will be lost if the information is not provided" and "T = the time available before the disaster will occur" and directions that "torture should be permitted where the application of the variables exceeds . . . the numerical point at which torture is acceptable."[13] But unlike the Philosophy 101 hypotheticals that are intended to refine the student's moral sense, these formulae are intended to facilitate the legal expansion of torture. Also unlike Philosophy 101, in which the philosophy professor's political powers are benign, these lawyers integrate rote Philosophy 101 arguments into legal interpretations in order to direct state power. Whatever the lawyers lack in philosophical sophistication and grace, they make up for in access to state power, which they are now using in a real-world experiment.

The lawyers ignore that utilitarian reasoning requires a considerable amount of certainty as to the consequences of actions. They ignore the fact that there is no reliable source for the empirical data needed to make the utilitarian arguments they make. The proponents have to invoke some secret reserve of classified information as to the prevalence of ticking time bomb-type scenarios that we are supposed to believe are rather common. Ultimately, the resort has to be to a "trust me" on the facts.

Not only does the pro-torture, lesser-of-two evils, lawyering approach rely on information that does not exist, it ignores the information that does. Much about the American abuses seems calculated more to satisfy sexualized interests or pure sadism than to elicit reliable information. Even if torture could be justified with a ticking time bomb scenario, we know it has not been limited to those scenarios. And even if it has provided information relevant to international security, we know that the international outrage at American torture has fueled resentment and violence and made us all less secure rather than more secure. Fear of the moral slippery slope was not invented in a classroom but through historical reflection. Torture never happens just once or only in isolated instances. Yet somehow this well-known information is never part of the consequence-analysis the argument calls for, while all varieties of speculative or secret information are essential to it.

Torture, thus, gets legalized under these interpretations by insisting on excessively technical statutory readings; ignoring the moral and historical contexts in favor of the pseudo-scientific appeal of utilitarian calculus; and invoking unverifiable information while dismissing facts that are known world-wide. What connects these strategies is the rhetorical appeal to language that involves precise terms and mathematics-like certainty and objectivity.

This rhetorical style ensures that there is no appeal to anything more fundamental than the words describing the law, except the need to secure the nation. It is an argument about survival on any terms as the undeniable good served by the lesser of any two evils. Rather than appealing to moral principles, it alleges facts. Its language is technical. Rhetorically, it is a campaign against naiveté, and the confident precision of its terms is part of its persuasiveness. Its rhetorical demands are seriousness and sobriety about the situation. It is wholly indifferent to human rights principles, which are rejected as utterly unsuited for the present debate even though they are the principles that ground the American legal system. However, as of September 11, these legal principles and those who propose them are deemed effete.

The style also reveals something about those who use it. It presents the law in mechanical, technical terms suggesting the law is a machine. This justifies the cold tone since a machine is not swayable by appeals to human dignity. The machine marches on its programmed tracks. It presents the lawyer's job as an objective one: describing the track the machine is on and when it can be expected to arrive at which station. More deeply, this rhetorical style insulates the lawyer from any personal responsibility for his work. It gives the lawyer a self-perceived defense of "obeying orders," which does not work for soldiers but is expected to work for lawyers who give the ultimate endorsement to the soldiers' torturing. It presents the lawyer as just doing his job, reporting the facts and nothing but the facts as to what the law requires. It provides to the lawyer the same cover for moral guilt that the torturer seeks when he asks for the lawyer's blessing: the lawyer is no moral monster for opining that torture is legal but rather is only the sober technician carrying out his job.[14]

VIOLENCE AND JURISPRUDENCE

> *Legal interpretation is (1) a practical activity, (2) designed to generate credible threats and actual deeds of violence, (3) in an effective way. . . Legal interpretation, therefore, can never be 'free;' it can never be the function of an understanding of the text or word alone.*
>
> Robert M. Cover, Chancellor Kent
> Professor of Law and Legal History, Yale University[15]

It is demoralizing for American lawyers to be revisiting the legality of torture. It is scandalous that individuals can be trained and practice as lawyers and rise in the professional ranks to the places from which they can advise the president and still have the impression that torture could be legal so long as it is called something else. It is as shocking as if slavery had been legalized simply by calling it "permanent employment." Of all the issues one might have recently thought well-settled into the dustbin of legal history, the prohibition of torture was certainly one.

For all its shamefulness, the topic is useful for reflecting on our understanding of the law and lawyers' relationships to it. Though our energies as lawyers would be better employed in devising methods to implement the prohibition, for the time being they have been derailed into justifying the prohibition. Nevertheless, having to take stock of ourselves on such a basic issue provides us with a good perspective for pondering basic issues, far more useful than beginning with speculations as to the inner workings of judges' or legislators' minds or the nature of language or society.

The legality or illegality of torture focuses our attention on the connection between law and violence. This connection is always there. Reducing, managing, controlling violence is the genesis of the law. The law organizes the threat of violence into predictable patterns. When a judge decides that this or that person is guilty or this or that will is invalid or this or that corporation shall win or lose its day in court, the judge has decreed that the state may bring violence upon the situation to take property in one person's possession and give it to another or, in criminal cases, to put someone in someone else's possession. Every dispute about the law is a dispute as to who shall be subjected to the state's threat of violence and who shall benefit from it. By the very nature of the craft, legal interpretation always takes place in a field of potential violence.[16] The law substitutes just and reasonable violence for idiosyncratic, unjustifiable violence. Torture as a specific legal question raises the general question as to the ways in which violence is managed by the law. It is the question of how official violence is to be channeled, organized, and brought to bear on an individual in pursuit of some greater collective good.

What kind of violence does American law channel, organize and manage? The torture prohibition is emblematic of the commitment of the law to non-brutality. It is not simply a rule. It is, in the words of Jeremy Waldron of New York University School of Law, an icon of the whole law, an archetype.[17] As such, it represents, embodies, and reflects something shared by every part of the American legal system and is not just the feature of this or that particular statute. It is a commitment that the law shall not wield its power through "abject fear and terror."[18] It is a commitment to recognizing human dignity.

The relationship of violence to the legal need to prohibit torture reflects something even more fundamental about the legal system: how the system's legitimacy is eventually tested. The legitimacy of a legal system is not simply a product of its insiders and how they assess the persuasiveness of this or that legal argument. Legitimacy is something conferred from outside the system by all those affected by it, rather than something guarded by insiders who control it. A sense by outsiders that the legal system is losing legitimacy raises the risk of unmanaged violence, and managing the risk of violence is the purpose of the legal system. Ultimately, lawyers are kept in check not by their mutual assurances as to the appropriateness of their legal reasoning but rather by the threat that laws considered unjust by those outside the legal guild ultimately increase violence. This increased violence is inherently revolutionary, always threatening to overthrow both the system and its protective guild—perhaps slowly, perhaps suddenly. With the claims of legality attached to American torture, the decrease in the international assessment of American political legitimacy is also a decrease in the legitimacy of the American legal system, each decrease increasing the risk of violence.

Footnotes to Torture

> *Not since the Nazi era have so many lawyers been so clearly involved in international crimes concerning the treatment and interrogation of persons detained during war.*
>
> Jordan J. Paust, Law Foundation Professor, University of Houston;
> Former Judge Advocate General Corps Lawyer, U.S. Army[19]

While the popular perception of lawyers tends to be one of a courtroom actor, and legal theorizers tend to imagine the lawyer as judge, the resurrection of torture as a legal issue shifts the analysis from these showier roles to the quieter, often invisible role of the lawyer as office advisor. It was neither courtroom drama nor judicial intervention that led to torture being deemed legal under American standards. It was the lowly legal opinion memorandum.

The legal opinion memorandum is the method by which office lawyers advise their clients, though they are really doing more to advise themselves. Other than its conclusion—reduced to a go or a stop to the client's plans—a written legal opinion is not really addressed to the cli-

ent. Unlike the boisterous courtroom arguments of litigators persuading
judges and juries, a written opinion is a quiet stringing-together of definitions to persuade the opinion's *author*. It is the professional's research
paper filed away to remind him at any future time how it was he decided
to say yes to his client. It is an introverted product of the profession's
more introverted wordsmiths, differing little from any academic essay in
the humanities except that it is intended to provide a map for targeting
or evading the violence of the legal system in the client's favor, should
the need ever arise. Fortunes and liberties are traded on the backs of
these essays, as clients wager this way or that based on their faith in the
lawyer's cleverness. The lawyer is well-paid for the cleverness in justifying a foregone conclusion or, at least, justifying something substantially
similar in practical terms.

For the most part, legal opinion memoranda and the office lawyers who
write them remain outside of popular awareness, but their memoranda
have substantial consequences in the legal system. Clients rely on the
conclusions, which means that clients take action based on them. For the
vast majority of memoranda, there is never a day of doctrinal reckoning.
They remain filed away. It is only when the client collides with an adver-
sary or a regulator that someone searches the files to find the legal map,
and only when the collision gets to—or at least near—a courtroom that
the memorandum's theories are tested. The functional audit rate, so to
speak, of memoranda is so low that both lawyers and clients can carry on
for years without the legal reasoning being tested. This roulette dynamic
can encourage lawyers to adopt ever more aggressive and idiosyncratic
lines of reasoning, and can provide the clients with an increasingly un-
warranted sense of confidence. Almost all legal opinions result in client
action, but very few of them are ever tested doctrinally.

If our understanding of the law begins with the courtroom arguments
rather than the office memoranda, we envision a competition between two
interpretations of the law. We then analyze the outcome of that competi-
tive process and what tends to make it more or less reliable. This usually
leads to analyzing the role of the judge as the relevant decision maker,
and this leads to analyzing the professional norms of persuasiveness and
both legitimate and illegitimate judicial biases.

The torture memorandum, however, directs our attention to the lesser-
theorized and more common mode of legal decision making. Rather
than two lawyers publicly in front of a judge, we see a lawyer privately
with a client. The client talks a while, and then the lawyer talks a while.
These conversations remain protected from public scrutiny. If the conversations conclude with the need for a legal memorandum, the lawyer

fills the desktop with books and the pot with coffee, shuts the doors and begins the work of persuading himself how he might one day publicly champion what his client has privately told him the client intends to do. Unlike the litigator-based model of legal philosophy, this model has no single decision maker and certainly no impartial one. Rather, this model involves a lawyer and client negotiating between themselves what risks either or both of them are willing to take. The client's risks may be property or freedom, while the lawyer's risk is one of reputation and malpractice suits.

Unlike the litigation model of lawyering, in the office model of lawyering the legal advice is one of the first links in the chain of causation. While a courtroom lawyer's interpretation of the law is an *ex post facto* prosecution or defense, the office lawyer's memo interpretation is one intended to give birth to certain facts—the client's behavior in relying on it. The American government memorandum that torture is not "torture" was not an argument in a court to defend someone from prosecution for "torture." Rather, it was permission to torture. Unlike courtroom arguments, legal opinion memoranda of this sort are seeds for future action. And it is the lawyer who chooses how best to sow what the client hopes to reap.

POLITICAL CONCLUSIONS AND PROFESSIONAL ARGUMENTS

> *Nagem Sadun Hatab, a 52 year old Iraqi, died in US custody on 6 June 2003 in Nasiriya, Iraq, as a result of "asphyxia due to strangulation." The autopsy also found bruising and six fractured ribs. Army investigators said that he had been kicked by soldiers on 4 June. The next day he was reportedly lethargic and covered in feces. The jail commander ordered that he be stripped and he was left naked outside in the sun and heat for the rest of the day and into the night.*

Amnesty International Report[20]

Legal opinion writing involves the lawyer's whole personality, not just a textual skill set. It involves the lawyer's risk-aversion, the lawyer's understanding of the client, the client's objectives, and the client's risk-aversion. It involves the lawyer's political understanding of the relationship of the client to governmental constraint, that is, the law. It involves the lawyer's moral sense that both the client and the client's objectives are consistent with the lawyer's values. It involves the lawyer's understanding of public policies. Ultimately, whatever forces are at play are brought to bear on a handful of legal interpretations devised by the lawyer to persuade the lawyer that the client can or cannot proceed.

The lawyer's interpretation of the law is how the lawyer votes for what the law is to mean. The legal system is closed in that only those admitted into the guild are given the right to have their votes heard. Only a lawyer's opinion on the law counts. A non-lawyer and a lawyer may have the same arguments and the same conclusions, but the non-lawyer is not permitted to voice them either in private with a client or in public with a judge. All of the similarities a legal opinion has to humanities essays come to an end this way: the lawyer's conclusions matter in a specific way that no one else's does. Even in a democracy, only the citizens vote.

Much as America's being democratic means Americans are accountable for their laws in a way in which citizens of nondemocratic nations cannot be, American lawyers must be held accountable. Whatever level of responsibility Americans generally share for American law, American lawyers share a greater responsibility as they are the ones with the exclusive occupational right to voice or ignore the law. The international community should pressure Americans for failing to eliminate torture in their name. And American citizens should pressure American lawyers to eliminate torture from their interpretations. The lawyers decide what the law requires or prohibits. It is lawyers who opined that torture was not "torture." And with those legal opinions, seeds for future state behavior were sown. True enough, those legal opinions were not sufficient for torture. But they were necessary for the legitimacy-destroying claim that American torture was legal.

The ability to control, even if not unfettered, confers moral responsibility. Lawyers have exclusive control of legal interpretation. We cannot pretend, if we ever could, that lawyers interpret the law for their client the way one interprets a foreign language for one who does not know it. Lawyers construct legal interpretations with all sorts of conscious and unconscious personal assessments, and are morally responsible for what follows when someone acts upon their interpretation.

This claim of moral responsibility is more radical than it might at first seem. It means that the lawyer is not the mere messenger of the law. However, the legal profession is designed on the premise that the lawyer *is* the mere messenger of the law. A legal wall of responsibility is erected between the lawyer and client. The lawyer is not responsible for the client's objectives, only to ensure that the client is advised on how best to legally pursue them. But the torture memorandum makes clear that the condition of "how best to legally pursue them" is not much of a constraint. In practice and in critical theory, the lawyer's skills to expand or contract what can be "legally pursued" are well known. Those skills are also well compensated. Yet, the wall separating the lawyer's and the client's moral identities theoretically remains.

The lawyer's exclusive occupational right to interpret the law ought to imply more than moral responsibility. And in some situations it does. Powerful and wealthy clients know that if they rely on the lawyer's legal opinions and suffer some sort of loss, they can be made whole by suing the lawyer for malpractice. These clients understand that the lawyer is wagering with legal interpretations, and they are sufficiently sophisticated to make sure the lawyer's bets are backed with the lawyer's own wealth rather than theirs. They insure their reliance on the lawyer's advice with the lawyer's assets. If they follow the advice and lose money, they take the money from the lawyer (or the lawyer's malpractice insurance provider, as the case may be).

Despite the fact that sophisticated legal clients know—and rely on—the potential personal liability of the lawyer when assessing the lawyer's legal interpretations, claims for making lawyers personally liable for their legal interpretations are understandably disfavored by the lawyers' guild. At most, the guild permits a lawyer to be liable for technical deficiencies in interpretation, that is, for failing to cite this or that authority or to recognize this or that distinction between the authorities cited. For example, even though Judge Jay S. Bybee has been overwhelmingly criticized by the American bar for his torture memorandum—with the dean of Yale Law School calling it "the most clearly erroneous legal opinion I have ever read"[21]—the vilest punishment proposed for him is removal from the guild, disbarment, being stripped of the right to make a six figure annual salary.[22] If, under American law, a soldier can be executed for torturing a victim to death, why not execute the lawyer who gives permission to torture?

Suggesting that lawyers might be imprisoned or executed for endorsing torture is more than an appeal to rough justice. It is grasping for some means to reign in the advice that American lawyers give when they know their advice will be acted on. This is not about prosecuting a lawyer who has defended a torturer. It is about prosecuting a lawyer who has consciously persuaded himself that torture was not "torture," knowing that once he had persuaded himself then someone was quite likely to be tortured.

Other than forcing lawyers into the same risks of those they advise, how can we force lawyers to use the best of all their personal resources and energies when interpreting the law, rather than hiding behind a fictional separation between themselves and their interpretation? How do we force lawyers to integrate more rather than fewer of their faculties into their reasoning? How do we force lawyers to give the best advice they can, other than putting them into the situation in which they are advising themselves? The advice we want lawyers to give is the description of what they would do if they were put in the client's situation with exactly the same risks of loss and punishment. How do we enforce moral responsibility for legal opinions? How do we force lawyers to respect the law? *What is the safety net?*

If a lawyer would not asphyxiate a detainee, then he ought not to give permission for someone else to do so. If a tax lawyer can lose her life savings for erroneously interpreting the intricacies of the tax code for a wealthy client, ought we to object to imprisoning a lawyer for erroneously claiming the American law endorses torture?

This empties the notion of professional and personal separation. But the division between the two has grown so great that there appears to be nothing some American lawyer somewhere would not be willing to advise as legal. Indeed, the division has grown so great that very powerful American lawyers advising the American president have opined that torture itself is legal so long as it is given another name. At what point of moral outrage over the disconnect between professional and personal separation do we question the consequences of the disconnect? What else would have kept American lawyers from advising torture was legal? *How else can American lawyers be forced to internalize the risks of their legal interpretations?*

If we reject claims of the image of a law as a machine and lawyering as an objective job for a technician, we must also reject the separation between the professional and personal. To tweak the slogan: the professional is political. Our personal judgments as to the morality of torture are what drive our professional conclusions as to its legality. Ultimately, then, we must admit that any professional debate is political. It's those who categorically oppose torture struggling professionally against those who would permit it in our names, at least sometimes, at least in the scariest of situations, at least when it is in our best interests as determined by the governmental interrogation apparatus.

The ultimate question for each lawyer is, *Am I willing to be an officer of a legal system that endorses torture?* If not, I am obligated to argue that torture is illegal. Just as Americans struggle to preserve the international political legitimacy of the United States by struggling to make clear that we as a people do not condone torture, American lawyers must struggle to preserve the legitimacy of our legal system by insisting that it not legalize torture no matter what it is called.

We cannot abide the defense that a soldier was just obeying orders. We cannot abide a lawyer's claim that the conclusion endorsing the morally horrific resulted from obeying the orders of a law impervious to morality. No lawyer believes the lawyer's job is simply reporting the facts and nothing but the facts as to what the law requires. We cannot provide cover for the guilty by continuing to defend a separation between the professional opinion of the lawyer and the lawyer. Lawyers who endorse torture ought to be prosecutable for torture consequent to their endorsement. This is not a tricky issue. Just as no one has a legitimate reason to know where on the continuum an intrusion one degree short of rape may be found, there is no legitimate reason for a lawyer to draw legal distinctions along the continuum of maiming and mutilating defenseless men and women in American care. Any lawyer doing so should personally assume the risk of error. The chilling caution of strict liability seems especially appropriate.[23]

MORAL AND LEGAL ABSOLUTES

> *I say that to take the straight beautiful bodies of men and women and to maim and mutilate them by torture is a crime against high heaven and the holy spirit of man. I say that it is a sin against the Holy Ghost for which there is no forgiveness.*
>
> F. S. Cocks, United Kingdom delegate urging the adoption of the 1950 European Convention on Human Rights[24]

So long as we refuse to accept the legal legitimacy of the lesser-of-two-evils moral analysis of torture, we are taking an absolutist position. Without invoking religious or metaphysical ideas, we are left appealing to preserving human dignity without being able to argue non-circularly as to what "human dignity" is. That may be fine. That may be as far as we can think about it. We may need to say that we can reduce the idea to nothing simpler, nothing more persuasive. But we need to be content with that. We ought not to be tempted to search for empirically conclusive grounding for our claims because none will ever be established. We cannot, for example, rest our moral conclusion against torture on the unverifiable claim that it never produces information that could save lives. We cannot assume the prohibition of torture does not have some costs.[25] This is not to say that we ought not to marshal factual evidence that torture increases violence rather than decreases it, but that we ought to accept that the essence of moral claims is a wagering as to which way is the best way forward. A wagering that reflects as much evidence as there might be, but a type of judgment that always involves a material degree of uncertainty. We do not have the luxury of awaiting empirical assurances. We are forced to decide with some doubt as to what the future will bring as a result of our moral decisions. We may believe it is obvious that respecting human dignity decreases violence across time. But we must admit that this is our moral hope, not an empirical conclusion. This is a hope involving a conscious choice of moral identity and not a reporting of empirically verifiable claims.

Legal absolutes are even more problematic than moral ones. The law never maps perfectly onto morality, and for good reason. For one, unlike moral theories, the law must not only be concerned with articulating standards but also devising consequences for transgressions. It must define degrees of culpability, codify extenuating circumstances, and institutionalize mercy for the guilty and not just sympathy for the victim. The current parade of American soldiers charged with abuses and the absence of charges against higher authorities also reminds us that guilt may be shared and often unequally so.

Just as we accept self-defense as an excuse for killing while prohibiting murder categorically, as a legal matter we must accept some defenses for individuals who torture.[26] These types of defenses, however, can be transformed into a systematic approval of torture, if we let them. It is one type of claim to defend a confused soldier who intentionally maimed a particular prisoner for what seemed a good reason at the time, and another type of claim that there is good reason for an army to systematically maim prisoners. We must remember that the essence of defensive justifications of violence is that they cannot be premeditated but rather always involve a sense of acting-in-the-moment, a denial of time or opportunity for reflection or devising a less violent response. Indeed, only the least degree of useful violence can ever be justified defensively.

These are the factors missing from the United States government's endorsement of torture as the lesser-of-two-evils in its war on terrorism. The government lawyers' torture memo transformed a defensive plea of self-defense and necessity—the lesser-of-two-evils defense—into an offensive strategy. The detailed analysis approving torture was a premeditation, an advance rationalization of wholesale violence that appealed to the narrow criminal defense legally available for individuals acting in the heat of immediate moral confusion. This does not make the defense wrong. It means the torture memo was wrong.

There is a lurking question here: if certain extenuating circumstances may defend an individual from the criminal charges of torture, why limit those circumstances to ones involving immediate moral pressures and confusion? Wouldn't we be better off allowing a systematic analysis? Wouldn't the individual soldier be better off knowing that the evils had already been weighed and calculated? Of what help is it to the individual to be pushed into the inconsistency of legally prohibiting torture but

allowing narrow legal defenses to it? Wouldn't it be better to institutionally resolve the tensions between the absolute prohibition and the
defensive authorization? After all, aren't we more likely to arrive at a
better resolution when we do it that way—without pressure, institutionally, methodically—than when we force the individual into the heat of
the moment?

This is the conclusion of those who advocate torture. What begins
as institutionalizing mercy for the guilty who find themselves forced
into unthinkable binds becomes the institutionalized endorsement of
the unthinkable. This approach is the one taken by the United States
government. The torture memorandum deferred to the president's moral
calculations as to the lesser-of-two-evils, insisting he had the right to
make these decisions on behalf of all Americans.

The law recognizes that humans find themselves in situations beyond
their wisdom and beyond their abilities. The law cannot impose on an
individual the obligation to risk being murdered by a midnight intruder
rather than to resist with deadly force, nor can it impose an obligation
that the individual interview the intruder as to his plans, weapons, and
motivations prior to deciding whether or not to shoot him. The law
compromises by respecting the imperfections of human abilities when
responding to overwhelming situations. If it turns out the intruder was a
harmless neighbor with dementia searching for his long-dead mother, the
law forgives the killing just as it would if the intruder had been equipped
to murder. Defenses for violent crimes recognize that reality forces us at
times to make decisions beyond our limits. These are situations without
time or other resources that would allow the weighing or other investigation of alternatives. These are defenses of despair, not calculation.

To institutionalize a torture-approval process, however, is to apply all
of the institution's abilities in the calculation of whom to torture. This
is not a situation involving a prerational, biologically based response of
fear, panic, or defense, but rather an institutionalized rationalization. This
is not a situation in which alternatives cannot be investigated, but rather
a process of weighing alternatives. This is not a begrudging acceptance
that the world forces individuals into inhuman choices, but rather the
intentional creation of inhumane situations. The legitimate defenses to
individual criminal charges are based on limits that inhere in individuals but are not found when there is ample time for group reflection and
response.

To return to the prior suggestion, the question is which legal approach
do we believe will lead to lesser violence over the long term? On the one
hand is a legal system that occasionally grants mercy to some sympathetic

individual who in the heat of some inhumane situation intentionally maims another. On the other hand is a legal system that institutionalizes governmental resources in a process of deciding which individuals are to be intentionally maimed. The difference between granting mercy to the guilty and permission to the guilty is the difference between respecting and violating human dignity. This is the difference between the two approaches. Over the long run, it is hard to believe that the first approach generates more violence but harder to believe that the second approach does not. The first approach belongs to a more legitimate legal system than the second precisely because it will lead to less rather than more violence. There is, of course, empirical uncertainty in this claim. There is no legal laboratory in which we can independently try the alternative laws and confidently conclude the results. This is the wager of moral decision. This is the choice of national identity chosen individually: on which side am I willing for us to err? From that choice flows the legal reasoning and, ultimately, the gamble that torture is more likely to destroy us than preserve us.

NOTES

1. *Amnesty International Index*. "Torture and Ill-Treatment in the 'War on Terror'": ACT 40/14/2005 available at www.web.amnesty.org/library/print/ENGACT400142005 (last visited September 7, 2006).

2. For a discussion of the legal prohibitions of torture beyond those contained in written agreements, see, e.g., Robert K. Goldman, "Trivializing Torture: The Office of Legal Counsel's 2002 Opinion Letter and International Law against Torture," *Human Rights Brief* 12.1 (2004): 1–4; Sanford Levinson, "'Precommitment and Postcommitment': The Ban on Torture in the Wake of September 11," *Texas Law Review* 81 (2003): 2013–53.

3. 18 U.S.C. Section 2340 (2000).

4. Richard Norton-Taylor and Suzanne Goldenberg, "Judge's Anger at US Torture," *Guardian Unlimited* (February 17, 2006) available at www.guardian.co.uk/guantanamo/story/0,,1711833,00.html (last visited September 7, 2006).

5. Memorandum from Jay S. Bybee, Assistant Attorney Gen., to Alberto R. Gonzales, Counsel to the President (Aug. 1, 2002) (the "Torture Memo") available at www .humanrightsfirst.org/us_law/etn/gonzales/memos_dir/memo_20020801_JD_%20Gonz_ .pdf#search=%22jay%20bybee%20torture%20memo%22 (last visited September 8, 2006).

6. Although Jay S. Bybee signed the memorandum, others were involved in drafting it. John Choon Yoo was substantially involved in the drafting of the memorandum. The addressee of the memo was Alberto Gonzales. After the memorandum was written, Bybee was appointed by the president to the U.S. Court of Appeals for the Ninth Circuit (the Senate confirmed him to this lifetime appointment within two months, though the memorandum was apparently unknown to members of the Senate at the time). Mr. Gonzales was appointed by the president to become the Attorney General of the United

States. Professor Yoo returned to his position as a member of the faculty at Boalt Hall School of Law, University of California, Berkeley.

7. Levinson, "'Precommitment and Postcommitment,'" 2013.

8. *Amnesty International Index*, "Torture and Ill-Treatment in the 'War on Terror.'"

9. A criminal act that is *malum in se* is an act wrong in itself, an act that is "inherently and essentially evil" (e.g., murder). In contrast, a crime that is *malum prohibitum* is wrong merely because the law forbids it (e.g., driving violations).

10. Ariel Dorman, "Untying an Ethical Question on Torture—Happiness for All Is One Justification," *San Francisco Chronicle* (May 9, 2004) available at www.sfgate .com/cgiin/article.cgi?f=/c/a/2004/05 /09/INGPD6FP5L1.DTL (last visited September 7, 2006).

11. For a technical criticism of the narrowing of the definition of "torture" in the Torture Memo in order to expand its use, see Louis-Philippe F. Rouillard, "Misinterpreting the Prohibition of Torture under International Law: The Office of Legal Counsel Memorandum," *American University International Law Review* 21 (2005): 9–41. 23–30.

12. "Torture Memo," 46. "Necessity" is a defense to criminal charges that alleges the accused was forced to act under duress and had no legally sanctioned alternatives; for example, killing another in self defense.

13. Mirko Bagaric and Julie Clarke, "Not Enough Official Torture in the World? The Circumstances in Which Torture Is Morally Justifiable," *University of San Francisco Law Review* 39 (2005): 581–616, quotation on 613–14.

14. This "defense" is made explicitly by some. See, e.g., Eric Posner and Adrian Vermeule, "A 'Torture' Memo and Its Tortuous Critics," *Wall Street Journal* July 6, 2004: A22.

15. Robert M. Cover, "Violence and the Word," *Yale Law Journal* 95 (1983): 1601–1629, quotations on 1611, 1617.

16. Cover, "Violence and the Word," 1601.

17. Jeremy Waldron, "Torture and Positive Law: Jurisprudence for the White House," *Columbia Law Review* 105 (2005): 1681–1750, quotations on 1722–1723.

18. Waldron, "Torture and Positive Law," 1726–27.

19. Jordan J. Paust, "Executive Plans and Authorizations to Violate International Law Concerning Treatment and Interrogation of Detainees," *Columbia Journal of Transnational Law* 43 (2005): 811–63, quotation on 811.

20. *Amnesty International Index,* "Torture and Ill-Treatment in the 'War on Terror.'"

21. W. Bradley Wendel, "Legal Ethics and the Separation of Law and Morals," *Cornell Law Review* 91 (2005): 67–128, quotation on 68. Calling it a legal analysis of which no one "could be proud," on page 68, Wendel cites several sources identifying not only ethical lapses but blatant incompetence in the preparation of the memo, such as the statement by Harold Hongju Koh, Dean, Yale Law School, that: "in my professional opinion, the August 1, 2002 OLC Memorandum is perhaps the most clearly erroneous legal opinion I have ever read," quoted in "Confirmation Hearing on the Nomination of Alberto R. Gonzales to be Attorney General of the United States Before the S. Comm. on the Judiciary," 109th Cong. 158 (2005), available at www.access.gpo.gov/congress/ senate/senate14ch109.html (last visited September 8, 2006); Kathleen Clark and Julie Mertus, "Torturing the Law: The Justice Department's Legal Contortions on Interrogation," *Washington Post* June 20, 2004: B3 (criticizing "stunning legal contortions" in the

memo); Adam Liptak, "Legal Scholars Criticize Memos on Torture," *New York Times* June 25, 2004: A14 (quoting Cass Sunstein's opinion that the legal analysis in the memos was "very low level, . . . very weak, embarrassingly weak, just short of reckless"); Ruth Wedgewood and R. James Woolsey, Op-Ed., "Law and Torture," *Wall Street Journal* June 28, 2004: A10 (concluding that the memos "bend and twist to avoid any legal restrictions" on torture and ignore or misapply governing law).

22. See Richard L. Abel et al., "Lawyers' Statement on Bush Administration's Torture Memos," available at http://www.afj.org/spotlight/0804statement.pdf (last visited Feb. 2, 2006). See also Richard B. Bidler and Detlev F. Vagts, "Speaking Law to Power: Lawyers and Torture," *American Journal of International Law* 98 (2004): 689; Marisa Lopez, "Professional Responsibility: Tortured Independence in the Office of Legal Counsel," *Florida Law Review* 57 (2005): 685–716.

23. Strict liability is a legal standard that imposes responsibility even when the accused has exercised the customary level of care. In tort law, it is applicable with respect to abnormally dangerous activities, such as possessing wild animals or explosives. In criminal law, it means that no "guilty" intention is required to commit the crime. For example, an adult having sex with a teenager under the age of consent is the crime of statutory rape even if the adult had no reason to believe the teenager was below the age of consent (in fact, even if the adult had been deceived into reasonably believing the teenager was an adult). The purpose of strict liability is to chill inherently dangerous, risky, or destructive behavior. It is not a common legal standard, and has never applied as a standard of care in giving legal advice.

24. Waldron, "Torture and Positive Law," 1710.

25. Levinson, "'Precommitment and Postcommitment,'" 2013, 2029; also see Bagaric and Clarke, "Not Enough Official Torture in the World?" 588–90.

26. See above, regarding necessity defenses to criminal charges.

12

Torture Makes the Man

Darius Rejali

"Don't be pussies," urged an American interrogator in Afghanistan in 2003.[1] I explore here why we might think violence, and torture in particular, requires and generates a kind of manly strength. Briefly put, this is the view that only a real man knows what needs to be done and doing torture is the evidence that one is a real man. Interviews with Brazilian torturers suggest that torture has a rich and varied relationship to manliness, and this theme crops up regularly in anecdotal interviews of other torturers too.[2] Still, such interviews are rare, and so one must turn elsewhere to understand the logic of this set of relationships.

I'm going to take a kind of back road to this puzzle, swinging through some literature now forgotten about torture and manhood during the Franco-Algerian war, and swing back at the end to the particular way this attitude has now appeared in the United States. This is critical because literature from the Franco-Algerian conflict, especially Jean Lartéguy's *Les Centurions*, decisively set the terms in which even Americans now imagine what is at stake in torture. The famous "ticking time bomb" story appears for the first time in *Les Centurions*, and Lartéguy deploys it to advance the view that it is democratic life that makes men weak, particularly soldiers, and that being tortured and in turn torturing others is an antidote to this weakness, allowing men to return to themselves as men and overcome the weaknesses engendered by democratic life.

Of course, the notion that democracy corrupts human beings or that the demand for equality undermines manliness is an old one—one can find examples from Plato to, most recently, Harvey Mansfield.[3] But the question is whether violence and torture can shore up one's manhood in the face of this corruption. Lartéguy claimed it could and, not surprisingly, French critics of torture held the view that it could not. They used torture to tease out a fear behind the White Man's use of torture, revealing the figure of a person who fears he has been weakened by civilization and embraces torture as his salvation. This, Frantz Fanon recognized, was the figure of the classic masochist as sketched out in nineteenth century writings of Sacher Masoch, writings that also drew similar connections between manhood, torture, and democracy.

What is critical is that Lartéguy's novel revived these themes in a decisively modern way, and set the framework for a kind of thinking about torture and democracy that, evidently, many still find inescapable. The sad part, of course, is that, in fact, torture does not and cannot make the man—it leaves behind broken victims and burned out and traumatized interrogators, and that is all that it leaves behind.[4]

In 1960, a war journalist and former *para*trooper, Jean Lartéguy wrote *Les Centurions*, a novel about French *para*troopers during the Franco-Algerian War.[5] The novel's protagonist was Boisfeuras, a *para*trooper ("*Para*") tortured by Nazis and again by the Viet Cong, who taught him the real meaning of strength and weakness. Boisfeuras then went on to fight in Algeria against terrorists. In one scene, Boisfeuras brutally and repeatedly slaps the beautiful Aicha, a thinly veiled Djamla Bouhired, to find bomb detonators. "I love you and hate you," Aicha says afterwards. "You've raped me and I've given myself to you; you are my master and I shall kill you; you hurt me terribly and I want to start all over again."[6] Boisfeuras, the torturer, is the real man.[7]

As a man who knew how to apply force, Boisfeuras was a man Muslim women could love no matter how much they hated him, and one that Muslim men learned to respect. Democracy and liberalism have not made him weak. In the pivotal scene, a dentist named Arouche plants fifteen ticking bombs to explode in crowded stores the next morning. Boisfeuras, the *Para*, has been born again from the prisons of the Gestapo and Vietnam. After describing his torture by the Gestapo, Boisfeuras tortures Arouche, and "by the time the dentist was carried off on a stretcher, in the early hours of the morning, he has confessed everything; none of the fifteen bombs went off."[8] In the history of torture, there is only one account of coerced interrogation working faster than this. In Alan Dershowitz's novel, *Just Revenge*, the prisoner confesses to being a Nazi after being slapped powerfully across the face just once.[9]

It is not clear what Lartéguy's inspiration was for the ticking time bomb scenario. He may have based it on what he wished Police Prefect Teitgin had done to the Communist terrorist Yveton, but never did. During the Battle of Algiers in 1957, Yveton claimed he had placed a bomb in the gasworks, but Teitgin refused to torture him for the information; Yveton, it turned out, was bluffing. Or perhaps Lartéguy drew on Police Prefect Lambert's exculpatory story of the grenade thrower of Oran. Lambert, as we now know, ordered the brutal torture of forty people, including a pregnant woman. But in public he claimed that the police had merely interrogated a young Arab who claimed he had a stockpile of grenades and who had confessed after being slapped around a bit. Control and professionalism were presented for conditions where there were none; sleek retail torture for wholesale brutality. And the people of Oran did not look too closely, for that would disclose the real nature of violence; what they wanted was the symbolic violence and satisfaction that torture provided them.

Misrecognition (*mesconnaissance*) is the sociological process by which people habitually pass off one kind of situation as another.[10] For life to go on, we proceed in *this* way. People misrecognize because they are invested in the way they think about themselves and the lives of others. Any other way of proceeding would be unthinkable or, at least, deeply disconcerting. Misrecognition lies at the borders of consent and coercion, just beyond or beneath consciousness and yet not an ideology. People become partners in confirming each other's misrepresentation of the world, even if one person ends up somewhat worse off than before.

Les Centurions supplied the scenario that substituted the symbolic violence of the ticking bomb scenario for the messy, wholesale process of torture during the Algerian war. Many things in the novel happened as the *Paras* imagined they should have. In the real Battle of Algiers, *Paras* tortured Djamila Bouhired/Aicha, the famous female FLN member; in the novel, she was just slapped around until she fell in love (Lartéguy in fact wrote in defense of the soldiers accused of torturing Bouhired).[11] In the real battle, General Aussaresses strung up and hanged with his own hands Si Millial/Ben M'Hidi, the organizational head of the FLN in Algiers; in the novel, Si Millial/Ben M'Hidi slit his wrists in despair. And, of course, Boisfeuras applied torture morally and selectively to collect ticking bombs literally within hours of a true confession, although even those who have seen the famous *movie* of the battle and accept it implausibly as a real description of events know that no event like this occurred.

Les Centurions won the Prix Eve Delacroix in 1960 and sold half a million copies. It won praise for its military realism, and French *Paras* embraced the novel because it seemed Boisfeuras spoke for them. Columbia Tristar adapted it for a major Hollywood movie, *Lost Command*, in which Anthony Quinn (as the *Para*) squares off against George Segal (as the Terrorist). American servicemen praise the novel today and one can find it on military reading lists alongside real classics such as Sun Tzu's *The Art of War*.

Lartéguy's story has also appeared on many TV shows and movies—most recently on Fox's *24* and in *NYPD Blue*. In both cases, producers frame torture and the ticking bomb scenario around the theme of manliness. In *NYPD Blue*, Sippowitz, the main torturer, has to take one of his colleagues aside and explain the ropes to him. The cop who couldn't handle it turns out to be the most insecure, indecisive and possibly emotional of the characters on the show. Likewise, in *24*, tough experts advise a fearful, insecure, anti-torture vice president who has suddenly been forced to take power when the strongly pro-torture president was seriously injured. They give him spine, while down the ranks, Kiefer Sutherland seems to have a level of success with torture of which most torturers can only dream.

These shows express values that have been more or less explicit in American newspapers since 9/11, as politicians and pundits express deep doubts about elementary parts of American civilization. "Radical terrorists will take advantage of our fussy legality, so we may have to suspend it to beat them. Radical terrorists mock our namby-pamby prisons, so we must make them tougher. Radical terrorists are nasty, so to defeat them we have to be nastier."[12] Behind this is the same kind of raw anxiety that drove Lartéguy's novel: the worry that we have become sissies and our enemies know it.

And Lartéguy's novel, and the story of the ticking time bomb, fills one with reassurance. Only real men will have the courage to torture. Ultimately the ticking time bomb is not simply a scenario that furnishes a justification for torture. If that was the case, it would have disappeared long ago since such cases are so uncommon. Indeed, after decades of monitoring torture, the only known case that plausibly fits its general *para*meters was finally documented in 2004. No, among Americans today, as among Frenchmen fifty years ago, this thought experiment is not so much a description of a likely real scenario, but a rite of manhood, a moral test of character. That is why many soldiers, lawyers, and professors—usually all men—are drawn to it. Only real men will say "yes" to the question "will you torture in this case?", affirming it with their life.

If nothing else, what Lartéguy's novel demands, what Boisfeuras achieves, and what every American who embraces the ticking time bomb scenario as their own will wants, is to be recognized for making the right, manly decision and so being the proper moral agent in democratic life. This is why Lartéguy's novel fills up our modern imaginary. What accounts for its power is in part how it is rooted in themes of political manhood, weakness and strength.

This is not an anachronistic reading on my part. The issue of manhood and democracy was very much at issue in discussions of torture during the Algerian War. Opponents of the colonial war called torture a "Nazi virus"[13] and the French government bristled at the "scandalous comparison" to the Gestapo,[14] but some French embraced the Gestapo's disciplinary reputation, sometimes to invoke fear ("This is the Gestapo here!") and sometimes with regret. "Since I was young, I have dreamed of being in the SS, but I missed the boat, I wasn't old enough. They at least, they knew how to work; they weren't amateurs," said one French torturer.[15]

Older interrogators noted the irony. "I was tortured by the Nazis; now I do it myself."[16] Younger ones were more forthright. In 1956, long before the Battle of Algiers, General Bollardière describes how one young cavalry officer observed, "In Algiers now, there is nothing but genuine chaps, *paras*, the Legion, fine big blond fellows, stalwarts not sentimentalists." Horrified, Bollardière replied, "Doesn't that remind you of anything, *des grands gars blond, pas sentimentaux* [big blond guys, not sentimentalists]?" The officer replied, "If I had been in Germany at that moment, I too would have been a Nazi."[17]

Is this merely a fetish over shiny, shiny boots and talismans of strength? Or is there something deeper here? Does torture make the man? It's a theme that didn't escape the critics of the Algerian war. Jean Paul Sartre argued that indeed torture was all about masculinity and recognition. For Sartre, "the torturer pits himself against the tortured for his 'manhood' and the duel is fought as if it were not possible for both sides to belong to the human race."[18] Torture is not war, where individuals struggle for victory and recognition as masters and slaves, as in the classic Hegelian confrontation. Torture arises *after the defeat* of one side, and it is born in hatred. The tortured victim must not simply be defeated (for he is already in ropes and cuffs) but negated. He must lose his human dignity and be rendered into a lower animal. In effect, the interrogators say something not unlike, "You are a rat! But you are the worst kind of rat, the kind of rat that pretends to be a human being, and only through torture do we learn what an execrable specimen you really are; only then do we see you in your true ratness."

In this sense, torture is the expression of racial hatred. But at the same time, the torturer cannot go all the way, for he fears that deep in this hated animal is a secret, a truth about the situation, and he fears it. He wants to know why this semi-human will not recognize him, why he continues to resist. The torturer doesn't just want information or betrayal. According to Sartre, he wants "the secret of everything," so that he can be assured of his own omnipotence.[19] Masculinity and recognized dominion over the earth are fused together in torture. But recognition is precisely what constantly escapes him with each act of violence. For either the rat is truly a weak, sniveling rat (and who would want the recognition of a rat?) or the rat is truly a man, equal to his torturer in every way, equal in nobility and strength, whose accusation can be read in his eyes: "It is not I who is behaving like a beast here."

The true secret is that no human being can give up his freedom any more than he can give up his subjective awareness of the world. And so the tortured will either resist or die. Resisting need not be fighting; the very fact that the tortured continue to live onwards after torture is a walking accusation against the torturer, a persistent source of frustration and anger for those who want nothing more than for the tortured to disappear.

Frantz Fanon, another critic of torture during the Algerian War, advanced arguments quite similar, although considerably more grounded in historical and psychological analysis than Sartre's. Fanon uses the analysis of torturers to trace out the distorting effects of colonialism on colonizers. This analysis has received considerably less attention than the other side of Fanon's argument—his (and Sartre's) justification of revolutionary violence. But whereas the argument for revolutionary violence can be justly criticized (as I argue elsewhere),[20] Fanon's analysis of torture is thought provoking and deserves some serious reflection.

In *Black Skin, White Masks*, Fanon describes a research project in which he performed a set of associational tests with some 500 Europeans of various nationalities. He waited until he was certain of their trust, and at some point in the test inserted the words *Negro* and *Senegalese soldier*. He observed that *Negro* brought forth "biology, penis, strong, athletic, potent, boxer, Joe Louis, Jesse Owens, Senegalese troops, savage, animal, devil, sin." The phrase *Senegalese soldier* evoked "dreadful, bloody, tough, strong." And one in fifty reacted to the word *Negro* with the word "Nazi" or "SS." There was in other words for some an even stronger association with the biological power of endurance and the brutal exercise of force. As one of Fanon's informers said, these troops were "our Black devils during the war."[21]

This was not unique to Fanon's informants. A noted scholar of Nazism, Enzo Traverso, explains that the association of German violence with African violence stretches back to World War I. In France, Doctor Edgar Berillon explained German cruelty by their racial characteristics (shape of skulls, smell and toxicity of their excrement) and their moral and psychological qualities (servility, lack of self-control, and warrior fetishism). He compared these characteristics to those of "primitive peoples" and suggested that German war atrocities had no equivalent "except among the semi-savage peoples of central Africa and the Congo."[22] The Germans, for their part, responded to such accusations with irony, recalling all their Nobel prizes and officially urging the French and British to stop using primitives, Africans, in European wars. "In the interest of humanity and civilization, colored troops should no longer be used in the theatre of war in Europe."[23] German propaganda during World War I presented the world conflict as "a fight to defend the people of an ancient culture against both the assault of Slavic and semi-barbaric hordes in the East and the threat in the West of the multiracial Franco-British armies which were infiltrated by savagery owing to the presence of colored soldiers and cannibals. The land of Kant and Beethoven saw itself under threat from cannibalistic tribesmen in uniform."[24]

Senegalese soldiers are deeply associated with raw brutality among Fanon's sources. And this is not the only place they are invoked for this purpose. The image of the Senegalese also appears in Fanon's account of a French torturer he treated in *The Wretched of the Earth*. In a striking and often quoted *exempla*, Fanon sketches the struggle of the torturer to win manliness through violence and how it all seems to go wrong. The torturer describes how tiring it is to torture. Given how much effort is involved, no torturer hands his prisoner to the next interrogator and lets the other chap have a go because if the individual cracks, "the other chap would get the honor and glory." So "you're competing with others and at the same time your fists are getting ruined. So you call in the Senegalese, but they either hit too hard and destroy the creature or else they don't hit hard enough and it's no good."[25]

This torturer took these problems home. He gradually came to dislike being contradicted and noise irritated him. He wanted to hit everyone all the time. And he began striking his children. One night, he beat his twenty-month-old baby with unaccustomed savagery. But what really scared him was when his wife criticized him for hitting his children too much. "My word, anyone'd think you were going mad." He then threw himself on her, beat her, tied her to a chair, saying to himself, "I'll teach her once and for all that I'm master in this house."[26]

Fortunately, he was returned to himself by his crying children and sought professional help. He was most worried about what he did to his wife. "It's certain that there's something wrong with me. You've got to cure me doctor." His police superiors refused him sick leave and he refused psychiatric treatment in an institution, so Fanon and his staff had to treat him at work. The problem was that work, that is, torture, was precisely what was driving the violence, and the man knew this "perfectly well." Since he could not stop torturing, and he could not resign, he asked Fanon "without beating about the bush to help him to go on torturing Algerian patriots without any prickings of conscience, without any behavior problems, and with complete equanimity."[27]

In short, this torturer wanted to live the life of Lartéguy's Boisfeuras, a man cool, poised, professional and respected, and he hoped psychological treatment would help him achieve this. But Fanon clearly believed this was impossible. The torturer was caught in a web of colonial associations that made him struggle for his manhood and recognition. And these were visibly manifest in his work conditions. Here he competed with other Frenchmen seeking to steal his glory, faced hardened and implacable Algerian prisoners, and seemed weaker than brutal Senegalese soldiers who did the dirty work. Behind this was, Fanon argued, a deep fear of the colonized peoples as peoples who are more rooted and stronger than sentimentalist Europeans.

To be specific, in *Black Skin, White Masks*, Fanon argues that white men fear the Negro but they fear him differently than they fear the Jew. The Jew is feared for his potential acquisitiveness and intellectual aggressiveness. Negroes are feared for their tremendous sexual powers, copulating in all times and all places. Government and civil services are at the mercy of Jews, but women are at the mercy of Negroes: robust slaves and eroticized black athletes. No anti-Semite, Fanon says, "would ever conceive of the idea of castrating the Jew. He is killed or sterilized. But the Negro is castrated."[28] The Negro represents a biological danger and the Jew an intellectual one. In the white man's mind, they inhabit two different registers of fears and the two cannot meet. Can you imagine, Fanon asks, an erection on Rodin's *Thinker*? It would be "a shocking thought" and one "cannot decently 'have a hard on' everywhere."[29]

So, Fanon asks, within this imaginary, if the white man hates the black man, "is he not yielding to a feeling of impotence or of sexual inferiority?"[30] And what is it that is generating this sense of sexual inferiority? Fanon speculates it is European civilization itself. "Every intellectual gain requires a loss in sexual potential. Civilized white man retains an irrational longing for unusual eras of sexual license, of orgiastic scenes, of unpunished rapes, of repressed incest."[31] What is going on is that the White Man has projected onto the Negro his own desires, as if the Negro really had them.

Fanon speculates that something like this undergirds a series of otherwise inexplicable acts by white men; for example, "men who go to 'houses' in order to be beaten by Negroes; passive homosexuals who insist on black partners."[32] He adds to this the American white man's obsession to identify "himself with the Negro," including creating white "hot jazz" orchestras, white blues and spiritual singers, white authors who vocalize the Negroes' grievances, or whites who perform on stage in blackface.[33]

All this, Fanon observes, reproduces "the classic scheme of masochism."[34] The masochist and the torturer, far from being completely different people, are the same person. When white women in the sexual act cry, "Hurt me!" they are merely expressing this idea: "Hurt me as I would hurt me if I were in your place." And when they fantasize rape by a Negro, its variant is "I wish the Negro would rip me open as I would have ripped a woman open."[35]

The masochist and the torturer represent, in Fanon's analysis, the crisis of white democratic masculinity. White liberalism created European male masochism in the colonies. On the one hand, it encouraged supremacist "feelings of sadistic aggression towards the black man."[36] Yet at the same time, the democratic culture of the home country stigmatized those feelings. Colonialism then placed a restraint where erotic relations were homoerotic and economic relations were cruel. When the colonialist finally embraced torture, he was looking to regain his manhood even if it meant rejecting the weak values of his democratic culture back home. Torture did indeed make the man, or try to. The problem was that it perpetually failed.

What is important about Fanon's study of torturers is not so much his psychological claims about the nature of repressed desire as the powerful network of associations he finds linked together in the colonial imaginary. These themes are far older than the Algerian conflict. Indeed, one can find them spelled out quite explicitly in the works of the Austrian novelist, Leopold von Sacher Masoch, the man after whom the condition "masochism" is named.

In *Venus in Furs* (1870), Sacher Masoch told the story of Severin, "a passionate and idealistic nobleman caught between the dictates of reason, domination and control—everything society told him a man should be—and his own peculiar passion for submitting to the cruelty of dominant women."[37] The tale briefly put is this: Severin hands the narrator a manuscript entitled, *Confessions of a Supersensualist*:

> In it he relates a love affair with the mysterious widow Wanda von Danjew, who philosophizes about love and cruelty, and whom Severin gradually draws into his sexual fantasies, training her in the ways of the dominatrix. As the fantasies of bondage, chastisement and slavery progress, Severin's love grows increasingly unrequited, and Wanda's cruelty grows ever more real. Throughout the *Confessions*, Severin struggles with his passions, until finally he receives a beating at the hands of Wanda's strangely

androgynous lover—a beating that will cause him to turn his back, presumably forever, on his masochistic pleasures. This tale is framed in a short narrative in which we meet Severin after he has been cured of his peculiar fancies. In becoming cured, he has become aggressive and dominating giving vent to the same old passions, but this time from the other side of the whip.[38]

This story became an iconic depiction of masochism. The novel furnished the basis for the diagnosis of masochism advanced by the Austrian psychologist, Richard von Krafft-Ebing. And Severin's masochism survives still in classic songs of Masochism, as in the lyrics of the Velvet Underground's song, "Venus in Furs" (1967):

Severin, Severin, speak so slightly
Severin, down on your bended knee
Taste the whip, and love not given lightly
Taste the whip. Now plead for me.[39]

But this is only one half of the classic masochist scheme. The other half, often overlooked, is Sacher Masoch's fascination with gross social injustices and violence in Eastern Europe in the fading days of the Hapsburg Empire. Even when he describes surreal scenes of demonic women with whips and cowering male submissiveness, he tries to persuade readers (and often succeeds) in suggesting that these aren't just fantasies but depictions of real social circumstances in Eastern Europe. He wanted to convey fidelity to a Slavic social milieu he took to be true, one of intensely natural peoples and intensely primitive sexuality—not a land of newspapers and bureaucrats. To be sure, anyone reading these novels seems to encounter a tedious repetition of scenes, but in a sense this was Sacher Masoch's point. In a world condemned to endless repetition of struggle, the only way forward was to extract maximum pleasure from oppression. Salvation existed only in "the work ethic, ascetic self-denial and a strong sense of duty."[40]

Often Sacher Masoch's novels were set among minorities and exploited groups, East European Jews and Ruthenian peasants for example, and these then provided tableaux in which he plunges his male heroes into delectable bondage while at the same time taking aim at these injustices. It was a liberal stance and championed repressed minorities—as Sacher Masoch saw it.[41] His novels revealed the "wretchedness and the economy of absolute monarchy," via the "decline of constitutionalism." He championed its "rescue through democracy" to the point where he imagined a "United States of Europe" and a "common legislation."[42]

But democracy also provides a limited salvation, for it makes men weak. There was, Venus says in the novel, a deep desire to rebel against civilization. Moderns have an "eternally restless, eternally unquenched desire for naked paganism."[43] Venus chides, "that love that is the supreme joy, that is divine serenity itself—those things are useless for you moderns, you children of reflection. That sort of love wreaks havoc on you. *As soon as you wish to be natural you become common.* To you Nature seems hostile."[44]

Christianity, nature, reason, modesty are all responsible for the masochistic urge. Modernity is a fatal historical condition. Man's over-cultivated glory and idealism flowers fully and woman can reveal herself as nature made her. In modernity, Man reveals himself to Woman's natural cruelty. As Venus says, "Yes, I am *cruel*—since you take so much pleasure in that word—and am I not entitled to be cruel? Man desires, woman is desired. That is woman's entire but decisive advantage. Nature has put man at woman's mercy through his passion, and woman is misguided if she fails to make him her subject, her slave, no, her toy, and ultimately fails to laugh and betray him."[45]

The moral, Sacher Masoch relates, is that "woman, as Nature has created her and as she is currently reared by man, is his enemy and can be only his slave or his despot, *but never his companion.*" This last, Severin adds, can only happen when "she has the same rights as he, when she is his equal in education and work."[46] This last addition is pious liberal faith but unconvincing given all else Sacher Masoch has said already.[47]

Ultimately, not only Wanda, but also Wanda's strangely androgynous lover, beat Severin up properly and so Severin at last "understood male Eros" at the hands of "the lioness [and] the lion."[48] Just to drive the point home, Wanda appears at the end to give a short homily on the healing properties of masochism for men. She begins by recounting a story of how courtiers in Syracuse created "a new torture instrument" for the tyrant of Syracuse.[49] A man was locked inside a huge iron bull that was roasted over a fire, and as the man cried, the noise sounded like the bellowing of a bull. Dionysus ordered the inventor to be the bull's first victim. One is either victim or master, and being the victim first is the best inoculation against further stupidity.

"Pleasure alone," she says, "makes existence worthwhile." Those who suffer or are needy embrace death willingly, but "the person who wants pleasure has to take life cheerfully, as people did in ancient Greece. He mustn't shy away from indulging [himself] at other people's expense, he must never feel pity. He must harness others to his carriage, to his plow, like animals. He must enslave people who feel, who wish to have pleasure like him; he must exploit them without regret for his service, for his delights. He must never ask whether they feel good about it, or whether they perish." Indeed, one must remember that if the people one has enslaved "had me in their control, they would do the same to me, and I would have to pay for their enjoyments with my sweat, my blood, my soul." This she goes on to say was the way the Ancient Greeks lived: "Enjoyment and cruelty, freedom and slavery have always gone hand in hand. People who want to live like Olympian gods must have slaves whom they throw into their fishponds and gladiators who fight during their master's sumptuous banquets—and the pleasure-seekers never care if some blood spatters on them."[50]

His bondage and education complete, Severin returns home a renewed man. "I learned something that I hadn't previously known and that now revived me like a drink of fresh water: *to work and to fulfill obligations.*"[51] Though outwardly the same landowning bourgeois he had been, he now had a profound inner strength born out of the realization that "we have the choice of being either hammer or anvil, and I was an ass to make myself a woman's slave. . . . The blows, as you see, were highly benefi-cial. The rosy supersensual fog has dissolved."[52] Nor, he says, would he hesitate to use the whip.

Submitting to masochism on this view was the opposite of degen-eracy, sentimentalization, namby-pamby moralism. And masochism on this view was a need to reassert one's masculinity by connecting it to life through acts of pain and suffering. What seemed so shocking in the imperialist colonial imaginary was that, in the course of colonial war, the technology of control that had been meticulously developed seemed to unravel so quickly. Discipline and order gave way and so there was a deep suspicion that perhaps civilization had wandered too far from its roots. Becoming a torturer in this sense was a logical response to this crisis of masculinity.

There is a long way from Sacher Masoch's late imperialist novels to Lartéguy's writings in the age of decolonization, but some themes carry over in striking ways. As in Sacher Masoch, Lartéguy plunges Boisfeuras into a historical situation in which his manhood and liberal temperament is tested. Boisfeuras is an officer captured after the fall of Dien Bien Phu. Through his Vietnamese torturers, Boisfeuras is "re-educated" just as Wanda educates Severin. And when he is released, he re-enlists and goes to Algeria, applying the lessons of his new education. And he has learned his lesson well. Aicha's avowal invokes the masochistic relationship anew. "I love you and hate you. You've raped me and I've given myself to you; you are my master and I shall kill you; you hurt me terribly and I want to start all over again."[53] For Lartéguy, as for Sacher Masoch, woman can be either mistress or slave. And lastly, should we forget it, Boisfeuras is still a champion of the weak. His mission is to defend innocent men, women and children from being blown to pieces by terrorists. He simply understands better than weaker, sentimental men what must be done.

While Boisfeuras shares a great deal with Severin, Lartéguy rejects critical components of the European world view that informed Sacher Masoch's account, such as Social Darwinism and vitalism. Lartéguy does not see life as a biological struggle between the races for living space and he did not feel the need to connect back to the biological space inhabited by the colored primitives in order to be strong again. Boisfeuras learns his lesson from Asians, not Africans. Communists and Fascists have a less prejudiced view of the nature of real power and unbending will. What remains then is the crisis of control in the face of losing real power, the diagnosis of its source (civilization), and the need to reconstitute that masculinity in the face of that diagnosis.

In this way, Lartéguy decisively modernized a powerful set of images of the late imperial era, preserving the core of them: torture does indeed make the man. And this accounts for the power of the scenarios he produces. For example, would you torture a terrorist if you knew he had planted a bomb and hundreds of innocents were going to die? This scenario reproduces the classic scheme without evoking Social Darwinism or vitalism. Either you do so, and prove you're a man. Or you do not, and then you show you are weak, because your values—democratic, enlightened, liberal, idealistic—made you weak. Behind the ticking time bomb scenario is the judgment, endlessly repeated in late 19th century literature, that civilization has somehow made us weak in the face of the challenges ahead of us. The ticking time bomb scenario in turn is a test of will and manhood, a test to entertain and engage in impossible thoughts despite one's socialization, and learn one's true nature.[54]

The phenomenological analysis I just provided has some obvious limitations. Torture and, for that matter, violence is not simply a dyadic relationship between two people who face each other. This simple scheme is forced on us by the use of the master-slave dichotomy, and bedevils all phenomenological analyses that draw on this schema. The dyadic understanding of violence hides the complex institutional and organizational context in which torture occurs, and there may be many different ways in which masculinity interacts with organizations that torture.[55] Using this schema as a way of understanding the empirical reality of torture may be deeply misleading and for this purpose positivist approaches may offer more nuanced tools.

But this analysis is enormously helpful nevertheless in revealing a grammar we use to make violence that is inflicted on us meaningful, and this grammar has a long cultural history. It helps reveal how Lartéguy breathed new life into this grammar, rejecting what had grown antiquated, and how the symbolic universe he created thrives on deep anxieties about modern civilization. It is no surprise that this set of images immediately appeared in the wake of 9/11. If nothing else, 9/11 demonstrated a powerful willingness of an implacable enemy to use the most sophisticated technologies of our civilization against us in horrifying ways. This enemy seemed rooted in an alien world, tough and hardened to pain. And it raised fundamental anxieties. Sippowitz on *NYPD Blue* and Kiefer Sutherland's character on *24*, like Boisfeuras, are the latest images that manage this crisis in control. This is why they displace all other accounts and justifications of torture. The ticking time bomb scenario bends all argument to its framework, preventing light from breaking beyond the edges to the realities of torture. Lartéguy's story exercises the power of a black hole in modern memory.

Phenomenological analysis also shows what an empty, defensive reaction it is. This is because Lartéguy's response is born from a condition of weakness, not strength. The ticking time bomb scenario expresses a characteristic reaction when we have a panicked sense of lack of control over a situation, contrary to what Lartéguy and other torture apologists imply. The conception of masculinity that informs the judgment, "Yes, I would torture," is based on deep doubts about the life one is living, about the values one is allegedly defending through torture, and ultimately, about one's own masculinity.

There is no question that these doubts are real. In the wake of 9/11 Americans *have* felt deeply misunderstood and underappreciated. All we want is to be recognized for what we are. We ask, "Why do they hate us?" and "What can we do to be loved and respected for who we are?" Perhaps, we think sometimes, they "hate us for who we are, not what we do."[56] As President Bush claimed in his speech before Congress on September 20, 2001, "They hate our freedoms—our freedom of speech, our freedom to vote and assemble and disagree with each other."[57]

It is seriously doubtful that Osama bin Laden even contemplated for a second that American society was just, good or progressive, any more than a school bully taking lunch money wonders for a second whether being smart might have some virtue. But, nevertheless, al-Qaeda touches on things that we value most about our society. Osama bin Laden is not just any enemy; he is a figure from our own past. Our founding question as a civilization is: can a society born of religious dissent and built on toleration survive? This is not my question or yours, but presumably a question for all Americans. Real enemies correspond to our own questioning myths, and bin Laden forces us to confront our deepest question as a civilization.[58]

Unlike traditional war, winning the War on Terror is not about winning more land or wealth. The War on Terror is about our way of life, our fundamental identity as a law-based, tolerant, democratic society. Those who oppose this kind of society believe that fundamentally such societies are scam games, and they disguise violent coercion with promises of freedom. They are not surprised we torture because they always predicted we would. It proves they were telling the truth all along.

And they have a point: if we cannot respect the rule of law, if we cannot fight with one hand tied behind our backs *and win*, who exactly are we? W. R. Kidd, whose book *Police Interrogation* was influential in shaping police behavior in the 1940s, spoke for many in the World War II generation who knew that torture was the method of the enemy. Shunning torture, Kidd wrote, "does not make us sissies. It takes more guts to control yourself and fight it out brain to brain that it does to slug it out. . . . If you resort to torture, you admit your victim is the better man." Kidd understood the importance of winning respect through interrogation, but he was certain that torture produced no respect. "When you 'break' a man by torture, he will hate you."[59]

The same point was made by Marine Major Sherwood Moran, the author of one of the "timeless documents" in the field of military interrogation in 1943.[60] Moran specialized in interrogating Japanese prisoners, widely regarded as fanatical and dangerous individuals from a hostile and alien culture, and Moran was exceedingly good at it. Among his striking observations, Moran made the point that those who tried hardest to break the morale of Japanese prisoners by humiliating him and forcing him to stand through interrogation not only hardened the prisoner's resistance but also usually ended up revealing their own fears to him and others, specifically, the "fear that the prisoner will take advantage of you and your friendship." Moran's philosophy, by contrast, was "know their language, know their culture and treat the captured enemy as a human being."[61]

But at the end of the Korean War, Americans began to wonder whether the enemy had a point, whether Americans were not indeed weak and easily taken advantage of due to this weakness. Unlike World War II, there was no decisive victory in the Korean War, and many Americans believed incorrectly that US POWs had shown uncommon weakness in the face of the enemy.[62] Conservatives blamed socialist subversion, while Liberals held that materialism had made Americans soft.

Although doubts about American valor have always existed in American history, the public embraced a myth that somehow their civilization had made them weak. Politicians and military officials were often sensitive to it. Harsh coercive programs like "countermeasures to hostile interrogation," "stress inoculation," or "Survival, Evasion, Resistance, Escape (SERE)" set out to shore up these alleged shortcomings in toughness and character, and unwittingly then served as conduits for torture training generation after generation.[63] Shortly after 9/11, President Bush again raised this powerful myth of potential American weakness in an interview. "I do believe," he said, "there is an image of America out there that we are so materialistic, that we're almost hedonistic, that we don't have values, and that when struck, we wouldn't fight back. It was clear that bin Laden felt emboldened and didn't feel threatened by the United States."[64] It was all too easy to see where this determination to overcome our self-perceived doubts would lead us. In 1966, a military historian warned portentously that efforts "to eliminate the weaknesses allegedly revealed in POW camps in Korea might well strain to the breaking point" the fundamental principles on which American civilization is based.[65]

Those who do not think we can win by means of these principles harbor deep doubts, not about the strength of al-Qaeda, but about the founding beliefs of our civilization. They worry that we have become sissies and our enemies know it. Nothing will shake their belief in torture's efficacy, no matter how much evidence is provided, because this belief is so wrapped up with their perception of themselves. It is in fact no surprise that the American interrogator in Afghanistan in 2003 urged his charges not to be pussies. For such men, Lartéguy's story shores up their resolution as it did for the French *Paras* in a moment of danger. This is a large part of its appeal today. But those who seek to cure their doubts by means of torture might do well to ponder what an Israeli fighter pilot said after he fell captive to his enemy. As he was sent to the torture chamber, he summed up his thoughts on whether torture produced manliness in one short sentence. "Screw all these bigmouths with their ticking bombs."[66]

NOTES

I thank the Carnegie Corporation for supporting the research leave that contributed to this article, which draws on a chapter from my *Approaches to Violence* (Princeton, forthcoming). It is published here by kind permission of the Princeton University Press.

1. Cavenaugh, cited in Chris Mackey and Greg Miller, *The Interrogators* (New York: Little, Brown and Co., 2004), 191. See also Mackey and Miller, 180–181.

2. Martha Huggins, Mika Haritos-Fatouros, and Philip Zimbardo, *Violence Workers* (Berkeley, CA: University of California Press, 2002), 81–135.

3. Harvey Mansfield, *Manliness* (New Haven, CT: Yale University Press, 2006).

4. For the trauma to torturers, see Richard McNally *Remembering Trauma* (Cambridge, MA: Belknap Press, 2003), 86; Huggins, Haritos-Fatouros, and Zimbardo, *Violence Workers*, 215–231; Mika Haritos-Fatouros, *The Psychological Origins of Institutionalized Torture* (London: Routledge, 2003), 88, 93, 95, 97, 101, 105, 113–116, 203; Frantz Fanon, *The Wretched of the Earth*. Trans. Constance Farrington (New York: Grove Press, 1968), 264–270.

5. Jean Lartéguy, *The Centurions*, trans. Xan Felding (New York: E.P. Dutton, 1962).

6. Lartéguy, *The Centurions*, 470.

7. For similar torrid scenes in other novels of this period, see Pierre Vidal-Naquet *Torture*. Trans. Barry Richard (Harmondsworth, England: Penguin Books, 1963), 146.

8. Lartéguy, *The Centurions*, 481.

9. Alan Dershowitz, *Just Revenge* (New York: Warner Books, 1999), 127–128.

10. Pierre Bourdieu, *Outline of a Theory of Practice*. Trans. Richard Nice. (Cambridge: Cambridge University Press, 1989), 21–22, 195–196.

11. Vidal-Naquet, *Torture*, 146.

12. Anne Applebaum, "The Torture Myth," *The Washington Post* (January 12, 2005): A21. For similar French observations, see Roger Trinquier, *La guerre moderne* (Paris: La Table Ronde, 1961); *Modern Warfare*, trans. Daniel Lee (New York: Praeger, 1964).

13. Edmund Michelet, cited in Vidal Naquet, *Torture*, 92. See also Patrick Kessel and Giovanni Pirelli, *Le peuple algérien et la guerre* (Paris: François Maspero, 1962), 41, 238, 455; John Ambler, *The French Army in Politics* (Columbus, OH: Ohio State University Press, 1966), 175; Pierre Vidal-Naquet, *La Raison d'état* (Éditions de Minuit: Paris, 1962): 148; Denis Lefebvre, *Guy Mollet face à la torture en Algérie, 1956–1957* (Paris; Bruno Leprine, 2001), 97; Comité Maurice Audin, *Sans Commentaire* (Paris: Editions de Minuit, 1961). 105; Michel Biran, "Deuxième classe en Algerie" *Perspectives Socialistes* (November 1961): 29.

14. M. Mollet, cited in Vidal-Naquet, *Torture,* 72. See also Alistair Horne, *A Savage War of Peace* (New York: Viking Press, 1977), 205; John Talbott, *The War Without a Name* (New York: Alfred Knopf, 1980), 94; and Jacques Massu, *La vraie bataille d'Alger* (Paris: Plon, 1972), 168–169.

15. *Paras* cited in Henri Alleg, *La Question* (Éditions de Minuit: Paris, 1961), 36; and Jean-Pierre Cômes, *"Ma" guerre d'Algérie et la torture* (Paris: L'Harmattan, 2002), 70. See also Alleg, *La Question*, 98; Horne, *A Savage War of Peace*, 203; Kessel and Pirelli, *Le people algérien et la guerre*, 55, 652.

16. *The Gangrene*. Trans. Robert Silvers (New York: Lyle Stewart, 1960), 59. See also Déodat Puy-Montbrun, *L'honneur de la guerre* (Paris: Albin Michel, 2002), 286, 310; Pierre Le Goyet, *La Guerre d'Algérie* (Paris: Perrin: 1989): 124.

17. Cited in Horne, *A Savage War of Peace*, 203.

18. Jean Paul Sartre, "Introduction," in Henri Alleg, *The Question* (New York: George Braziller, 1958), 30.

19. Jean Paul Sartre, "Introduction," 29.

20. See Rejali, *Approaches to Violence* (Princeton, forthcoming).

21. Frantz Fanon, *Black Skins, White Masks*. Trans. Charles Lam Markmann, (New York: Grove Press, 1967), 166–167.

22. Edgar Berillon, cited in Enzo Traverso, *The Origins of Nazi Violence*. Trans. Janet Lloyd (New York: New Press, 2003), 92.

23. Traverso, *The Origins of Nazi Violence*, 92.

24. Traverso, *The Origins of Nazi Violence*, 92–93.

25. Fanon, *Wretched of the Earth*, 268–269.

26. Fanon, *Wretched of the Earth*, 268.

27. Fanon, *Wretched of the Earth*, 269–270.

28. Fanon, *Black Skins, White Masks*, 162.

29. Fanon, *Black Skins, White Masks*, 165.

30. Fanon, *Black Skins, White Masks*, 159.

31. Fanon, *Black Skins, White Masks*, 165.

32. Fanon, *Black Skins, White Masks*, 177.

33. Fanon, *Black Skins, White Masks*, Note 38, 176–177.

34. Fanon, *Black Skins, White Masks*, 176.

35. Fanon, *Black Skins, White Masks*, 179.

36. Fanon, *Black Skins, White Masks*, 177.

37. John K. Noyes, *The Mastery of Submission* (Ithaca: Cornell University Press, 1997), 5.

38. Noyes, *The Mastery of Submission*, 5.

39. Cited in Noyes, *The Mastery of Submission*, 7.

40. Noyes, *The Mastery of Submission*, 55.

41. Noyes, *The Mastery of Submission*, 53–54.

42. Leopold von Sacher-Masoch, cited in Noyes, *The Mastery of Submission*, 53.

43. Leopold von Sacher-Masoch, *Venus in Furs*. Trans. Joachim Neugroschel (New York, NY: Penguin, 2000), 4.

44. Sacher-Masoch, *Venus in Furs*, 5, 18.

45. Sacher-Masoch, *Venus in Furs*, 5–6.

46. Sacher-Masoch, *Venus in Furs*, 119.

47. See for example, Sacher-Masoch, *Venus in Furs*, 47.

48. Sacher-Masoch, *Venus in Furs*, 96–97.

49. Sacher-Masoch, *Venus in Furs*, 114, 40.

50. Sacher-Masoch, *Venus in Furs*, 115.

51. Sacher-Masoch, *Venus in Furs*, 117. See also the example, pp. 94–95, of the painter who finds his art again through masochism.

52. Sacher-Masoch, *Venus in Furs*, 119.

53. Lartéguy, *The Centurions*, 470.

54. And in this respect, it represents, not a little, certain readings of Nietzsche's Eternal Recurrence of the Same.

55. Huggins, Haritos Fatouros, and Zimbardo, *Violence Workers*, 81–135.

56. Victor David Hanson, "They Hate Us for Who We Are, Not What We Do," *Chicago Tribune* (January 18, 2005): http://www.victorhanson.com.

57. George W. Bush, "Address to a Joint Session of Congress and the American People" (September 20, 2001): http://www.whitehouse.gov/news/releases/2001/09/20010920-8.html.

58. "Friend and Enemy, East or West: Political Realism in the work of Osama bin Laden, Carl Schmitt, Niccolo Machiavelli and Kai Ka'us ibn Iskandar." *Historical Reflections* 3 (2004): 425–443.

59. W. R. Kidd, *Police Interrogation* (New York City: R.V. Basuino, 1940), 49.

60. Stephen Budiansky, "Truth Extraction," *Atlantic Monthly* (June 2005): 32.

61. Budiansky, "Truth Extraction," 35.

62. Albert Biderman, *March to Calumny* (New York: Arno Press, 1979), 115–134; 189–214; 221–223; 265–271; Peter Karsten, "The American Democratic Citizen Soldier: Triumph or Disaster?" *Military Affairs* 30.1 (Spring 1966): 34–40; H.H. Wubben, "American Prisoners of War in Korea: A Second Look at the 'Something New in History' Theme," *American Quarterly* 22.1 (Spring 1970): 3–19.

63. Jane Mayer, "The Experiment," *The New Yorker* (July 11 and 18, 2005): 63–71; M. Gregg Bloche and Jonathan H. Marks, "Doing Unto Others as They Did Unto Us," *New York Times* (November 14, 2005): A21.

64. President George W. Bush, cited in Bob Woodward and Dan Balz, "'We Will Rally the World.'" *The Washington Post* (January 28, 2002): A01.

65. Karsten, "The American Democratic Citizen Soldier," 39.

66. Ronny Talmor, "How a Bomb Ticks," in B'Tselem, *Legislation Allowing the Use of Physical Force and Mental Coercion in Interrogations by the General Security Service* (Jerusalem: B'Tselem, 2000), 71. First appeared in *Tarbut Ma'ariv* (October 1, 1999).

13

Feminism's Assumptions Upended

Barbara Ehrenreich
(Originally published May 16, 2004 in the Los Angeles Times*)*

EVEN PEOPLE WHOM WE MIGHT have thought were impervious to shame, like the Secretary of Defense, admit that the photos of prisoner abuse in Abu Ghraib turned their stomachs. The photos did something else to me, as a feminist: they broke my heart. I had no illusions about the US mission in Iraq, whatever exactly it is, but it turns out that I did have some illusions about women.

Of the seven US soldiers now charged with sickening forms of abuse in Abu Ghraib, three are women: Pfc. Lynndie England, Specialist Sabrina Harman, and Specialist Megan Ambuhl. It was Harman whom we saw smiling an impish little smile and giving the thumbs sign from behind a pile of naked Iraqi men—as if to say, "Hi mom, here I am in Abu Ghraib!" We've gone from the banality of evil . . . to the cuteness of evil.

It was England we saw dragging a naked Iraqi man on a leash. If you were doing PR for al Qaeda, you couldn't have staged a better picture to galvanize misogynist Islamic fundamentalists around the world. Here, in these photos from Abu Ghraib, you have everything that the Islamic fundamentalists believe characterizes Western culture, all nicely arranged in one hideous image—imperial arrogance, sexual depravity . . . and gender equality.

Maybe I shouldn't have been so shocked.

We know that good people can do terrible things under the right circumstances. This is what psychologist Stanley Milgram found in his famous experiments in the 1960s, which found most people willing to follow orders and deliver what they believed were painful electric shocks to others. In all likelihood, England, Harman and Ambuhl are not congenitally evil people. They are working class women who wanted an education and knew that the military could be a stepping stone in that direction. Once they got in, they wanted to fit in.

And I shouldn't be surprised either because I never believed that women are innately gentler and less aggressive than men. I have argued this repeatedly—once with the famously macho anthropologist Napoleon Chagnon. When he kept insisting that women were psychologically incapable of combat, I answered him the best way I could: I asked him if he wanted to step outside . . .

Like most feminists, I have supported full opportunity for women within the military—one, because I knew women could fight, and, two, because the military is one of the few options around for low-income young people. Although I opposed the first Gulf War in 1991, I was proud of our servicewomen and delighted that their presence irked their Saudi hosts. Secretly, I hoped that the presence of women would eventually change the military, making it more respectful of other people and cultures, more capable of genuine peacekeeping.

That's what I thought, but I don't think that any more.

A lot of things died with those photos. One of them was the last justification for the war with Iraq. First, the justification was the weapons of mass destruction. Then it was the supposed links between Saddam and Osama bin Laden—those links were never discovered either. So the final justification was that we had removed an evil dictator who tortured his own people. As late as April 30—two days after the photos surfaced—George Bush was exulting that the torture chambers of Iraq were no longer operating.

Well, it turns out they were just operating under different management. We didn't displace Saddam Hussein; we simply replaced him.

And when you throw in the similar abuses in Afghanistan and Guantánamo, in immigrant detention centers and US prisons, you see that we have created a spreading regime of torture—an empire of pain.

But there's another thing that died for me in the last couple of weeks—a certain kind of feminism or, perhaps I should say, a certain kind of feminist naiveté.

It was a kind of feminism that saw men as the perpetual perpetrators, women as the perpetual victims, and male sexual violence against women as the root of all injustice. Maybe this form of feminism made more sense in the 1970s. Certainly it seemed to make sense when we learned about the rape camps in Bosnia in the early 90s. Rape has repeatedly been an instrument of war and, to some feminists, it was beginning to look as if war was an extension of rape. There seemed to be at least some evidence that male sexual sadism is connected to our species' tragic propensity for violence.

That was before we had seen female sexual sadism in action.

But it's not just the theory of this naïve feminism that was wrong. So was its strategy and vision for change. That strategy and vision rested on the assumption, implicit or stated outright, that women are morally superior to men. We had a lot of debates over whether it was biology or conditioning that gave women the moral edge—or simply the experience of being a woman in a sexist culture. But the assumption of superiority, or at least a lesser inclination toward cruelty and violence, was more or less beyond debate. After all, women do most of the caring work in our culture, and in polls are consistently less inclined toward war than men.

I'm not the only one wrestling with that assumption today. Mary Jo Melone, a columnist in the *St. Petersburg Times,* writing on May 7: "I can't get that picture of [Pfc. Lynndie] England out of my head because this is not how women are expected to behave. Feminism taught me 30 years ago that not only had women gotten a raw deal from men, we were morally superior to them."

Now the implication of this assumption was that all we had to do to make the world a better place—kinder, less violent, more just—was to assimilate into what had been, for so many centuries, the world of men. We would fight so that women could become the generals, the CEOs, the senators, the professors and opinion-makers—and that was really the only fight we had to undertake. Because once they gained power and authority, once they had achieved a critical mass within the institutions of society, women would naturally work for change.

That's what we thought, even if we thought it unconsciously, and it's just not true. Women can do the unthinkable.

You can't even argue, in the case of Abu Ghraib, that the problem was that there just weren't enough women in the military hierarchy to stop the abuses. The prison was directed by a woman, General Janis Karpinski. The top US intelligence officer in Iraq, who was also responsible for reviewing the status of detainees prior to their release, was Major Gen. Barbara Fast. And the US official ultimately responsible for managing the occupation of Iraq since last October is Condoleezza Rice. Like Donald Rumsfeld, she ignored repeated reports of abuse and torture until the undeniable photographic evidence emerged.

What we have learned from Abu Ghraib, once and for all, is that a uterus is not a substitute for a conscience, and menstrual periods are not the foundation of morality.

This doesn't mean gender equality isn't worth fighting for its own sake. It is. If we believe in democracy, we believe in women's right to do and achieve whatever men can do and achieve, even the bad things. Women deserve equality not because we are special, but because we are human.

Gender equality cannot, all alone, bring about a just and peaceful world. In fact we have to realize, in all humility, that the kind of feminism based on an assumption of female moral superiority is not only naïve; it is also a lazy and self-indulgent form of feminism. Self-indulgent because it assumes that a victory for a woman—a promotion, a college degree, a right to serve alongside men in the military—is ipso facto—by its very nature—a victory for all of humanity. And lazy because it assumes that we have only one struggle—the struggle for gender equality—when in fact we have many more. The struggles for peace, for social justice and against imperialist and racist arrogance, cannot, I am truly sorry to say, be folded into the struggle for gender equality.

What we need is a tough new kind of feminism with no illusions. Women do not change institutions simply by assimilating into them, but only by consciously deciding to fight for change. We need a feminism that teaches women to say no—not just to the date rapist or overly insistent boyfriend—but, when necessary, to the military or corporate hierarchy within which she finds herself. In short, we need a kind of feminism that aims not just to assimilate into the institutions men have created over the centuries, but to *infiltrate* and subvert them.

To cite an old, and far from naïve, feminist saying: "If you think equality is the goal, your standards are too low." It is not enough to be equal to men, when the men are acting like beasts. It is not enough to assimilate. We need to create a world worth assimilating into.

14

Totalitarian Lust: From *Salò* to Abu Ghraib

Eduardo Subirats
(Translated by Christopher Britt Arredondo)

1. The Bastille

IN HIS *DIRECTORIUM INQUISITORUM*, a 1503 treatise on inquisitorial interrogations and tortures, Nicolau Eimeric formulated a golden rule. According to this theologian, torture should never be conceived simply as an arbitrary game of cruelty nor as an institutionally sanctioned crime to be committed in God's name. On the contrary, the techniques and instruments of torture are specifically and rationally dependent on an ultimate transcendental value; and it is precisely this interior significance of torture that bestows on the torturer the highest theological dignity. In this manner, Eimeric voiced his radical opposition to the common interrogational practice of breaking the bones of "defenseless people," since this practice lacked any rational function. He proposed, rather, the use of technologies that were bound to socially relevant individuals, such as doctors, soldiers, and priests who practiced heresy. In these cases, torture was to be designed according to principles that were theologically differentiated for each class of dogmatic transgression. Torture, in sum, was to be considered an instrument of spirituality; as well it should be to this day.[1]

To reduce torture epistemologically to the category of a pure technological problem, or to confine it sociologically to corrupt administrations and tyrannical political systems, or yet again to restrict it juridically according to some more or less virtuous, more or less virtual principle of human rights: all of this and its like exposes nothing but the desire to misunderstand torture. Torture is one among many expressions of human dominance. It therefore needs to be considered in relation to other contemporary manifestations of the power of the modern state: for example, the technical-scientific destruction of ecosystems; the economic strategies of global genocide; or programs for nuclear and biological extermination. And yet torture is not one more among these various forms and instruments of civilizing domination. Torture is the most privileged spiritual expression of this power.

It would be similarly mistaken to trivialize torture as collateral damage or as the undesired consequence of cleanly operating apparatuses of political or military domination, be they fascist or neo-liberal. The methods and instruments of torture should be understood, rather, as means of central importance because they reveal the sub-structures of the moral, epistemological, and political systems that put torture into practice. This is then perhaps the place to recall two classic interpretations of torture. "Die Waffen sind nichts anderes, als das Wesen der Kämpfer selber," wrote G. W. F. Hegel in his *Phänomenologie des Geistes*. Weapons are the essence of their bearers; they reveal the nature of the rational consciousness of the civilization that uses them; and they make manifest the significance of the bloody spirit of universal history.[2] Torture is the intimate expression—the erotic and charismatic expression—of the logos of domination. It is for this reason that it is concealed. The other interpretation to have in mind here is *In der Strafkolonie*, where Franz Kafka describes the tortured body as a surface on which the rational system of the law is encoded, thus defining the concentration camp as a metaphor of modern civilization.

Torture is a microcosm. Hence, its considerable theological, philosophical, and political value. The physical and chemical techniques of destruction of the person—from the grappling irons and mutilations put into practice by the Holy Christian Brotherhood, to the electrical charges, drugs, violent contusions, prolonged asphyxia, aggressive sensorial stimulation, and sexual violation practiced in centers of military intelligence throughout the Cold War—in short, what we see before us today is not, as the institutional watchdogs of human rights are inclined to proclaim, the vision of an inexpressible and incomprehensible horror. It is the exact opposite: the calculated expression, at once rational and necessary, that defines modernity, the global capitalist system, or Western civilization as such. This is the expression that reveals the profound logos of modernity. It is, to be precise, the same expression that once led the Marquis de Sade to explore, in his memories of imprisonment, the nexus between torture and civilizing rationality.

The literary configuration of sadist torture in *Les 120 journées de Sodome* is particularly revealing given our contemporary panorama of wars, genocides, and the humiliating mockery of the globalized electronic masses. First of all, the criminal intent of Sade's imaginary secret societies forced them into a situation of social exclusion and legal defiance, which Sade represented metaphorically by means of the mystical image of a fortified castle hidden far away in an inaccessible place. But Sade did not formulate the secretive confinement of his libertines as a negative condition and necessary punishment for participating in criminal associations. His use of extra-territoriality did not delimit an illegal or irregular situation from either a juridical or moral point of view. On the contrary, he used it to define metaphorically a state of exception on the basis of which the legal and moral order of a rational and revolutionary system of domination might be constituted. In this regard, Sade's libertines are the instruments that execute the final moral and political consequence of the philosophical and historical reason of the *Grande Revolution*: the same rationality that instituted the guillotine and the revolutionary dictatorship of Robespierre: the same rationality that erected the sacrificial altars of liberty and threw open the doors to the Napoleonic wars: the same rationality, in sum, that inaugurated a new era of colonial usurpation, exploitation, and genocide. This violence configures the new rational republican order in the same sense that the political theories of Thomas Hobbes or Carl Schmitt treated a state of exception as a condition for the establishment of a totalitarian state.[3] And it is in this sense also that today we pay witness to a process of military expansion and domination that has culminated in the public torture and extermination of prisoners of war at Guantánamo and Abu Ghraib.

The moral exemplarity and juridical function of the sadist libertines explains the redundant affection that Sade attaches to logical rigor, to geometric order, to strict norms and formal hierarchies. What is more, the moral and juridical function that Sade assigns to his libertines also explains the visualization and vigilance of their criminal acts or performances. And it explains as well the punctilious praise for a system of total administrative control that indiscriminately includes both the moral conduct and the pleasure-seeking of victims and their victimizers alike.[4] For this reason also, the secret sadist society is a visionary anticipation of the totalitarian organization inherent to contemporary global military and political bureaucracies, as Max Horkheimer and Theodor W. Adorno noted some time ago in their *Dialektik der Aufklärung*.[5]

Nevertheless, Sade's philosophy does more than explain the legally constituting function of violence that either precedes or remains beyond the law. Sade was not an ideologue. Nor was he a theorist of the modern or postmodern totalitarian state. His literary work, rather, underscores the logical and epistemological premises as well as the politico-economic and moral consequences of the new political and metaphysical order of the Revolution. By means of tediously repetitive performances of criminal pleasure and the industrial rationalization of rape, torture, and crime, Sade reveals the logical sub-structure of the simultaneously liberal and totalitarian, enlightened and destructive, progressive and apocalyptic system of modern civilization.

There are two fundamental characteristics that define the spiritual and civilizing significance of torture. One is political. In extremely crude terms, it can be formulated as the criminal exemplarity with which certain sectors that are at the vanguard of political and military organization of a legal state publicly proclaim their own seditious power as the source of a new de facto local or global order. It is for this reason that torture—whether of the sort practiced during the colonial Inquisition of the sixteenth century or of the kind practiced in the colonial penitentiaries of the current Global War—must hide its primitive, bloody, and sacrificial brutality from society while, at the same time, making sure to exhibit itself as a public demonstration of a power that is as absolute as it is arbitrary. The case of Giordano Bruno, who was subjected over six years to interrogations and torture in the secret prisons of the Vatican only to be burned alive at the stake after his tongue had been removed, illustrates this doubly archaic dimension of torture. But in its exemplary old inquisitorial form as well as in the technically dignified form it has achieved today under the sway of the new theology of totalitarianism, torture also reveals a theological characteristic: it exposes the ultimate reason and final consequences of lofty doctrines such as the universal redemption of mankind by means of ecclesiastic conversion (Paul), or by means of economic development and the cultivation of democracy as a spectacle (which are the theological ends of the colonial wars of the twenty-first century).

On the basis of these theological and political characteristics, Sade's work provides a primordial revelation: the very same rationality that once sustained the enlightened republican ideals of liberty and equality served to perpetuate the nihilistic significance of Christian morality and its crystallization in the apparatus of the state. Oppression and destruction, rape, violation, humiliation: these were its final rational postulates. It is in this sense that *Les 120 journées de Sodome* anticipates the so-called "dialectic of enlightenment," the Janus-faced grimace of a revolutionary rationality that simultaneously incorporates a totalitarian political and military machinery and a genocidal principle of annihilation.

2. *Salò*

Salò, o le 120 giornate di Sodoma, by Pier Paolo Pasolini, is first and foremost the intellectual testimony of an age of imperialist wars, mass media abuse, and genocide.[6] The film specifically narrates the practices of sexual violation, torture, and execution carried out by fascist European states during the wars of the 1940s. But Pasolini does more than document a real case of organized crime: he juxtaposes it to a critique of late-modern civilization as a totalitarian system. In addition to providing this political perspective on the ecclesiastical organization of state-sanctioned crime, *Salò* provides a denunciation of the moral nihilism that impregnates the modern philosophy of Sade, Nietzsche, or Klossowski, and it does so precisely by using these thinkers' most critical philosophical illumina-tions. Pasolini denounces this modern nihilism by placing philosophical citations in the mouths of the fascist victimizers in his film. Interest-ingly, these victimizers are surrounded by a décor that pays homage to the sacred icons of the Futurist vanguard, from Fernand Léger to Carlo Carrá. Thus *Salò* provides a denunciation of torture; but at the same time it interprets torture as the secret writing of a modernity that legitimizes and disseminates torture as a language. Last but not least, this film also announces the coming of a new global fascism: the global fascism that is staring us in the face today.

This important film presents four definitions of torture or, rather, four aspects of its institutional practice. To begin with, *Salò* describes torture as lust, linking it to destruction, humiliation, and sacrificial death. In effect, Pasolini stages the Holy Trinity of libidinal excitation, sexual violation, and murder and combines these three moments with narcissistic fantasies of omnipotence. He treats these as the signs of that same collapse of humanity that Freud had announced decades before in his diagnosis of modernity as a culture of violence. With its final sequence of scenes, *Salò* highlights this collapse, offering images of women and men who have been violated and mutilated in a macabre dance of absolute power.

The second definition provided by this film associates torture with freedom. To be more exact, *Salò* defines torture as the supreme expression of freedom. There simply is no moral ideal of sovereignty, irregardless of how paranoid or absolute its will-to-power may be, that can express with greater transparency the emancipation of the self from any and all legal or political fetters; there is no better expression of independence from human customs and norms; no clearer expression of a hegemony that recognizes no limits to its technical and imaginative prowess; there is, in the final analysis, no principle of domination that can be applied in a manner that is so innocent, so absolute, and so impeccable as occurs in the relation of the torturer and his victim. As one of the libertines of Pasolini's film proclaims, it is only through torture that the transcenden-tal liberty of techno-scientific and moral reason can be realized both as a fantasy of omnipotence and as the lust for a true *an-arkhia* (the state prior to the law and constitutive of the law).

The third meaning of torture developed in *Salò* is aesthetic. But perhaps it would be more accurate to speak here of the multiple aesthetic functions of torture. In this regard, it might also be useful to recall the profuse imagery of violations and mutilations, massive bombings and assassinations that distinguish the little screen of the global village in these final years of transition toward the new world order of the twenty-first century. This aesthetic dimension, or more precisely this performative dimension, merits special attention.

In Sade's *Les 120 journées*, torture and assassination were presented in the format of a baroque setting. These were crimes perpetrated in order to be seen; the libertine as actor and the reader as voyeur participated equally in the resulting pleasure. Pasolini takes up this spectacular dimension. And he does so under a variety of aspects. The aestheticization of horror is one of these. The exemplary genocide of *Salò* takes place in an elegant Palladian villa, decorated with many of the masterpieces of the artistic vanguards. The ambience is decidedly refined, literary, philosophical. In this sense, the film anticipates the aestheticization of horror today through mediated *mise en scènes*: the victims of Guantánamo clinically uniformed in orange suits, transported in stretchers to their torture cells, a somber spectacle that condenses genocidal violence into the clinical precision of instruments of advanced biotechnology.

Still, Pasolini also treats this aestheticization of terror in another sense: he duplicates it reflexively. Reconstructing the scenes of torture as a play within a play, and using the procurers as sadist narrators, he surreptitiously introduces that same distance and defamiliarization (*Befremdung*) with regard to the representation that Brecht had formulated as a means to artistic clarity. This reflexive duplication in Pasolini's movie engages in a polemical fashion with the two most elemental characteristics of the representation of violence in the global village: first, the fictionalization, neutralization, and evaporation of the reality of violence; and second, the hyper-realistic and pornographic exaltation of violence (pornographic, that is, in the sense of the pornographic industry of crime, sexual sadism, and violence that characterizes the Hollywood aesthetic). By reason of this defamiliarizing, reflexive, and clarifying function, Pasolini's *Salò* was, and continues to be, a prohibited film, unlike the pornography and violence currently produced by the globalizing mass media.

The fourth meaning of torture examined by *Salò* is political and civilizing. It concerns the constitution of a totalitarian power. In this respect, it proves useful to remember that *Salò* provides a vision akin to the one that Kafka develops in his *Strafkolonie*. In both instances, torture is revealed as a kind of coded writing on the bodies of the victims;

the torturers derive pleasure from writing this secret coded language, which is in effect an inaugural system of oppressive norms that gives rise to an ideal totalitarian society. From the first to the last images of his film, Pasolini shows—and in this sense he is faithful to the example of Sade—the intimate relation between torture on the one hand and, on the other, ecclesiastic morality, military machinery, and financial power. Or, to put it more precisely, Pasolini demonstrates how torture is the interior dimension of the neutral and autonomous machinery of fear and trembling, according to which political philosophy, from Hobbes to Schmitt, has defined the modern absolutist and totalitarian state.[7]

3. THE CIVILIZING PROCESS

Salò is interesting not only in the sense that it denounces the crimes of historical fascism, but also because it anticipates the fascism which yesterday belonged to tomorrow, as Barth David Schwartz points out in his biography of Pasolini.[8] Torture as totalitarian lust; torture as an expression of liberty, sovereignty, and imperial power; torture as a spectacle and the encoded language of power: these are the contemporary dimensions of torture as an instrument of civilization.

Pasolini described this instrumental function of torture by means of the architecture of initiation that structures his film: Salò is divided into a series of successive "circles" through which the victims must pass on their way to their final sacrificial consummation. These circles allude to Dante's Inferno, and as occurs in the Commedia, the significance of their content is allegorical. The first of these circles, the "Girone delle manie," stages an artificial system of stimuli and constant lustful excitement. This system is replete with the most extreme fantasies and incentives, from masturbation to execution. It is however a system of incitation and excitation that generates increasing gradations of frustration; this frustration, in turn, leads the victimizers and their victims alike to embrace a destructive and self-destructive aggression. It is with this metaphor that Pasolini concludes his first critique of neo-liberal and postmodern fascism: a provocative system of consumption, which, regardless of whether it is dedicated to sexual trafficking, the corporate production of ecologically devastating seeds, or trafficking in arms, generates progressive degrees of violence, the exponential growth of hunger, epidemics, death, and the indefinite expansion of war.

In the next circle, the "Girone della merda," Pasolini exposes the necessary consequence of this first capitalist cycle of libidinal hyper-excitation, frustrating emotional discharges, and the subsequent accumulation of lethal energy. As unarmed spectators, we behold this new circle unable to cope with the final degradation of humanity. The film stylizes this degradation poetically, with successive scenes of the military imposition of a collective suicide, and images of people swallowing blades, crouching in humiliation, and feverishly gulping down their own excrement.

Blood is the last of the circles of initiation to a totalitarian civilization. With this symbol, which is at once vital and sacrificial, *Salò* represents torture as a process of mutilation of the organs of erotic union and biological generation. At issue is a kind of torture that is simultaneously political and sexual: precisely the sort of torture that the fascist regimes of the so-called Cold War in Colombia, Chile, or Argentina practiced and that continues to be practiced under the auspices of torture's new setting—the "War on Terror." This blood symbolism also designates torture as a paradigm for the terminal destruction of the human being. Yet Pasolini adds to this another ingredient of considerable relevance to the industrial and mediated culture of the twenty-first century: the trivialization of human pain and agony by means of violent, destructive, and lethal spectacles. This is Pasolini's conclusion concerning totalitarian lust.

The final sequence of scenes in *Salò* is particularly enlightening in this regard. In a prison that is open to the skies above, the victims are subjected to mutilations and tortures that are lethal. But one of the libertines contemplates this deathly scene from an enclosed balcony and through the double prism of a set of binoculars. The camera reproduces this privileged perspective, highlighting in a detailed close-up the expressions of desperation and discouragement of the victims' faces. The screams of the victims cannot be heard, however. Instead, a sacred exaltation of sensuality, eroticism, and beauty plays in the background; it is Orff's *Carmina Burana*. Suddenly, the libertine inverts the position of his binoculars. The camera shifts from distant and diluted images of mutilated bodies to an intimate and clean image of the libertine being masturbated by one of his soldiers. The film shows this voyeuristic and masturbatory victimizer seated with his back to the camera. He is, consequently, an anonymous viewer. His narrative function is identitarian. He represents the spectator of mass media. He is us. Pasolini reconstructs this electronic "us" as an accomplice of a self-destructive power.

The spiritual constitution of this mediated collective consciousness in the era of the global war is distinguished by three characteristics. First: the fictionalization of reality. With Abu Ghraib, this mediated trivialization of reality has reached the extreme of jumbling the photographs of the real victims together with images produced and distributed by the industry of pornography. Such a hybridization of fiction and reality does not only signify the weakening of reality in the sense of "la guerre qui n'a pas eu lieu." Of much greater importance is the profound dimension of this semiotic exchange of simulacra and representations: the linguistic, moral, and libidinal continuity of, on the one hand, the consumption of electronic pornography by the masses and, on the other, the totalitarian lust of torture and assassination on a massive scale that plays itself out every evening on prime-time television.

Abu Ghraib is a symbol of the civilizing process in an age of spectacles in still another sense: its fragmented spaces; the deformation and de-personalization of its victims; the signs of a military terror which, in part, exhibits its hyper-modern technocratic efficiency and, in part, demonstrates the schizophrenic structure of a power that shifts forms, generates schizoid subjects, and provokes rationally uncontrollable conduct. It is what Michel Foucault announced in his welcoming salutation to Gilles Deleuze's *Anti-Oedipe* as a deleuzian era yet to come.

The third and final aspect that crystallizes around this voyeur of *Salò*—this voyeur that is us—results directly from the previous two: the electronic evaporation and schizophrenic deconstruction of reality. At issue is our own collective state of catatonic rigidity, intellectual and emotional coldness, and practical as well as communicative lack of validity. It is a generalized state of somnambulism, in which it becomes impossible to comprehend the reality of the spectacle and construct meaning out of our damaged existence.

NOTES

1. Nicolau Eymerich, Francisco Peña. *Le manuel des inquisiteurs* (Paris: Mouton Éditeur, 1973), 207 and following.

2. G. W. F. Hegel. *Die Phänomenologie des Gesties*. A: 320.

3. S. Carl Schmitt. *Der Begriff des Politischen* (Berlin: Dunker & Humblot, 1963), 34 etc. Giorgio Agamben, *Homo sacer: sovereign power and bare life* (Stanford: Stanford University Press, 1998.), 30 etc.

4. The Marquis de Sade. *The 120 days of Sodom, and Other Writings*. Compiled and translated by Austryn Wainhouse and Richard Seaver (New York: Grove Press, 1966), 240 etc.

5. Max Horkheimer und Theodor W. Adorno. *Dialektik der Aufklärung* (Frankfurt: S. Fischer Verlag, 1969), 88.

6. Pier Paolo Pasolini. *Salò, the 120 Days of Sodom* (1975).

7. Carl Schmitt. *Der Leviathan in der Staatslehre des Thomas Hobbes* (Stuttgart: Klett-Cotta, 1982), 51.

8. Barth David Schwartz. *Pasolini Requiem* (New York: Vintage Books, 1995), 637.

15

Information and the Tortured Imagination

Thomas C. Hilde

> The natural argument developed in hundreds of pulpits was this: If
> the Allwise God punishes his creatures with tortures infinite in cruelty
> and duration, why should not his ministers, as far as they can, imitate
> him?
>
> —Andrew Dickson White, *A History of the Warfare of
> Science with Theology in Christendom*, 1896

THE LOGIC OF TORTURE is such that the practice of torture necessarily entails
its institutionalization. The way in which the moral argument for torture is
structured is such that torture's product—in the present case, information
or intelligence—also ultimately necessitates a redescription of reality that
breaches the very logic of information-gathering. When such power of
redescription lies in the hands of exclusive political actors, regardless of
their intent, truth is written by power residing at the boundary of political
tyranny if not crossing it. We shall see that necessary assumptions—necessary to deflect any charge of brute oppression or sadism—embedded in
the argument for torture as a means of information-gathering underscore
the argument's absurdity, that the logic of institutional torture contains
the germ of its own absurdity. Worse, it also contains the seeds of a
pseudo-reality bound up with political tyranny.

In this essay, I will dispose of the current argument that torture is an
"exceptional" but ethically justifiable practice for seeking information.
This argument's emblematic version is the ubiquitous "ticking time
bomb" scenario, a test case of our moral limits that is actively encouraged
by several high-profile academic, legal, and political figures. I conclude
that torture necessarily becomes, by its own logic, an institution. This
gives the lie to claims for torture as a means of information-gathering for
the greater good. The conditions and qualifications necessary in concoct-
ing a moral argument for torture must themselves be rigorous. The time
bomb scenario, however, additionally requires a radical redescription of
actuality, beyond mere hypothesis, in order to fit the torture argument.
This is precisely what current proponents of torture do or, rather, where
the consequences of their logic lead. The humanist project of presenting
testimonials of torture to public consciousness is morally important. But
the goal of eliminating the practice requires demonstrating that its logic is

197

incoherent, since many policymakers are enthralled by this logic. Rather than dismissing the argument outright as an implausible hypothetical, we need to show how it normatively structures the practical elements of torture. This can then provide stronger moral as well as practical demands for eliminating torture, which I think is the only reasonable and ethical objective.

I will not directly consider questions of human nature, torture as a form of sadism and so on. Certainly, torture is barbaric. But I wish first to examine the argument for torture on its own terms; namely, torture as a method of valuable intelligence-gathering or information-seeking. The institutionalization of torture, while perhaps a structural by-product, rests on the claim that some information is of greater moral gravity than the individual torture victim's pain or even death. I will show that this argument for torture runs aground of practical limitations which are generally excluded from the current "torture debate," framed as it is as a legal debate about what is possible according to extant international and domestic law. The implications are considerable. I suggest that, akin to the logic of torture from the Middle Ages through the Modern period, in order to justify the contemporary practice of torture one requires an *a priori* script of a fantasy.

TORTURE AND THE TICKING TIME BOMB

There are two basic moral positions in the current discourse on torture. The two principal positions are variations on the themes of: 1) Torture is wrong, immoral, or evil; and 2) Torture is wrong, but it may be used in exceptional circumstances to counter a greater evil (although some apparently think it is simply "fun").

I will consider the second view regarding the instrumental use of torture. Presuming that torture is not an end in itself, we must ask what the purpose of torture is. Suppressing dissent, forcing renunciation of beliefs, extracting confessions, forcing denunciation of others, punishing, intimidating a wider population, humiliating and terrorizing, and gathering information are all historical objectives of torture.[1] It is important to understand that the uses of torture are diverse and complex, although in this essay I focus on the current stated objective of torture as information gathering, which philosopher and legal theorist David Luban has remarked, in an essay excoriating recent legal arguments, remains the sole conceivable rationale for torture in liberal ideology.[2] Luban suggests that the "liberal ideology" of torture is such "that the sole purpose of torture must be intelligence gathering to prevent a catastrophe; that torturing is the exception, not the rule, so that it has nothing to do with state tyranny; that those who inflict the torture are motivated solely by the looming catastrophe, with no tincture of cruelty; that torture in such circumstances is, in fact, little more than self-defense; and that, because of the associations of torture with the horrors of yesteryear, perhaps one should not even call harsh interrogation 'torture.'"[3]

In the current situation, the "war on terror,"[4] one might argue that the objective of torture is to force one group to submit to another's will, to intimidate, to oppress. There is some evidence for this claim. Naomi Klein, in an article in *The Nation*, cites a US NGO Physicians for Human Rights manual for treating torture survivors: "perpetrators often attempt to justify their acts of torture and ill treatment by the need to gather in-formation. Such conceptualizations obscure the purpose of torture. . . . The aim of torture is to dehumanize the victim, break his/her will, and at the same time, set horrific examples for those who come in contact with the victim. In this way, torture can break or damage the will and coherence of entire communities."[5] In this sense, torture as a means of waging war has the same objective as terrorism as a means of waging war—both intend not merely to cause the death or pain of individual victims, but to create terror in a larger population. Regardless of hidden intentions and socio-psychological tendencies,[6] the preeminent explicit justification for torture in the "war on terror" is information-gathering, especially information that might practically counter some threat of greater moral gravity than the torture of an individual.

In the United States, we have entered into a discussion based on very real practices (Abu Ghraib, Baghram, Guantánamo, etc.) and their very real public images (Abu Ghraib), which have given a peculiar saliency to attempts to justify the "exceptional circumstances" clause of the sec-ond position mentioned above. Some of the most high-profile American jurists, politicians, lawyers, and philosophers have rushed to the side of the U.S. administration's contorted defense of torture as a regretfully necessary reality.[7] These justifications, Luban maintains, amount to patent "intellectual fraud."[8] Part of the defense involves rendering the Abu Ghraib case one of the actions of "a few bad apples" or, in other words, a case of sadism in which particular individuals may be blamed rather than the institution and chain of command of which they are a part. The main defense of the broader use of torture involves a claim to morally significant information, as noted above in the liberal ideology of torture.

Let's consider the main claim. In legal terms, it is often called the *necessity argument*, the claim that a criminal act is justified because it was necessary to prevent a worse act.[9] In moral terms, the argument is a basic utilitarian one. Its main example is the "ticking time bomb," a scenario popularized and normalized on the American television show, *24*.[10] This scenario is perhaps most famously used in the contemporary context by Alan Dershowitz.[11] The scenario runs like this: a bomb (usually nuclear) is set to go off that will kill thousands of innocent people. You have captured the terrorist who planted the bomb or who possesses information that will lead to finding the bomb. You are limited for time. Do you torture the information out of the terrorist or do you allow the bomb to explode? The answer is the result of a simple utilitarian calculation: one weighs one individual's pain versus the deaths of thousands of people. As Luban notes, the argument is designed to get the absolutist, the one who holds position number 1 above, to grant that there are exceptions to the absolute sanction against torture. The scenario relies on a notion of *meaningful* information (as opposed to raw data) that may be plausibly considered more morally significant than the act of torture. Further, however—and this is the tricky part—a highly implausible scenario (in fact, it is generally thought not to have existed[12]) with an arguably reasonable utilitarian judgment (torture the individual terrorist; save the thousands of innocents) is then used to justify the broader use of torture. It relies on a false postulation that if the absolute sanction against torture cannot be consistently supported, then everything goes, and what is then interesting about torture are the benefits it might generate.

Note that there are three crucial elements here: 1) the torture victim is "bad"; 2) the objective of torture is information; and 3) the torture victim and the particular scenario are individualized so that we can easily calculate the cost-benefit numbers. I will examine these in turn, but the third point is a particular view of the first two points which conceals the actual logic of torture, discussed in the following section.

First, the bad terrorist, it is sometimes assumed, forgoes the right to be treated with the basic human rights accorded to any other human being. In fact, labeling an individual a "terrorist" before having any idea of guilt is a value statement. Any discussion of the issue of human rights is complex and will be set aside here.[13] But, in any case, this view of the terrorist surrendering rights normally assigned to all shares a parallel with a Kantian argument regarding capital punishment.[14] The Kantian argument runs like this: the murderer surrenders any claim to participate in the moral community when he violates the universal rule—the categorical imperative—that would apply to others whom he has terrorized or tortured. He has used others as means in the most despicable way, and has thus, through his action, opted out of the rule that one should not use others as means. The penalty aspect then comes from the traditional *lex talionis* or "eye for an eye," ultimately through a system of due process of law. That is, the murderer has, through his actions, sanctioned his own execution.[15] In the case of the terrorist, he has also intentionally committed an act that violates the universal norm against killing. He thus excludes himself from laying claim to a right against violent harm which he himself has denied others. The result, for some, is that any harsh treatment of the murderer is justified. Although she ignores the philosophical argument, Heather MacDonald, for instance, asserts the typical line (while defending interrogation as "nontorturous stress"): "to declare nontorturous stress off-limits for an enemy who plays by no rules and accords no respect to Western prisoners is folly." Ridiculing "the fantasies of the international law and human rights lobbies," she places the moral burden on the evil character of the terrorist.[16] The implicit message of this kind of assertion is that any treatment of such evil beings is justified, including what the US government has called "alternative interrogation." Even for the Kantian in the case above, however, the spell of vengeance which allows for abuse of the criminal is a barbaric basis for punishment. This is part of the reason why, perhaps absurdly, the system of capital punishment in the United States involves state executions but not "cruel and unusual punishment."

The bad guy assertion does not apply to Abu Ghraib or Guantánamo anyway because, as US generals have admitted and the International Red Cross has documented, perhaps some 80–90% of "detainees" were caught up in the wrong place at the wrong time.[17] Without knowledge of any "guilt" in the first instance, a justification for torture based on the combined Kantian-*lex talionis* claim used in capital punishment arguments has no basis whatsoever. The legitimacy of punishment requires proven guilt, but guilt is far from proven in a case in which an estimated 80–90% of suspects are innocent of being terrorists. Torture—if analogous to punishment in this argument—is then utilized as a means to *establish* guilt. This is tantamount to saying that guilt comes in the form of forced confession or verifiably accurate information. On one hand, torture notoriously yields confessions for crimes not committed. On the other hand, guilt as an *outcome* of torture—verifiably accurate information—belies the supposed strength of the ticking time bomb case, which presumes the guilt of the torture victim *prior* to torture. In the particular cases of Abu Ghraib and Guantánamo, in fact, the majority of the detainees are innocent of being the bad guys. "'We of course had to make snap judgments in the battlefield,' said one administration official involved in reviewing Guantánamo cases, who spoke anonymously to avoid angering superiors. 'Where we had problems was that once we had individuals in custody, no one along the layers of review wanted to take a risk. So they would take a shred of evidence that a detainee was associated with another bad person and say that's a reason to keep them.'"[18] If torture is used as a means of gathering information, including the information of whether or not the detainee is a terrorist, the Kantian argument collapses for it requires this information in advance of the act. In the case of Abu Ghraib and other detention centers, therefore, the widespread use of torture techniques cannot be justified by denying rights and humane treatment to detainees. In fact, the Kantian argument ends up applying perhaps even more forcefully the other way around—against the torturers. Indiscriminate torture, if not all torture, is a moral and legal crime on any ethical account. It must be understood here that torture is not individualized—a single bad guy over and against thousands of innocents—but rather quickly becomes an institution through its systematic application. In the case of Abu Ghraib, it is an indiscriminate institution. It may very well be the case that many of the people tortured in the Iraq War and the "war on terror" are innocent.[19] Yet, the justification that proponents muster is to torture in order to protect the innocent.

Second, the objective described in the ticking time bomb scenario is information or, more precisely, "actionable intelligence." As above, the argument depends on knowing in advance that the torture victim possesses the information that is sought and that he will not yield the information by any other means. The conditions necessary to make this case, however, end up reducing it to an absurdum.

In an argument *for* torture under "exceptional circumstances" where information "seems to be an appropriate aim," Fritz Allhoff lists four conditions to supplement the ticking time bomb argument: 1) that torture should only be used to gain information that could prevent future threats; 2) that there is a "reasonable expectation that the captive has knowledge of the relevant information"; 3) that there is a "reasonable expectation" that the captive's information "corresponds to an imminent and significant threat"; 4) that there is "reasonable expectation" that "acquisition of the information can lead to prevention of the terrorist act." Allhoff states, "If all four of these conditions are satisfied, then torture would be morally permissible."[20]

Allhoff's conclusion relies on an *a priori* assumption of the conclusion itself of the ticking time bomb argument: that the information is of greater moral significance than the act of torture (information "seems to be an appropriate aim"). The argument begs the question by beginning with what is supposed to be concluded. That is, we might only conclude that the information is of greater moral gravity once we have tortured to gain the information. This is reason enough to reject the argument. Furthermore, preventing "future threats"—the sole justifiable use of torture in Allhoff's argument—is wide open to political interpretation, as we have seen in the "war on terror" and in the justification for the Iraq War. Does a future threat require that it be "imminent"? "Significant"? What is the character of the threat? Potential mass violence? Political oppression? A foreign political arrangement that runs counter to one's own political or economic preferences? Suppose the terrorist does not cooperate under torture. If the threat is indeed morally significant, does this then also allow for the torture of the terrorist's children? Will you volunteer for that job? Should an entire population be tortured in search for the alleged ticking bomb? Does a future threat justify indiscriminate torture, casting a broad net, until one finds someone with the requisite information that both finds the "bomb" and justifies the torture, apologies to all the innocents?

Let's look briefly at the listed conditions because they are widely presumed and depend on two notions that are important in the time bomb framework: "exceptional circumstance" and "reasonable expectation."

What qualify as "exceptional circumstances," the grounds for the necessity argument and the time bomb argument? The answer would have to be a great risk of significant loss of life, but also the knowledge of this risk or knowledge of a very high probability. In order to serve as a context for the argument, the risk would have to be concrete rather than hypothetical. There is much to be debated here about what qualifies as an exceptional circumstance. I mention this to note that each torturing state has used this same characterization of the situation as seething with a vague, ill-defined enemy whose presence serves to justify any actions taken against it and its scions. In Argentina and Chile, it was the dire threat of communism. In Burma, it is the threat of disorder in the state. In medieval Europe, it was heresy. In Algeria, it was the threat to colonial power. In Cambodia, it was "enemies of the state." In Germany, it was the threat of racial and cultural impurity. In the United States, it is the "war on terror." Exceptional circumstances are circumstances constructed by fear and menace. In the history of politics the menacing threat—whether actual or perceived—is always utilized as a means to consolidate power in the name of unifying and mobilizing the people in the face of the menace. It can also be used in an argument based on a hypothetical situation as a means of persuasion apart from argumentation. Since the time bomb argument is purely hypothetical, and a hypothetical is a legitimate form of argumentation, we need not make too much of the exceptional circumstances condition in judging the validity of the argument. But it is crucial to point out that the notion is designed to confuse the distinction between hypothesis and actuality. As discussed in the final section below, this provides the germ for a fantasy world of torture akin to medieval uses of torture.

Note the qualification of "reasonable expectation" attached to the conditionals in Allhoff's claim (and note also the expression's curious inverse relation to "reasonable doubt," used in judicial cases). What is the nature of "reasonable expectation"? What is the nature of reasonable expectation in a climate of fear? Moreover, what does reasonable expectation mean in terms of information, the keystone of torture's justification? Allhoff is correct in his assessment that these would be necessary conditions for torture if one grants the first premise that torture may be justified in the quest for information of greater moral significance than the act of torture. But we have seen that that premise is simply an assertion. Moreover, even if we do grant the assertion, the "reasonable expectation" qualification requires prior knowledge that the torture victim—the "terrorist"—is indeed a terrorist, indeed possesses the "relevant" morally significant information, and indeed will not yield this information except under torture. This in turn entails that there is some means of having uncovered this prior information and that the torture victim is thereby guilty of possessing the information. While this is a possibility, it nevertheless dilutes considerably the justification of torture as a means of gathering information in that, again, the torturer would be required to know already with near-certainty the information that he seeks through torture. The sole remaining information that might still support the argument would be the precise location of the "time bomb."

Apart from the implausibility of the scenario and of reasonable expectation that a torturer will gain this knowledge, there are several practical strikes against this one remaining ingredient in the argument. I will mention two. First, as soon as one of their own is captured, terrorist groups as a matter of strategy abandon their locations and plans under the assumption that the captured cell member could very well yield to torture. Second, it is uncertain whether information gained from torture is good or bad until it is verified. Much is made of information from torture being unreliable and the practice therefore ineffectual, although this does not stop some commentators, such as Richard Posner, from speculating that "it is hard to believe that it is always and everywhere ineffectual; if it were, we would not have to spend so much time debating it."[21] Such remarks imply that the simple existence of torture means that it is effective in some sense. Is torture therefore justified by its very existence?

Recall, however, that it is the outcome of *meaningful* or *true* information (or, if one prefers, "actionable intelligence") leading to the prevention of a greater harm—saving the lives of thousands—that the ticking time bomb argument relies upon. How can one know that the information is meaningful or have a "reasonable expectation" that it will be so?

Some may find this discussion repulsive, since it grants for argument's sake the assumption of torture as a justified means of gathering information. Let me be clear that what I am seeking to show is that this claim is itself a fallacious (though widespread) assumption in the "war on terror," and that the logic of the practice of torture bears this out. If, as Luban suggests above, the liberal ideology of torture does not allow sheer cruelty, but only information-gathering, we must turn to a discussion of information.

TORTURE, INFORMATION, AND INSTITUTIONALIZATION

The time bomb argument is bogus. It suffers from the same defect of most ends-justify-the-means claims. That is, it adopts an unquestioned fixed supposition or end by which the means to achieve it are simply to be manipulated in its service. The scenario hardly qualifies, then, as a model of either morality or truth-seeking, for the only question is which means to use, or, in other words, which "facts" will prove the supposition or end. Torture becomes a "successful" means in that the torture victim will usually confess to anything the torturers desire, thus confirming the supposition. The argument is a prescription for describing reality as whatever the torturers wish it to be.

The time bomb argument, nevertheless, attempts to justify in practice torture as an information-gathering method. That the argument itself does not justify the practice has not stopped proponents of torture "under exceptional circumstances" from pretending that it does. It simply becomes an argument of "good enough," an argument from evasive ignorance or perhaps indolence. The practice of torture, the worst thing that human beings do to one another, requires more support than "good enough" to justify it. Furthermore, the actual use of torture at Abu Ghraib, Guantá-namo, Baghram, and elsewhere is still premised on the notion that there is valuable intelligence to be gleaned from torture, even if it does not meet the scenario of the ticking time bomb. But the time bomb scenario raises a further smokescreen over the logic of torture when an entity seeks to gain "actionable intelligence." The time bomb scenario suggests that torture is used individually and discriminately given the broad play in the "reasonable expectations" conditions (which, in their strict interpretation, are likely impossible to meet). The logic in the practice of torturing for information entails institutionalization of a program of torture, which is a much more radical political question than torturing one clearly bad terrorist bursting with critical information. Institutionalization follows from the use of torture as a means of gathering information. And this is a function of the problem of misinformation in verifying actionable intelligence and how the problem might be resolved.

Intelligence is gathered in a number of ways: through satellite reconnaissance, monitoring communications, extensive monitoring of open sources such as newspapers and internet sites, the securing and use of agents on the ground, and so on. Intelligence-gathering is viewed as a way of uncovering "truth," and many analysts view this mission, at least in principle, as a noble calling. A former intelligence official, J. E. Drexel Godfrey, puts it like this, "intelligence is rooted in the severest of ethical principles: truth telling. After all, the end purpose of the elaborate apparatus that the intelligence community has become is to provide the policymaker with as close to a truthful depiction of a given situation as is humanly possible. Anything less is not intelligence."[22] My own anecdotal experience with the intelligence community suggests that there is wide agreement on the idea that intelligence-gathering is a matter of truth-seeking, and that when the "truth" of intelligence is utilized, distorted, and manipulated in the service of pre-established political goals this is because policymakers choose to do so, not intelligence-gatherers. Scandals in the intelligence community usually have to do with the "politicization" of intelligence.[23] Of course, intelligence-gathering requires inference, judgments about what qualifies as valuable information, and interpretative frameworks in order to be the collection of anything but raw data. *Evaluation* of the "facts" runs all the way down, and we could certainly dispute the assumed strong distinction between fact and value implicit in the self-description of the intelligence-gatherer's enterprise. "Information," after all, "is a kind of message, where the message is selected from a set of possible messages."[24] But I want to look more closely at how the practice of torture could yield actionable intelligence or meaningful information.[25] Of course, it may very well be the case that torture is an unnecessary means for collecting whatever information is sought and that other methods are adequate. In fact, the method that seems to have actually yielded results in the "war on terror" is buying off turncoat informants. In spite of the speciousness of the time bomb argument, however, proponents have justified torture ostensibly in the name of collecting valuable and meaningful information. The process by which such information could be verified is thus crucial as both an ethical and practical matter.

Suppose that an individual terrorist, based on "reasonable expectations" that he has significant information, is tortured for the information. How does one know when one has meaningful or true information? Under severe pain, torture victims often admit to anything to halt the pain, regardless of their guilt of possessing significant information. We thus have two problems here: the "guilt" of the torture victim and the verisimilitude of the information. Since a torture victim might *admit* to anything, torture cannot be a means to establish guilt (setting to the side the moral issue of torturing a potential innocent). Since the torture victim might admit to *anything*—whether intentional misinformation or not—some further element is required to verify whether the information is either false or "actionable." If one already possesses whatever knowledge forms a "reasonable expectation" that the torture victim has significant information, one could then perhaps correlate the torture information with this previous knowledge in order to verify it. The problem is that this would appear to render torture moot as a practical matter. The torture information must be previously unknown (but somehow of great moral gravity) in order to justify the act of torture. It is therefore unclear whether or not it is meaningful information until one has tortured, gained information, and then somehow verified the information. Standing alone, whatever an individual torture victim says cannot otherwise be meaningful information. And, thus, unless captured red-handed, likely obviating the "need" for torture, even the guilt of the torture victim is in constant question.

Perhaps the principal means of verifying information from a tortured individual is to corroborate the information in a context of other information from other tortured individuals. Although practiced elsewhere, one particular example comes to mind. An old friend of mine, an investigative journalist, recently recounted to me his time spent in Burma/Myanmar with Burmese journalists. Each of the journalists had been tortured by the Myanmar government. All of them had some point in their personal account of torture where they simply do not remember. This moment was one in which the journalist could not remember anything, a moment in which, they surmised, information poured out of the tortured psyche. Under the delirium of torture, such information is unlikely to be coherent. Discussion turned to the nature of government torture. It became clear, although this is anecdotal, that the military regime of Myanmar maintains a database comprised of information gained through torture. The problem, of course, is that information from individual torture victims must be correlated and verified or falsified in order to be serviceable. The raw information must be triangulated, so to speak. The Myanmar government would torture *many* people in order to evaluate various individual bits of information and compare them with other bits of information (or misinformation) in order to build a coherent account of actual information. The database serves to find patterns in the mass of information and misinformation. All the data from the individual torture victims—whether "good" or "bad" information—is logged into the database. Given that individual misinformation is indistinguishable from individual information, it becomes necessary to look for repeated patterns of information rather than attempting to verify or falsify bits of data. The more comprehensive the data, the more complex the patterns. If one tortures indiscriminately and broadly, one therefore has more complex patterns with which to work and a better understanding of what is meaningful in the information. Patterns of information by themselves are meaningless. But they serve to corroborate and verify trustworthy information and infer other patterns. A descriptive story can be interpreted and assembled from the resulting patterns, regularities, constancies. This is where information can become meaningful, although not necessarily verisimilar.

The Myanmar case illustrates the possibility that torture *never* involves a calculation regarding the one versus the many except in hypothesized fantasies. The torturer cannot determine whether information is potentially useful without the practice of torture being widespread. This indicates that torture as a means of information-gathering necessitates the institutionalization of torture as a practice. Further, it suggests that the more extensive the practice, the larger the institution, the more successful it will be.

What does institutionalization entail? I will mention three points. First, rather obviously, it entails the broad use of torture. Individual torture makes little sense from the perspective of seeking information. Torturing broadly, including torturing innocents, follows from a justification of torture as an information-gathering method precisely because it allows for verification and thus renders information actionable intelligence. As I have said, this requires a systematic practice. A systematic approach involves methodology, a legal regime (which we have seen developed by the current US administration and its cadre of lawyers), training of interrogators, training of medical staff, buildings, supplies, a supply system, etc. As Luban asks, "Should universities create an undergraduate course in torture? Or should the subject be offered only in police and military academies? [Luban cites the infamous School of the Americas.] Do we want federal grants for research to devise new and better techniques?

Patents issued on high-tech torture devices? Companies competing to manufacture them? Trade conventions in Las Vegas? . . ."[26]

Second, institutionalization entails that the "torture debate" is framed wrongly from the outset to the extent that this debate takes place between those who focus on the horror of torture and the crass cost-benefit utilitarians who are convinced by time bomb arguments. While others have said the same thing about torture as intelligence-gathering, about its institutionalization, it is important that we understand that institutionalization is the logical outcome of individual torture as portrayed in and encouraged by the time bomb scenario. Individualized torture is precisely where the time bomb case and similar arguments focus the "torture debate." Permit me to use current rhetoric to underscore the point: institutionalization of torture is the foundation of a "torture nation." It is doubtful that such a shift in the character of a nation is worth the price of battling an ill-defined war with obscure objectives. In any case, institutions—especially institutions in a democracy—are matters of the public good and the embodiment of a democratic public's values and hopes. To relegate their creation to a process of secrecy and dubious means is to redefine radically the political landscape as much as the moral landscape along anti-democratic lines. This is what is truly at stake in the torture debate, but it is largely passed over in silence by the official arbiters of the debate.

Finally, institutionalization of torture as information-seeking entails a system of truths with potentially little correlation to actuality. As such, institutional torture, contrary to its rough and ready instrumental rationality, wavers at the edge of fantasy in which prior assumptions—whether accurate or mistaken—brought to the act of torture may be indefinitely confirmed and reconfirmed by the torture victim and subsequent torture victims. We are compelled again to ask the pragmatic question of what job torture does. A historical illustration of torture and how it manufactures reality underscores this point.

TORTURE AND FANTASY

Between the thirteenth and eighteenth centuries, torture of those accused of "superstitions" and other heresies spread throughout Western Europe (the Spanish Inquisition lasted in the Americas into the nineteenth century). In the grip of paranoia that witches threatened the security and unity of the Church, hundreds of thousands of people, the majority women (due to their inherent susceptibility to demonic possession), were accused of witchcraft, interrogated under torture, and often executed. They were burned alive, drowned, hanged, and disemboweled under the guidance of the infamous *Malleus Maleficarum*.[27] Confessions under torture often involved providing names of other witches, thus ensuring the perpetuation of the persecutions. Among the many accusations made against witches was their diabolical consort in the satanic agency of foul weather. Since the Greeks, weather phenomena had been attributed to supernatural entities. Over the course of early Christianity, bad weather, though originally taken as a sign of God's wrath, gradually became associated with airborne demons. By the 15th century and the papal bull of Pope Innocent VIII, *Summis Desiderantes* (1484), which commanded the hunt for witches, the synthesis of human agency in the form of the witch and demonic forms of weather was complete.[28] Lightning, thunderstorms, high winds, sleet, hail were the doing of the human agents of demons. "Out of the old doctrine—pagan and Christian—of evil agency in atmospheric phenomena was evolved the belief that certain men, women, and children may secure infernal aid to produce whirlwinds, hail, frosts, floods, and the like. . . ."[29] Witches were tortured to exact confessions of their dark manipulations of the weather and then either to repent or suffer execution, sometimes both. Various scholars during the period attempted to explain that there were more coherent accounts of foul weather, but risked and sometimes suffered their own fate on the stake as heretics.

Under torture, of course, one will say anything. In saying anything—perhaps, in the delirium of torture, believing anything—the tortured witches provided a stream of fantastic tales of their devilish manipulation of weather.

> The poor creatures, writhing on the rack, held in horror by those who had been nearest and dearest to them, anxious only for death to relieve their sufferings, confessed to anything and everything that would satisfy the inquisitors and judges. All that was needed was that the inquisitors should ask leading questions and suggest satisfactory answers: the prisoners, to shorten the torture, were sure sooner or later to give the answer required, even though they knew that this would send them to the stake or scaffold. Under the doctrine of "excepted cases," there was no limit to torture for persons accused of heresy or witchcraft; even the safeguards which the old pagan world had imposed upon torture were thus thrown down, and the prisoner *must* confess. The theological literature of the Middle Ages was thus enriched with numberless statements regarding modes of Satanic influence on the weather. Pathetic, indeed, are the records; and none more so than the confessions of these poor creatures, chiefly women

and children, during hundreds of years, as to their manner of raising hailstorms and tempests. Such confessions, by tens of thousands, are still to be found in the judicial records of Germany, and indeed of all Europe. Typical among these is one on which great stress was laid during ages, and for which the world was first indebted to one of these poor women. Crazed by the agony of torture, she declared that, returning with a demon through the air from the witches' sabbath, she was dropped upon the earth in the confusion which resulted among the hellish legions when they heard the bells sounding the *Ave Maria.* It is sad to note that, after a contribution so valuable to sacred science, the poor woman was condemned to the flames. This revelation speedily ripened the belief that, whatever might be going on at the witches' Sabbath—no matter how triumphant Satan might be—at the moment of sounding the consecrated bells the Satanic power was paralyzed. This theory once started, proofs came in to support it, during a hundred years, from the torture chambers in all parts of Europe. . . ."[30]

These were confessions constructed not only from the inquisitors' fantasies, but from the witches' hallucinatory contradictions and paradoxes. So another case went, "[King James I] applied his own knowledge to investigating the causes of the tempests which beset his bride on her voyage from Denmark. Skilful use of unlimited torture soon brought these causes to light. A Dr. Fian, while his legs were crushed in the 'boots' and wedges were driven under his finger nails, confessed that several hundred witches had gone to sea in a sieve from the port of Leith, and had raised storms and tempests to drive back the princess." Notice that a fantastical delirium confirming the suspicions of church and secular rulers explained a prior conception of weather. Delirium confirmed the fantasy of the "sacred theory of meteorology" through tortured and uncontrollable imaginations and, hence, became confirmation and further development of a presumed, antecedent reality. Apart from the political uses of torture and the stake, the delirium of the witch was, combined with inherited myths, the science of weather. The goal was not to achieve more precise explanations of meteorological phenomena, but to preserve the sacred authority of the Church. As such, torture had a kind of utility: the confessions confirmed authority. It also had a logic by which it could repeat its authoritative description of the world. It is not as if we can call the products of medieval torture "information" for there was nothing objective and independent of the minds of the torturers to be explained. Truth was a function of fantasy, corroborated simply to the extent that it fit an existing set of beliefs. Torture itself would lead the victim to this corroboration, since it was the only way to end the suffering. But I do not want to make too much of this in the case of witches. Discerning objective truth was not the aim of medieval torture.

We can hardly fault inhabitants of the late Middle Ages for holding an unscientific view of meteorology and a mythology of witchcraft. While we can bemoan the fanaticism and barbarity of the persecutions and inquisitions from our present perspective, we must also be wary of anachronism. The point of this historical digression is to show a structural pattern that is common to institutional torture.

> "I said he was important," Bush reportedly told [former CIA Director of Central Intelligence, George Tenet] at one of their daily meetings. "You're not going to let me lose face on this, are you?" "No sir, Mr. President," Tenet replied. Bush "was fixated on how to get [al Qaeda "chief of operations," Abu Zubaydah] to tell us the truth," Suskind writes, and he asked one briefer, "Do some of these harsh methods really work?" Interrogators did their best to find out, Suskind reports. They strapped Abu Zubaydah to a water-board, which reproduces the agony of drowning. They threatened him with certain death. They with-held medication. They bombarded him with deafening noise and harsh lights, depriving him of sleep. Under that duress, he began to speak of plots of every variety—against shopping malls, banks, supermarkets, water systems, nuclear plants, apartment buildings, the Brooklyn Bridge, the Statue of Liberty. With each new tale, "thousands of uniformed men and women raced in a panic to each . . . target." And so, Suskind writes, "the United States would torture a mentally disturbed man and then leap, screaming, at every word he uttered."[31]

What do we make of this? The goal is Abu Zubaydah's "truth." The method is torture—the modern waterboard as opposed to the medieval *strappado*.[32] The outcome is Keystone Kops. And, of course, a man whose mind has been left in the torture chamber. Note that the individual Zubaydah's information is useless; in this case, as a result of the torture (thus defeating its supposedly justifying end of generating information). In place of medieval stories of the weather, Zubaydah gives the interroga-tors stories about nonexistent but anticipated ticking bombs. The torture itself engenders fantastical information and hysteria that corresponds to the fantasized hypothesis of the time bomb. Everything takes place in an endogenous world of unreality while an institution grows like an excrescence around the unreality, slowly obviating moral justification once the practice is entrenched within the institutional system, and finally burrowing into political culture. Like the inquisitions, like Stalin's purges, the excrescence then turns inward to feed on itself.

There is nothing wrong with a little fantasy in our lives. Some of our most pleasant experiences involve fantasies. But fantasy can create a moral and political climate that demands actions that harm, maim, and destroy. What the medieval torture system and contemporary "alternative interrogation" have in common is a social administration that generates for common consumption "truth" in the conventionalist sense Nietzsche famously described as a "flexible army of metaphors, metonymies, anthropomorphisms" that becomes "fixed, canonical, and binding."[33] The truth here, however, corresponds to the method itself—whose pragmatic value is doubtful—rather than to the exogenous reality the method purports to explain. We must face the very real possibility that the actual objective of institutionalized torture is not, in the end, information-gathering to counter existential threats, but the perpetuation of an end in itself.

NOTES

1. Amnesty International. *Torture in the Eighties* (London: Amnesty International, 1984). 4–6.

2. David Luban, "Liberalism, Torture, and the Ticking Bomb." *Virginia Law Review.* 91 (2005): 1425–1461.

3. Luban, "Liberalism, Torture, and the Ticking Bomb," 1439–1440.

4. I am doubtful that the so-called "war on terror" is indeed a war, but rather ultimately an attempt to consolidate power in the executive branch of the US government. However, I will use the expression "war on terror" in the loose sense in which it is commonly used.

5. Naomi Klein, "Torture's Dirty Secret: It Works." *The Nation.* May 30th, 2005. http://www.thenation.com/doc/20050530/klein.

6. For a discussion of the psychology of torture, see Mika Haritos Fatouros, *The Psychological Origins of Institutionalized Torture.* (London: Routledge, 2003).

7. See Michael Hatfield's essay in this collection.

8. Luban, "Liberalism, Torture, and the Ticking Bomb," 1427.

9. Luban, "Liberalism, Torture, and the Ticking Bomb," 1427.

10. See also Darius Rejali's discussion of the ticking time bomb in this collection. For a discussion of the condescending assumptions the time bomb scenario implies about its audience, see Elaine Scarry, "Five Errors in the Reasoning of Alan Dershowitz," in Sanford Levinson, ed. *Torture: A Collection.* (Oxford: Oxford University Press, 2004). 281–290. For more, see also Scarry's *The Body in Pain* (New York: Oxford University Press, 1985).

11. Alan M. Dershowitz, *Why Terrorism Works* (New Haven: Yale University Press, 2002).

12. See Stephanie Athey's essay in this collection on the case of Abdul Hakim Murad.

13. See Raymond Geuss' discussion of human rights for a position with which I generally agree. Geuss, *History and Illusion in Politics* (Cambridge: Cambridge University Press, 2001). Section 3.

14. Excluded from this discussion is the debate over who qualifies as a "terrorist" and who is a "freedom fighter." These terms are themselves politically charged and may shift over time depending on changing political views and historical events. The definition of "terrorist" is notoriously slippery, since "terrorism" refers to a tactical means while "terrorist" includes implicit reference to particular ends and/or the supposed identity of the person or group in question. The latter is a distinction usually determined by the individual's or group's enemy.

15. See Jeffrey Reiman, "Against the Death Penalty," in S. Luper, ed. *Living Well* (New York: Harcourt Brace and Co., 2000). 553–562.

16. Heather MacDonald, "How to Interrogate Terrorists," in Karen J. Greenberg, ed. *The Torture Debate in America*. (Cambridge: Cambridge University Press, 2006). 89, 95.

17. *Report of the International Committee of the Red Cross (ICRC) on the Treatment by the Coalition Forces of Prisoners of War and Other Protected Persons by the Geneva Conventions in Iraq During Arrest, Internment, and Interrogation*. Section 1.7. February, 2004.

18. Carol D. Leonnig and Julie Tate, "Some at Guantánamo Mark Five Years in Limbo." *Washington Post*. January 16th, 2007. A01.

19. See, for instance, discussion of the case of Khaled Masri in Dana Priest, "Wrongful Imprisonment: Anatomy of a CIA Mistake." *Washington Post*. December 4th, 2006. A01.

20. Fritz Allhoff, "An Ethical Defense of Torture in Interrogation," in Jan Goldman, ed. *Ethics of Spying*. (Lanham, Maryland: The Scarecrow Press, 2006). 132–134.

21. Richard A. Posner, "Torture, Terrorism, and Interrogation," in Sanford Levinson, ed. *Torture: A Collection*. (Oxford: Oxford University Press, 2004). 294.

22. J. E. Drexel Godfrey, "Ethics and Intelligence," reprinted in Goldman, ed. *Ethics of Spying*, 2. [Originally published in 1978].

23. For one discussion, see Robert M. Gates, "Guarding Against Politicization: A Message to Analysts," reprinted in Goldman, ed. *Ethics of Spying*, 171–184. [Originally published 1992]).

24. Claude Shannon, "A Mathematical Theory of Communication." *The Bell System Technical Journal*. 27 (July 1948): 379–423. 379.

25. I am using a standard definition of information here as a mind-independent, objective entity, sometimes referred to as "data + meaning." For a sophisticated account of the varieties of information, see Luciano Floridi, "Is Semantic Information Meaningful Data?" *Philosophy and Phenomenological Research*. LXX (March 2005): 351–370.

26. Luban, "Liberalism, Torture, and the Ticking Bomb," 1446.

27. The *Malleus Maleficarum* ("Witch Hammer") is a text dating to 1486, authored by Heinrich Kramer and James Sprenger. It sought to prove the existence of witches and describe their activities. Its third section is a how-to manual on the identification, prosecution, torture, and execution of witches. The extent of the text's influence in Europe and the Americas is disputed and it had its detractors during the period. But it is generally agreed that the text is a key document in the persecution of witches. See the recently retranslated 2-volume set edited by Christopher S. MacKay. (Cambridge: Cambridge University Press, 2006).

28.   The inspiration for Pope Innocent VIII was Exodus 22:18, "Thou shalt not suffer a witch to live."

29.   Andrew Dickson White, *A History of the Warfare of Science with Theology in Christendom* (New York: D. Appleton and Company, 1896). Chapter XI, 3.

30.   Dickson White, *A History of the Warfare of Science with Theology in Christendom*. Church bells, at the time, were thought to help shake the air of demons.

31.   Barton Gellman, "The Shadow War, In a Surprising New Light." *Washington Post.* June 20th, 2006. C01.

32.   The variety and ingenuity of torture techniques was impressive. The strappado was common because it was one of the simplest techniques. Strappado involved hanging a person from a tree or rafter by their wrists tied behind their back. The rope was then raised and dropped repeatedly, dislocating the shoulders. Sometimes weights were added, a variation of the strappado called "squassation."

Modern waterboarding involves placing a wet cloth or plastic wrap over the horizontal victim's nose and mouth or a sack over the head and pouring water over it. Waterboarding is controlled drowning of the victim, inducing the gag reflex and an overwhelming sense of imminent death. Waterboarding has been used around the world. It may very well be the modern analog to strappado in that it is also a simple torture technique.

33.   From "On Truth and Lie in an Extra-Moral Sense." Cited in Richard Schacht, *Nietzsche* (London: Routledge and Kegan Paul, 1983). 73. Schacht's translation.

Notes on Contributors

CHRISTOPHER BRITT ARREDONDO teaches Spanish at George Washington University (Princeton University Ph.D., 1998). He is the author of *Quixotism* (2004) and is currently writing a book on exile based partially on research conducted while on sabbatical in Santa Marta, Colombia. He is the author of various essays that study the role of the intellectual in the formation of nationalist and pan-nationalist identities in Spain and Latin America. His principal areas of interest include nationalism, fascism, imperialism and post-colonial studies, and Hispanic perceptions of the U.S. and vice versa.

STEHANIE ATHEY is a visiting scholar at the Center for the Study of Human Rights, Columbia University, and associate professor in the Department of Humanities and Interdisciplinary Studies at Lasell College. Athey's scholarship is in the fields of race, gender, and cultural and literary representation. She has edited a collection on the art, armed resistance, and civil organizing of women in Africa, India, and the Americas, *Sharpened Edge: Women of Color, Resistance and Writing* (2003); she has also written articles on colonial discourse in the Americas, eugenic feminisms of the late 19th century, and the intersection of race and reproductive technologies.

ASHLEY CAJA is a senior majoring in Latin American Studies at the George Washington University.

PILAR CALVEIRO is a professor at la Benemérita Universidad Autónoma de Puebla (Mexico). She is the author of the influential book on the Argentinean "desaparecidos," *Power and the Disappeared* (1998), as well as *Family and Power* (2005) and *Politics and/or Violence* (2005).

CARLOS CASTRESANA is a public prosecutor of the Supreme Court of Spain and coordinator of the UNODC Project for Crime Prevention in Nuevo León, México. He is visiting professor and director of International Human Rights Programs in the Center for Law and Global Justice, University of San Francisco. Spokesman and president of the Union of Progressive Prosecutors in Spain, in 1996 Castresana authored and filed the lawsuits and subsequent reports on genocide, terrorism, torture, forced disappearances, crimes against humanity, universal jurisdiction, and extradition against the Military Juntas of Argentina and Chile beginning the Pinochet Case before the Spanish National Court.

ARTHUR DENNER is an independent scholar and freelance translator living in Princeton, New Jersey. His translations from the French include two other works by Tzvetan Todorov: *Facing the Extreme: Moral Life in the Concentration Camps* (New York: Metropolitan/Henry Holt, 1996) and *The Fragility of Goodness: Why Bulgaria's Jews Survived the Holocaust* (Princeton: Princeton University Press, 2003).

ARIEL DORFMAN is a Chilean-American writer and human rights activist who holds the Walter Hines Page Chair at Duke University. His books, written both in Spanish and

English, have been translated into more than 30 languages and his plays staged in over 120 countries. He has received numerous international awards, including the Lawrence Olivier Award (for "Death and the Maiden," which was made into a feature film by Roman Polanski). His novels include *Windows, Konfidenz, The Nanny and the Iceberg,* and *Blake's Therapy.* His latest works are a travel book, *Desert Memories,* and the plays "Purgatorio" and "The Other Side." He has also published a novel, *Burning City,* with his son, Joaquin Dorfman. He contributes regularly to major newspapers worldwide.

BARBARA EHRENREICH is a social critic, activist, writer, and Ph.D. from Rockefeller University. Her *Nickel and Dimed* (2002) was a bestseller in the United States. She is also the author of *Blood Rites: Origins and History of the Passions of War* (1991), *Complaints and Disorders: The Sexual Politics of Sickness* (with Diedre English) (1991), and ten other books of non-fiction and fiction, including the recent *Bait and Switch: The (Futile) Pursuit of the American Dream.* She also contributes to major political and literary magazines.

MICHAEL HATFIELD is a professor of law at the Texas Tech University School of Law (New York University School of Law J.D., 1996). He teaches a course in Law and Conscience, which explores issues of civil disobedience, religious expression, politics, and ethics. He researches and publishes in issues involving religion, politics, conscience, and the American lawyering culture.

THOMAS C. HILDE is a research professor at the University of Maryland School of Public Policy (Penn State Ph.D., 2001). He is editor of *The Agrarian Roots of Pragmatism* (Vanderbilt, 2000) and of *Pragmatism and Globalization* (Rodopi, 2008). Hilde is also the author of several essays on political thought, ethics, aesthetics, and policy issues. He directed the Environmental Conservation Education Program and the Applied Philosophy Group at New York University before moving to UMD. He writes on environment and development, international affairs, democracy, and pragmatism. He is also a Fulbright Senior Specialist.

ALPHONSO LINGIS is Emeritus Professor of Philosophy at the Pennsylvania State University. He has published *Excesses: Eros and Culture* (1984), *Libido: The French Existential Theories* (1985), *Phenomenological Explanations* (1986), *Deathbound Subjectivity* (1989), *The Community of Those Who Have Nothing in Common* (1994), *Abuses* (1994), *Foreign Bodies* (1994), *Sensation: Intelligibility in Sensibility* (1995), *The Imperative* (1998), *Dangerous Emotions* (1999), *Trust* (2003), *Body Modifications: Evolutions and Atavisms in Culture* (2005), and *The First Person Singular* (2006).

PAULA LUTTRINGER is an Argentinean who lives in Paris. She was "disappeared" for more than five months during Argentina's Dirty War. Her photographic series, *El Lamento de los Muros,* from which the cover photograph is taken, documents some of the hundreds of secret detention centers in Argentina during the 1970s and 1980s and some of the thousands of women who were disappeared, tortured, and often murdered in the centers.

REBECCA E. NATALONI is a senior at the George Washington University, where she studied Spanish and Italian Language and Literature. She also completed a year of study in Spanish Philology at the Universidad de Alicante, Spain.

WILLIAM NICHOLS is an assistant professor of Spanish at Georgia State University in Atlanta, Georgia. He focuses on issues related to twentieth-century Spanish Peninsular Narrative and Transatlantic Cultural Studies, specifically the relationship between politics, cultural production, and capital. He is currently revising a manuscript titled "Transatlantic Mysteries: Culture, Capital, and Crime in the 'Noir' Novels of Paco Ignacio Taibo II and Manuel Vázquez Montalbán."

ADI OPHIR is an associate professor at the Cohn Institute for the History and the Philosophy of Science and Ideas at Tel Aviv University. He is also a research fellow at the Van Leer and the Shalom Hartman Institutes in Jerusalem. His recent book in English is *The Order of Evils* (Zone Books, 2005). He currently studies "states of disaster": the role of modern states in mitigating large scale disasters, on the one hand, and producing them on the other.

DARIUS REJALI is a nationally recognized expert on government torture and interrogation. He is a Carnegie Scholar and professor of political science at Reed College. He is the author of *Torture and Modernity: Self, Society, and State in Modern Iran* (Westview, 1994), *Torture and Democracy* (Princeton, 2007), and *Approaches to Violence* (Princeton, 2008). Iranian-born, Rejali has spent his scholarly career reflecting on violence and, specifically, reflecting on the causes, consequences, and meaning of modern torture in our contemporary world. His work spans concerns in political science, philosophy, sociology, anthropology, history, and critical social theory. He has popularized his work in interviews and articles in magazines and newspapers including *Time*, *Newsweek*, *The New York Times*, and *Salon.com*, as well as in television appearances on CNN, Court TV, and Channel 5 (UK).

LAURA REXACH was born in San Juan, Puerto Rico. She is a senior majoring in finance at the School of Business at the George Washington University.

MARGARITA SERJE is a professor of anthropology at Universidad de los Andes (Bogotá). She leads a research group on Space and Society, studying the landscapes and territories historically considered as "frontier zones" and "no man's lands" and the conflicts between the state and the communities of the "red zones" of Colombia. She is the author of *El revés de la Nación: Territorios salvajes, fronteras y tierras de nadie* (Bogotá: Uniandes, 2005).

EDUARDO SUBIRATS is a professor in the Department of Spanish and Portuguese of New York University. He specializes in modern philosophy, aesthetics, critical theory, and colonial theory. His works study Spanish intellectual history, colonization, the Enlightenment, avant-garde theory, and artistic movements in Spain and Latin America. He currently contributes cultural and political articles in the Latin American daily press and is the author, among other books, of *Da vanguarda ao pós-moderno* (São Paulo, 1984–85–87–89; Madrid, 1985; Barcelona, 1989), *Culturas virtuales* (Madrid, 1988;

México, 2001), *A flor e o cristal* (Sâo Paulo, 1988), *El continente vacío* (Madrid, 1993; Mexico, 1994), *Linterna Mágica* (Madrid, 1997), *Memoria y exilio* (Madrid, 2003), and *Viaje al fin del Paraíso: Un ensayo sobre América latina* (Madrid, 2005). Subirats formerly taught at Princeton University and at universities in São Paulo, México, Caracas, and Madrid.

TZVETAN TODOROV is the author of *The Conquest of America* (1982), *Mikhail Bakhtin: The Dialogical Principle* (1984), *Facing the Extreme: Moral Life in the Concentration Camps* (1991), *On Human Diversity* (1993), *Hope and Memory* (2000), and several other books. He has also been Visiting Professor at universities including Harvard, Yale, Columbia, and UC-Berkeley.

REBECCA WITTMANN is an assistant professor of history at the University of Toronto. Her research focuses on the Holocaust, postwar German trials of Nazi perpetrators and terrorists, and German legal history. She has received fellowships from the Alexander von Humboldt Foundation, the Social Sciences and Humanities Research Council of Canada, the United States Holocaust Memorial Museum, and the DAAD (German Academic Exchange Service). She has published articles in *Central European History, German History,* and *Lessons and Legacies*. Her book, *Beyond Justice: The Auschwitz Trial*, was published in 2005 with Harvard University Press. She is currently working on her next project: "Nazism and Terrorism: The Madjanek and Stammheim Trials in 1975 West Germany."

Index